AGAINST THE CURRENT

AGAINST THE CURRENT

Paddling Upstream on the Tennessee River

Kim Trevathan

THE UNIVERSITY OF TENNESSEE PRESS
Knoxville

LIBRARY OF CONGRESS CATALOGING-IN-PUBLICATION DATA
Names: Trevathan, Kim, 1958– author.
Title: Against the current: paddling upstream on the Tennessee River / Kim Trevathan.
Description: First edition. | Knoxville: The University of Tennessee Press, 2021. |
Includes bibliographical references and index. | Summary: "Written twenty years
after his first expedition down the Tennessee River that was chronicled in *Paddling
the Tennessee River*, this new book finds Kim Trevathan paddling upriver, providing
him with different perspectives of the river, its surroundings, and an older and perhaps
wiser author. Trevathan's range as a writer is on full display here, with the everyday strug-
gles of navigating a canoe against wind and current, poetic musings on events and physical
beauty, and an obsessive concern for the environment"—Provided by publisher.
Identifiers: LCCN 2020032204 (print) | LCCN 2020032205 (ebook) |
ISBN 9781621906254 (paperback) | ISBN 9781621906261 (adobe pdf)
Subjects: LCSH: Tennessee River—Description and travel. | Tennessee River—
Environmental conditions. | Tennessee River Valley—Environmental conditions. |
Trevathan, Kim, 1958—Travel—Tennessee River. | Kayaking—Tennessee River.
Classification: LCC F217.T3 T739 2021 (print) | LCC F217.T3 (ebook) |
DDC 917.6804—dc23

LC record available at https://lccn.loc.gov/2020032204
LC ebook record available at https://lccn.loc.gov/2020032205

CONTENTS

ILLUSTRATIONS

PHOTOGRAPHS

MAPS

ACKNOWLEDGMENTS

Thanks to all family—mother, sister, brother, sister-in-law, nieces and nephews—for advice, inspiration, and support on the trip. Thanks to new friends and old who provided shelter, food, and other moral support: Mel Purcell, John Hewlett, Chris Alexander, Charles Ray, Charles Rose, David Whiteside, Martin Knoll, Ruthie Cartlidge, Rick Huffines, Phillip Grymes, Drew Crain, Mark Ellison, Terry Bunde, David and Jordan Wilburn, Phil and Tammie Zacheretti, Karen and Jeff Pewitt, John Becker, Vince Vawter, Charles Dodd White, April Ellen White, Neil Norman, Christina Seymour, Sam Overstreet, Barbara Wells, Dan Klingensmith, and Scott Steele. Special thanks to state park rangers Bob Holliday and John Bowen for valuable information and support. Thanks to Alan Jerrolds at Pickwick State Park and all the other rangers, campground managers, and workers who helped Maggie and me out. Thanks to the Corps of Engineers lock operators who shepherded us through nine dams.

Thanks to Maryville College and to the Appalachian College Association for its support.

Finally, I'm grateful for Catherine, Sam, and Anna for their gentle ribbing, loving concern, and sage advice.

AGAINST THE CURRENT

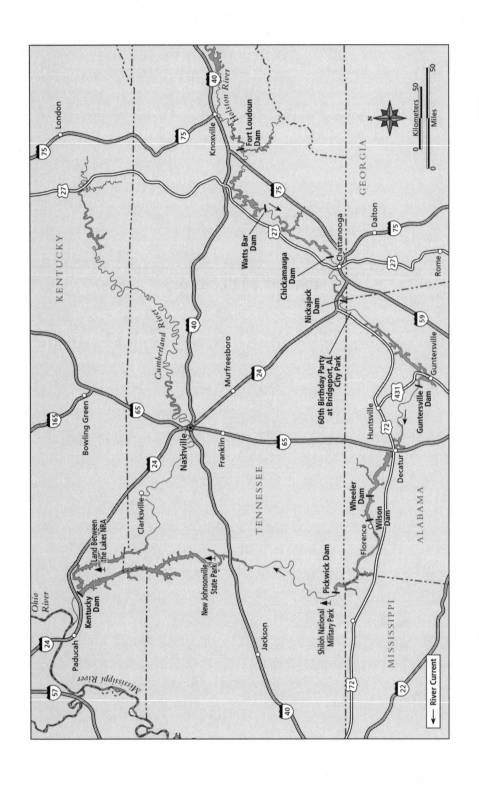

INTRODUCTION

EASY WATER, 1998

On a chilly October evening, a couple of hours after dark, I glided up to Broadway Wharf in Paducah, Kentucky, after sixteen straight hours of paddling, a forty-two-mile day. I was so tired I was hallucinating as I approached the end of this canoe trip down the length of the Tennessee River from Knoxville to Paducah. Family cheered as my dog Jasper, a mix of German shepherd and yellow Labrador, sailed over the bow and swam the last twenty feet to the boat ramp, ecstatic that the 652-mile trip was over. An hour before, squinting at an object backlit by security lights in front of a metal industrial building, I thought I saw an enormous statue of Neptune. It was not a statue of Neptune, not even close. It was not a statue of anything, rather a hallucination borne of exhaustion. I paddled past Neptune toward Broadway Wharf, knowing I was on the home stretch of the five-week voyage through the heat of late summer, over the flat water of nine lakes. I was so ready for the trip to be over that I had paddled that last day starting at three o'clock in the morning, including a lockage through Kentucky Dam.

After embracing my wife, mother, father, aunt, and in-laws, I began hauling my filthy gear up the ramp to their vehicles while Jasper danced around, greeting family and strangers alike. I dropped off a load of rubber dry bags and staggered back toward the canoe past a man sitting on a bench facing the river. He sipped from a tall can inside a brown paper bag.

"Canoe trip?" he said.

"Yeah."

"Where from?"

"Knoxville." I waited for the usual response: Knoxville? How long did it take you? Why didn't you put a motor on that thing?

"That ain't so great," he said. "Current must have carried you most of the way."

"Not really," I said. "It was a lot of work."

"That right?"

I headed back down the ramp toward my family.

I had expected congratulations, at least the familiar head-shaking "crazy" gesture I'd gotten from strangers all the way down the river. But I was too exhausted to retort anything that would make sense.

Emboldened by my silence, he shouted at my back, as I was retreating: "Try the Yukon next time!"

This guy put my 1998 trip into perspective, humbling forty-year-old me at a point when I was feeling so proud of what I had done. Then, as if aware that he'd dampened my little celebration, he added, "I do like your dog, though."

Twenty years later, instead of paddling the Yukon or some other exotic and dangerous river, I decided to paddle the Tennessee again, this time upstream from Paducah to Knoxville, from near where I grew up in western Kentucky to where I now live, the wrong way, if you will, against what passes for current on a dammed-up river. I had the same boat, an Old Town Discovery, about sixteen-feet long, but I had a different dog, a ten-month old puppy named Maggie, who at sixty-five pounds outweighed Jasper by twenty. I would turn 60 on the river that spring, in April. I was leaving in mid-March, at the beginning of the unusually wet and cold spring of 2018, and I truly did not know if I could complete this trip. I didn't know if I had the stamina, physical or mental, and I didn't even know if the Army Corps of Engineers would lock us through dams in a canoe going upstream. I worried about tornadoes, about capsizing the boat in such cold weather, and about whether Maggie, an exuberant pup, would run off or get me into some kind of trouble by jumping up and "hugging" someone who didn't want to be hugged.

I was concerned about where I would camp on the Tennessee, a working river where people navigate barges, work at industries, hunt, fish, ski, swim, party, and live (in boats and houses). There's not always a desirable and legal place to camp every fifteen miles. A handful of state parks and private campgrounds exist on the river, but most of the time, as I found out from the first trip, I'd be looking to establish my own camping spot, ideally a flat, relatively soft plot of uncluttered earth where I could land the canoe and not be bothered. Islands were optimal, but only about half of them were suitable because heavy vegetation or high, steep banks made them inaccessible. Land owned by the Tennessee Valley Authority (TVA), wildlife management areas, and national wildlife refuges were good places for me to consider, but great campsites often didn't appear when I needed them.

That February leading up to my launch date—March 15—as winter extended into spring and long, hard rains fell across the Tennessee Valley, I would look out my window in east Tennessee and wonder if I had it in me to even start out in an open boat accompanied by an unruly pup I didn't know all that well, a sleeping bag for a bed, and a leaky tent as living quarters. Loved ones who supported the first trip didn't think it a great idea. My girlfriend, Catherine, worried about meth addicts accosting me. Meth addicts weren't something I worried about on the 1998 trip, and I thought it unlikely that I'd run into any on the Tennessee River twenty years later. Then, at a pre-launch speaking engagement at New Johnsonville State Park, on the river in west Tennessee, I made fun of Catherine's worry in front of a small audience, and a couple confirmed having come upon someone cooking meth at Birdsong Creek, just a few miles upriver. Somebody else chimed in about a lab they'd found on the riverbank.

My mother—ninety-three years old, a tireless supporter of my writing and the one who got me started in so many ways—said she had told her friends about my trip, and they had asked if I was an "idiot." It may have been idiotic, but I was driven to go up the river because I was curious about a couple of things: how the river had changed in twenty years, and how the passing of two decades had changed me. Would I be able to withstand the cold, the wind, the aching and the soreness? Would I need to use my Uncle Ed's sixteen-gauge shotgun—the same one I'd taken in 1998—to scare off varmints or villains? Would a tornado swoop down and send us flying above the bluffs of north Alabama or skipping like stones at lethal velocity across the surface of Guntersville Lake?

Nobody was making me go, and many gave good reasons not to do it.

I listened. But I went ahead anyway.

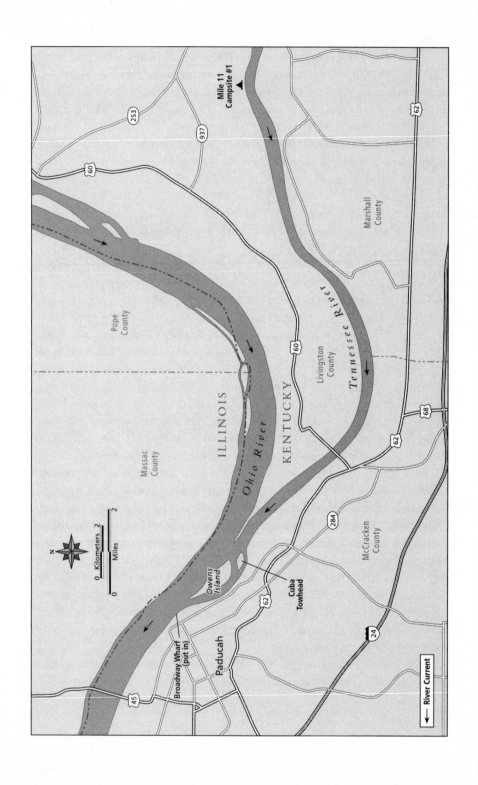

1

STAYING UPRIGHT

I stood inside Paducah's floodwall near the mouth of the Tennessee River and shivered as I stared out at its vast confluence with the Ohio. Pellets of cold rain stung my neck and face. Longtime friend Mel Purcell and I were the only ones there except for a few city workers using a crane to remove the two-story tall metal floodgates on this, the first day of spring 2018. February downpours had raised the Ohio twenty feet above normal. Kentucky Dam, twenty-two miles upstream on the Tennessee, had been spilling as much as 260,000 cubic feet per second, all of its twenty-four gates wide open, the tailwaters resembling a turbulent run of whitewater, rife with waves, whirlpools, and water that boiled and belched and bubbled up, as if about to explode. Kentucky Lake, behind the dam, had swollen to almost eleven feet above normal pool.

As I stood there trying to decide whether or not to launch, Mel danced around to keep warm, his hands jammed in the pockets of his sweatpants. Maggie watched us from my car, wet nose smearing the windows. The stiff north wind and the temperature—in the high thirties at mid-morning—made my adventure seem a lot less appealing than it had from the comfort of my house, as I made supply lists and studied maps. Where Mel and I stood, a half hour walk away from the Tennessee's Mile Zero, on the Ohio proper, workers were just beginning the process of dismantling the floodgates, which

In early March 2018, Kentucky Dam was discharging from all of its flood gates, creating a flow of 260,000 cubic feet per second. Photo credit: John Hewlett.

would allow you to drive a car to the water's edge. They wouldn't get to Broadway Wharf, my intended launching point, until the next day. So, unless I wanted to portage gear and canoe over a mile, the Tennessee, for the purposes of my adventure, was closed for business.

"Don't you check these kinds of things?" asked Mel. He had driven me here from our hometown, Murray, Kentucky, about an hour away.

I forced out a laugh. I expected such comments from a smart-aleck who had known me for over fifty years, who wasn't afraid to say aloud what was painfully obvious. Despite my meticulous preparations, it hadn't occurred to me that the floodgates protecting the city would still be up. After all, the Ohio had descended to near-normal in the last week or so. Maggie was ready for action, and I'd psyched myself up to begin a trip full of uncertainty, but common sense prevailed that day, the closed floodgates and the cold drizzle two clear omens not to launch when I didn't have to. Mel agreed to drop me off the next day for Launch Attempt Number Two.

If I'd known what the first five miles would be like, I never would have launched on that second day of spring. I might not have launched at all. Ever. The skies had cleared, but it was cool and windy, in the mid-forties, and nothing I'd done, or read, or heard prepared me for what awaited me.

Not launching on this cold day, with a fifteen to twenty mile-per-hour wind coming out of the north, at my back, would have been an option, but not a good one. I didn't want to ask Mel to bring me back to Paducah a third time. He'd do it, but I'd hear about it, too. Plus, the Ohio had descended to a reasonable level, and Kentucky Dam was forecast to spill around 100,000 cubic feet per second—the upper end of tolerable spillway volume for a canoeist to approach, I'd been told by a fishing guide. The lake behind the dam was at near-normal winter pool, exposing shoreline for me to camp on. All of this could change quickly with a heavy rain, so despite the chill and the wind, I felt I needed to take advantage of the forecast and the water levels.

The city workers in the process of removing the floodgate at Broadway Wharf didn't have the drive-through door open, but they let us walk in from the street where my car was parked, through the small doorway with canoe, dog, and gear—four trips of about 200 yards for Mel and me. After I told one worker about my plans, he said, "that's a lot of paddling." Understatement of the century.

Paducahans know about high water. In February 1937, before Kentucky Dam was built, what the Corps of Engineers called a 500-year flood rose up and covered ninety percent of the city with water. It was eight feet deep on Broadway Avenue. Ice chunks crashed through store windows. The river crested at over sixty feet, almost twenty-two feet above flood stage. Thirty-thousand of Paducah's 40,000 citizens were evacuated. The Flood Control Act of 1938 funded Paducah's three-mile-long, fourteen-foot-high flood wall, as well as an earthen levee system that extended nine more miles.

We got the boat loaded, frisky Maggie up near the bow, and I began pushing off with my paddle against the concrete ramp. Waves sloshed against the windward side of the plastic boat, some strong enough to sprinkle us, a cold launch-day christening. In an attempt to free us from the ramp, Mel put his foot on the gunnel and pushed down. Once a touring tennis professional who reached seventeenth in the world, you'd think Mel would be aware of the force he was capable of exerting. You'd think he'd know that pushing down on the top edge of a tippy boat would have consequences. He pushed down so hard with his foot that he nearly turned us over. At Mile Zero. I had to reach out with my right arm and brace against the concrete to keep us from capsizing. My entire arm, including my sleeve, was soaked

At Broadway Wharf in Paducah, Mile Zero, Maggie and I launched on the second day of spring, 2018. Photo credit: Mel Purcell.

and a half-gallon of water sloshed around in the bottom of the boat. Not the smooth start I was hoping for. And things would get worse.

In theory, a tailwind would seem to favor an old guy paddling upstream. It pushed me up the passageway between the industrialized right bank and two-mile-long Owens Island on my left. It, along with Cuba Towhead, a bit farther upstream, blocked the brunt of the north wind. The trouble with a tailwind is this: it is not constant, and it tends not to blow squarely at one's back. I had to fight to keep from being blown against the right bank, and by the time I got to the tip of Cuba Towhead, at an expanse of water where the Ohio and the mouth of the Tennessee merge, the wind was scraping whitecaps from the gunmetal surface, a phenomenon I would learn to dread on this trip. A fisherman in a small johnboat motored up and shouted over the wind: "I thought I was the crazy one." I wanted to chat, but the wind was having its way with both of us.

For the first five miles, the banks of the river are lined solid with barge-fleeting areas, places where towboats make up their loads and refuel. The bank is blocked by moored barges two and sometimes three deep. You have few gaps for an escape to the bank if you need to stop and rest from getting blown around like a paper cup. After a couple of miles I saw an opening and steered into a canal-like corridor between the line of barges and the bank, sheltered from the worst of the wind and waves. I assumed incorrectly that there would be another gap between barges where I could pass back into the main channel and continue on my way to Kentucky Dam. We pulled over to the bank for a stop at Jimar Paving Company, and Maggie, in her brand-new life jacket, promptly found something unspeakable to wallow in. She was experiencing the freedom of life without a leash for the first time, and her agenda was simple: discover rotten things she could sniff, eat, or wallow in. She also liked to dig and to run flat-out fifty-yard sprints, not always in a straight line. At this point in the trip, she had no idea how long we would be on the river, even though I had explained it to her. Like her, I was going full blast on this first day, but out of necessity, not choice.

I coaxed Maggie back onboard and continued onward in the corridor, passing under a walkway where my fishing rod, sticking up in the stern behind me, almost broke off. I lost one of my trusty lures, the Little Cleo, a silver spoon that I trolled with behind the canoe. I'd caught largemouth bass, smallmouth bass, striped bass, bluegill, catfish, drum, and even a couple of walleye with it. I had others, but it hurt to lose one out of such negligence, on the first day. After about a half-mile in the corridor, I was in the process of passing under an even lower walkway when Maggie abandoned ship. She bounded up onto the walkway above and accosted an employee on his way to work. As he politely fended off Maggie's friendly but aggressive advances, he told us we couldn't keep going the way we were. There was no opening to the river proper, and electrical lines snaking through the water might kill us. After I retrieved Maggie, we had to backtrack about a quarter-mile against the north wind, which took almost an hour of frantic paddling. This was my first experience with what I call the paddling treadmill. Maggie began to fidget and whine, as if doubting my competence.

Back in the channel, my goal was simple: stay upright. To accomplish this, I had to work the paddle constantly. Most of the time I paddled forward as fast as I could, looking like a human windmill. Watery swells rose up behind us and raised the stern, where I sat, and then lifted the bow, Maggie's spot, constantly tossing us up and down, as if on a teeter-totter. I had to use the two-bladed paddle as a rudder from time to time to steer the boat so that my back was square to the tailwind. Otherwise, we risked getting hit broadside by a wind that could tilt us over sideways.

Maggie staggered with the rising and falling, the yawing this way and that. I had no time to get a drink of water from the gallon jug under my seat, no time to grab a snack. I couldn't get my camera or phone out of a dry bag to take a photo. Workers at the barge terminals stared at us, but I couldn't stare back or wave or give the thumbs-up signal. A couple of times, the swells rose up so high that I was convinced the boat would flip over endwise, cartwheeling like George Clooney's fishing boat in *The Perfect Storm*. When I could keep the boat straight, water splashed over the bow as we dipped into the troughs. When wind pushed us sideways, water splashed mainly on me, and Maggie was getting wet from my frantic paddling. I thought we were going over for sure when the boat got turned broadside to the wind. But we stayed upright, and I paddled against the wind, toward the east bank, on my left, hoping the land and the moored barges would block the gusts. For some reason, it was even worse on the east bank, so I angled us back out into the middle of the channel.

Our immediate goal was the George Rogers Clark Bridge (Highway 60) visible up ahead, a boundary which marked a break in the barge terminals and, in theory, access to the bank as long as there was some place flat enough to land. No matter how hard I paddled, the bridge never seemed to get any closer. The tailwind kept shoving us, but it didn't seem to be moving us upriver. I would note this visual phenomenon—the distance mirage—many times on the voyage. I'd get excited about seeing a high-profile landmark up ahead—a bridge, a dam, some power lines—and then it would take an eternity to reach it. Staring at the object only made it worse, especially out in the middle of a lake, with no perspective on the bank going past, a better marker of progress.

I was exhausted after four hours of paddling. Breathing hard, my arms aching, I was feeling each of my fifty-nine years. I felt cramped, regardless of the fact that I'd set up the cushioned Old Town seat, with back support, and behind that I'd crammed the enormous rolled-up Paco Pad, a bright blue self-inflating luxury sleeping pad I'd bought for the trip. I could lean back and brace my feet against the thwart to pull strong strokes against the river, but I didn't know how long I could keep it up. I needed a break. Maggie had lain down, which stabilized the boat somewhat, but the swells and the wind kept pushing us this way and that as the river curved northeast. Up ahead, as I got closer to the bridge, it looked as if the water smoothed out and the whitecaps disappeared.

I was grateful for the old boat, which I almost didn't take on this trip. I considered a kayak, lower to the water and generally more efficient against current, but then I got Maggie, who grew into a larger dog than I thought she would, too big for the cockpit of a touring kayak. The Old Town was heavy—about eighty pounds empty—and it sat high out of the water, but I could load it down with gear, and we could move around in it, even stand up if we wanted to. Maggie often stood or pranced around from side to side. I stood for only a few seconds at a time, when I had to. For a canoe, the Old Town tracked well in flat water, which means that it maximized the efficiency of a paddle stroke, gliding a good distance from human propulsion. As today was proving, my canoe was stable in bad weather, difficult to turn over.

Canoes are old-school, a throwback to indigenous peoples and French fur traders, who not only floated downstream but also fought their way upstream long before we built the high dams on North American rivers. I liked this historical link with people propelling a boat with a paddle or a pole over long distances. I was in no big hurry; I wanted to go slow, to observe the details of the scenery, to see the changes from winter to spring.

A trolling motor might have come in handy, and I could have installed one on my canoe, but I did not want a motor, electric or gas/oil. I liked the idea of a cleaner voyage that left little imprint on the river and its banks. I liked the idea of propelling myself, the independence of it, and I think not having a motor on my canoe forced me to learn much more about the river, about the wind and the waves and the weather of the present and the future. I was close enough to the water to smell it, to reach out and touch it, and pulling through it in a canoe put me on intimate terms with the Tennessee. A motor would have made the trip easier, for certain, and probably safer, too. I would have been able to speed up in places I thought were less interesting, as if fast forwarding through a movie at the slow but important parts. A motor would have made unnecessary the strategies I would have to formulate regarding current and wind. In short, a motor would have dumbed-down the trip and made me like just about everyone else.

We stopped at Mile Eleven that evening, across from Wepfer Marine of Calvert City, a town where my father worked as a chemical operator for thirty years. At his company, General Aniline and Film (GAF), he worked a swing shift, a sequence of seven day shifts, seven afternoons, and seven midnights, with days off between shift changes. I don't think he slept much in his lifetime, and my shenanigans didn't make it any easier for him. He and my mother, a public librarian, made my life comfortable with their hard work and the solid upbringing they gave me. Despite current appearances, floating up a river in a canoe, I inherited their work ethic and gave everything I had to whatever I did. I'd tried many jobs—paperboy, house painter, window washer, dish washer, grocery stocker, landscaper, medical supply salesman, content provider for an immersive photography company—before settling in as a college writing teacher. What I'd done that first day on the river, one might consider work, even though I'd fallen far short of my goal, Haddock Ferry ramp at Mile Seventeen. It made me laugh a little to read a pre-trip diary entry where I wondered if I could "power on through" the first twenty-two miles, lock through the dam, and camp in Land Between the Lakes Recreation Area the first day. The first day!

I'd had enough paddling by five o'clock, and we pulled over at a sloped landing spot below a muddy, sheer bank thirty feet high. The strip of land below the bank, a mixture of mud and sand, had been underwater fairly recently, the level of the river below the dam—called "tailwaters"—having fallen from thirty feet to fifteen. My rubber boots sank ankle deep in the mud on the first few steps, but I was able to find a spot firm enough to pitch a tent and start a small fire. Maggie ate her dinner and ambled toward a rotting fish. I grabbed her by the collar and tied her to a big chunk of driftwood half buried in the mud. When I wasn't looking, she dragged the driftwood a few yards toward the lovely rotting fish. I don't think I could have budged this piece of wood. Her energy and force of will amazed me. I sat on a log, added boiling water to my packet of beef stroganoff, and closed it up to let it "cook." These dehydrated dinners were my sustenance for most of the trip, along with oatmeal, extra-crunchy peanut butter, tortillas, homemade trail mix, Clif bars, and apples. I could write up a weight loss plan: eat all the dehydrated food you want, everything from stroganoff to Mexican rice with chicken to biscuits and gravy. Eat portions for two, for three! Have gobs of peanut butter on flour tortillas. Have a tortilla any time you feel like it. Oh yes, and paddle at least twelve miles a day against current and wind. Guaranteed weight loss.

That night, camped somewhere between rural Livingston and Marshall counties, just a couple of miles south of the Ohio River, I cocooned myself in my sleeping bag as the temperature dropped below freezing, as it would several nights that spring. I admitted Maggie into the tent, without her stinking life jacket, and she got into her corner, sometimes nudging me with her bulk off a portion of the Paco Pad. She grumble-growled at me for space. This routine I called "aggressive snuggling." It would be a stretch to say that I slept well that night, but the bag and the tent kept me warm, and a hot water bottle, along with a last-minute purchase, a pair of down-filled booties, helped warm my feet, which had gotten wet in the splashy paddling that day.

All night, the Wepfer boys worked, the spotlights of their pushboats sweeping across the 500 yards of river between us. Barges and their spotlights would become fairly commonplace from here on to Kentucky Dam and beyond. In this stretch, between the Ohio and the dam, they ruled the river, especially this time of year when few others motored this section for fish or pleasure. I bet the Wepfer workers were wondering why the heck anybody would want to camp on this part of the river, in this kind of weather, but they were too busy to come over and find out.

2

LOCKING THROUGH

The next morning, awakened by birdsong, I did not want to emerge from my sleeping bag to put on frosty wet boots and break camp. I was grateful we had survived the previous day relatively unscathed, and looking back on it, I don't remember a time—including on whitewater—of such sustained terror. Capsizing was one of my biggest fears on this trip. Turning over in water this cold—around fifty-two degrees—could have been catastrophic, even deadly. First, I'd have to turn the boat upright while treading water, retrieve what gear was floating, and get back into the boat, no simple feat. I'd next have to paddle to somewhere that I could land the canoe, not an easy task on that first five miles, and bail out the boat. Then I'd have to dry out what got wet, including myself. I'd have to change clothes and get warm enough to stop shaking. Oh yeah—and I'd have to retrieve poor Maggie. Who knows where she would have ended up? Who knows what else I would lose?

That morning I was feeling weary from the exertion and stress of the day before. I consoled myself by telling Maggie that things would get a lot easier once we locked through Kentucky Dam and made it to Mile Fifty-five; we'd have a good break there, at my sister Melissa's lake-house, called "Hopetown," where, in the summer, she ran a camp for kids as part of her company, Daystar Counseling Ministries.

I started another driftwood fire on the mud beach and considered the challenges of the day ahead. Kentucky Dam was by far the busiest of the Tennessee's nine dams, and I was concerned about whether they would lock me through going upstream in a canoe. Going downstream in 1998, I had few problems locking through dams. Lowering a boat from one reservoir to the next resembled waiting inside a giant bathtub that was draining— peaceful, cool and shady—also a little smelly. To lock through boats going upstream, the operators had to raise the level in the chamber by pumping water in, which created turbulence. I had done a rehearsal, without Maggie, at Watts Bar Dam, in east Tennessee, and the process seemed as peaceful and uneventful as a downstream passage. The lock operator told me he'd given me "a slow lift." He was congenial and curious about my upcoming trip but could not say for certain whether I'd be able to lock through the other eight dams. The policy, he said, would differ for each dam.

Instead of calling dams a day or two ahead of my arrival and finding out the policy, I thought a better strategy would be to show up near the lock and call then. I'd rehearsed what I was going to say: "I'm in a canoe paddling upstream, and I was wondering if you'd lock us through." I liked the "wondering" part. I meant it to convey that I wasn't cocky enough to presume they would lock me through, and it was coy enough that I hoped it would disarm even the most by-the-book lock operator. But first I had eleven miles to paddle, and I had no idea when the prodigious current released from the dam would start pushing against me with greater force than it had so far. I'd be heading generally east and then south, but for now, in the early morning, no wind had risen.

As I was about to finish my cup of instant coffee, a squadron of geese flew past close enough that I could hear their wings beating the air. Without honking, they whooshed by me a few yards away, close to the water, as if I were part of their world and not an intruder. It was a good reminder of why I was doing this in the first place, for moments like those—rare, calming, and spontaneous. Understated beauty on a cold, cold morning, the sun rising just above the horizon, giving light but no warmth.

Launching, I ferried from our camp to the south side of the river to stay in favor of wind and current. I approached the *Betsy Wepfer*, a tug idling upstream of Wepfer Marine, and paused below the pilot house, wondering whether I could stay on the south side and pass alongside the barges or if they wanted me to cross back to the opposite bank.

"Keep doing what you're doing!" shouted a deckhand before I could ask anything.

This was heartening advice, which I took in a more general way than I'm sure he intended. A few miles farther upstream, I got scolded by a barge crew making up a load of coal. I was on the north bank and wanted to stay there, out of the wind, but up ahead was a fleeting area where a tow had angled his load so that the lead barges seemed moored to the bank I was favoring. I couldn't tell, but I figured there had to be a gap there between the front of his load and the bank, enough for a canoer to slip through. My motto was to "make every paddle stroke count," so veering off for a wide turn to the opposite bank around this guy was not what I wanted to do. When I got to within a couple hundred yards of the moored front barges, I began to see that, if there was a gap, it was a narrow one. A deckhand spotted me and told me I needed to turn around.

"Sorry about that," he said. "I don't mean to be a jerk, but you can't get through up there."

I turned around, and as I approached the towboat, the guy I took to be the captain came out and was a little firmer: "You never want to get between a load and the bank," he said.

We stopped at Haddock Ferry for lunch, my original destination for camping that first night. I'd scouted this place from the bank in January, before the big rains, because I knew that camping would be a major challenge on this muddy riverine section. I had noted the boat ramp, which generally meant public property, and a decent clearing near the river to pitch a tent. Now, the narrow little road to the ramp was closed, either washed out or covered with debris from the recent floods. My would-be camping spots were still underwater.

The current got stronger the closer we got to the dam, and for a long time I could see I-24, a mile below the dam. It was a sunny and warmer than the day before, with less wind, but the current had picked up. Suffering from the visual distance-mirage of the interstate bridge ahead, I paddled and paddled, but it never seemed to get any nearer. Around four o'clock I passed under the interstate, pulled into a little creek just upstream of the Highway 641 bridge, called the lock operator, and recited my rehearsed line.

"Sure, no problem," he said, "but it will be a couple of hours."

He was locking through a barge going upstream, the same direction as me, and he told me to tie up near the barge cells, round metal cylinders the diameter of grain silos. They were 100 yards from the bank toward the main part of the dam, near the tailwater current. I'd checked the TVA website that day: 90,000 cubic feet of water per second flowed from the generators and flood gates, just under the flow rate that the fishing guide had told me was safe. But where I was, near the north bank, very little current was visible on the lock side which was separated from the face of the dam by a wedge of land reinforced with big rocks called riprap. I asked the lock operator if I could paddle on up to the guide wall and tie up there.

"Okay," he said, "if you can make it up that far."

This didn't make sense to me. I'd have to "make it that far" if I were going to lock through. I paddled on up to the guide wall, about a quarter of a mile, no problem. What I'd forgotten from my scouting trips was that the right guide wall is only about ten feet long. I could not get behind it for shelter the way I had planned. We would be exposed to a lot of turbulence if the lock operator decided to let another barge come through going downstream. He said he would call me when he was ready for us. I tied off to the rocks and tried to calm Maggie, who wanted to jump out and explore the sloped wall of riprap.

After an hour, a guy motored up in a fishing boat and asked, "Seen any skipjack a-jumpin'?"

I said that I sure hadn't. I knew what a skipjack was and that some fishermen used them for bait to catch the monsters that lurked below dams, but I wouldn't know one by its jump.

A little later, just a few feet away from us, a tow's wheel wash troubled the waters like a Class V rapid, and I tried to calm Maggie and hold tight to the line that held us in place. I think this tow must have had such a big load going upstream that the crew had to break it up into sections, and was getting into position to finish the process. By half past six, as the sky began to threaten rain and the temperature dropped, I became concerned. It had been over two hours and nobody had called me.

I called the operator. A different guy than before answered. He said it would be a while longer and asked me if he had my correct number. He did not. I began to worry a bit about these guys. I waited another hour, until it was dark, and called again.

"Paddle on up to the doors," he said. "I'm ready for you."

I was already nervous about the way Maggie would act inside the lock. Would she fidget and whine and rock the boat? That's the last thing I wanted on the first dam. I imagined that these lock operators communicated with each other, and if we created a ruckus, he'd warn the others upstream about the rowdy dog with the geezer in the old green canoe. Approaching such a large-scale industrial structure in the dark only added to my horror and dread.

On the phone, the operator told us to tie up at the front bollard or bitt, a yellow-painted iron post that would rise (or descend) with the level of the water. Toward the front of the lock, for some reason, the turbulence wasn't as bad. Maggie was calm as we rose up around seventy feet to the level of vast Kentucky Lake, on the other side of the dam, calmer waters, I thought, the pathway to refuge at Hopetown in a few days.

As the water rose to the bottom of the iron gates in front of us, it rushed into cavities at the lower part of the barrier, sucking and splashing mightily. Maggie looked but did not react. So far, so good. Then, toward the end, the ungodly whirlpools spun faster all around us, and I tried not to look at them because they induced dizziness. I tightened my grip on the line around the bollard as the bow of my canoe whooshed back and forth, and I tried to keep the boat flat against the slimy, smelly wall. Toward the end of the process, the lock operator leaned over the wall a few yards above us.

"There are a bunch of barges wanting to lock through. What do you want me to tell them you're going to do?" he asked, tension in his voice.

"I'll head to the left, toward the bank."

He had some other things to say, but I couldn't hear because Maggie started barking as if to tell him off. One thing I heard was to stay away from the mooring cells.

The doors of the lock opened up from the center to a city of barges, their lights searching the water around them and sweeping across me as if I were an escaping prisoner. With my tiny headlamps shining forward and aft, I paddled hard to the left, toward a creek where Vulcan Materials (crushed stone, sand, and gravel) had a fleeting area. Paddling through the dark past the three or four barges, I could sense their impatience for me to be out of their way. I'd have to hug the bank, find a suitable place to land, and set up camp at night under a sliver of moon. Maggie, exhausted, had settled down as we passed Light House Landing and the port of Grand Rivers, whose lights seemed brilliant and infinite against the oblivion that surrounded us. I'd paddled at night enough times to know how it transformed everything, how you had to look twice at what lay ahead and not get overly excited. What looked like the Loch Ness monster passed a few feet in front of our bow, a twenty-foot long column of writhing water. This turned out to be a pair of cruising beavers and the wake they created with their powerful webbed feet. In another hour, around ten o'clock, we landed near the canal that connected Kentucky and Barkley lakes. I had officially arrived at the northern end of Land Between the Lakes (LBL), an undeveloped strip of land that the Forest Service managed, which lay between the Tennessee and Cumberland rivers, now lakes at this location. I fumbled around in darkness, setting up camp while Maggie sprinted up and down the beach tossing driftwood into the air. I fed her, got her into the tent, and ate my own dinner—peanut butter smeared across a tortilla—before descending into a deep sleep.

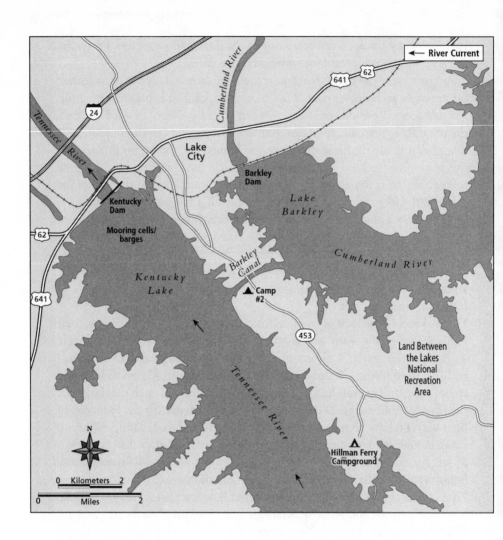

3

CLIMBING IN A BOAT

Aloud, authoritative voice awoke me, a know-it-all pontificating from the road above, one walker talking to another. When I sat up, my annoyance turned to panic: Maggie was gone. She'd somehow let herself out of the tent, perhaps to investigate the voice. I may have left the zipper open just a crack and she'd used her nose to open it wide enough to escape. The other possibility, that she had the wherewithal and dexterity to open a complicated double zipper system, made me worry about her potential for mayhem. Fortunately, she had not gone far. Just a few yards from the tent, she was digging into the sand with such energy that great gouts of it flew up behind her. To get her to stop, I filled her bowl with dog food from the five-gallon bucket and then sat on it to boil water for coffee. The hiker's voice grew fainter, and I thanked Maggie for not pursuing him and introducing herself.

Getting past that first dam, past the strong tailwater current and through the lock, was a big relief. Now we were on the longest and widest lake of the river, in territory where I had grown up—home turf—and I looked forward to some easy paddling for a couple of days, and then some rest under a roof at my sister's place.

I liked to think of myself as an adventurer on some modest level, the modesty arising from the fact that I wasn't paddling the Yukon or the

We were fortunate to find this campsite after dark on night two; in Land Between the Lakes, it faces the canal that links Kentucky and Barkley lakes.

Zambezi but traveling through familiar territory in an era of cell phones and emergency helicopters, unlike one of my canoeing heroes, Alexander MacKenzie. In the late-eighteenth century, he embarked on a trip into the unknown, toward one of the many blank spaces on Earth, the Northwest Territories of what is now Canada. MacKenzie led a fleet of canoes, with a crew of hardened voyageurs and native guides, to find the Northwest Passage from Montreal to the Pacific, which would open up maritime trade with Russia and China. He failed in his quest, turning back at the Arctic Ocean, which was frozen and impassable year-round. In his book *Disappointment River*, Brian Castner tells MacKenzie's story alongside the narrative of his own canoe trip down what is now known as the MacKenzie River, which showed little change since that first trip 200 years before. Though the hardships of MacKenzie's journey into the unknown dwarfed my own challenges, his exploration and others like it fascinated me. I envied these explorers and the time in which they lived, when we didn't think we knew everything.

Nobody fills in the blank spaces of the Earth any more. Hovering satellites have obliterated them; people hardly use the paper maps that showed those blank spaces. Still, looking at any kind of map—Google maps on a phone

We took a lunch break on the shoreline of Land Between the Lakes
near Hillman Ferry Campground, around Mile 29.

or the Army Corps of Engineers' Navigational Charts that I had open in
front of me in a waterproof clear plastic envelope—differed so much from
actually traversing a place on the ground or across water. This disparity
between representation and reality would play out again and again on
this trip. Crossing familiar waters where I had grown up, I was retracing
what memory had mapped for me, filling in the blank spaces of what I had
forgotten. Images from my past would emerge on this part of the voyage:
my father and grandfather taking me bank fishing before I could walk a
straight line or bait my own hook; motoring a small boat across the lake
and jumping off a rocky outcropping into the warm, deep waters where I
could lose myself in the silence below the surface; hiking late at night with
a gaggle of hooligans to the ruins of a hotel high above the lake and filling
the woods with smoke, shouts, and laughter. In one of my first memories of
Kentucky Lake, I was walking across it with Rusty Sims, my oldest friend,
when we were around the age of eight. We stomped on its frozen surface
at Pine Bluff, where his parents had a cabin. Rusty remembers us cradling
big chunks of riprap and slamming them down onto the ice. Who knows
why? We deserved a Darwin Award. I don't know if the lake froze all the

way across at this time, in the mid-1960s, but we wandered out 100 yards, unsupervised, unaware that we were seeing something that probably hadn't happened until then and probably wouldn't ever happen again.

Over the years, the more I learned about the Tennessee, the more connected to it I felt. I read about what the river was like before the dams, before the Tennessee Valley Authority's inception in the 1930s. I was able to talk to some old timers who knew the river before the dams. One, Charley Dickey, took a long paddling trip on the free-flowing river in 1936 and drank untreated water from it, unthinkable now. Much of what I learned about the river came from Donald Davidson's two-volume history, *The Tennessee*. He described a wild waterway that, before it was segmented by dams, meandered and boiled and shoaled up, making navigation difficult for early European explorers and settlers in flatboats, and later on for steamboats that freighted commerce. Below Chattanooga, where I was headed, strong currents in turbulent sections with nicknames like the Suck, the Pot, and the Skillet, confused and terrified navigators. For a time, the Chickamauga tribe fired arrows at whites like Colonel John Donelson, on his way to settle what would become Nashville, on the Cumberland River. Muscle Shoals, near Florence, Alabama, made the water boil up to form an impassable barrier at most river levels. The river was alive, animate and dangerous in ways long forgotten, its wild character a victim of progress. Wilson was the first dam built to help commercial traffic negotiate the shoals by controlling the water level below the structure. It was also built to power industry that supported the military in World War I. The pre-TVA river was known for catastrophic flooding, most notably in 1936. Floods still occur, but their severity has been mitigated because the dams allow manipulation of reservoir levels so that water can be stored and released in the rainy seasons (late fall/winter/early spring).

By virtue of being forgotten, a known place on the map can become blank again, at least obscured. The dams, having segmented the river into separate reservoirs, have not only allowed us to generate power and to prevent catastrophic flooding and improve navigation, but they have also obscured the Tennessee's character as a continuous river across the South that connects Appalachia with the Midwest. Many do not know where the dammed river begins and ends, what cities and states it flows through, why it has been important to cultures for hundreds of years of recorded history, and long before, in peace and in war, for commerce and recreation. Segmenting the Tennessee into nine lakes blocked the natural flow of the river and also created a barrier to our knowledge of it as a whole. A fisherman might know Kentucky Lake between the dam and Paris Landing, at Tennessee's northern border, but once the lake narrows into a more riverine section less hospitable for fishing and marina culture, its habitat and its wildlife typically become less familiar to that Kentuckian. People I met on this trip would stop referring to the river as a lake as soon as I got into Tennessee. Even though it still looked like a lake in Perryville—wide, calm, without visible current—the Park ranger at Mousetail Landing referred to it as the Tennessee River. Was he correct? Of course. And so is any Kentuckian who refers to it as Kentucky Lake all the way up until the lock at Pickwick Dam.

Segmenting the river and altering its geography and landscape into what Donald Davidson calls "the new river," obscured its history. Momentous events, some tragic and bloody, transpired on the old river, and ghosts like Ulysses Grant can still be conjured up as you travel upstream, shadowing Grant's route early in the Civil War. He and his troops were either marching or traveling by steamboat up the river, supported by ironclad gunboats during the battles of Fort Henry, Fort Donelson (on the Cumberland), and Shiloh, the bloodiest conflict in American history at that time. On my way upstream, I planned stops at Shiloh and at Johnsonville State Park, where Confederate General Nathan Bedford Forrest won an impressive but ultimately inconsequential victory late in the war.

On that third day, starting out from the site of Maggie's impressive escape, I could see the outline of Eggner's Ferry Bridge, sixteen miles upstream, a prominent landmark I would focus on for a day and a half. Starting out on Day Three, I could see only the tops of the main span girders wavering in the haze. This was visible evidence that in going upstream, I was rising in elevation, climbing in a boat. This kind of thing would be more obvious on a river whose headwaters begin in the mountains and descend dramatically with rapids and waterfalls before flattening out in a valley, such as the Little River in east Tennessee, which emerges in the Smokies at an elevation of 5,100 feet and bottoms out at 814 feet, where it meets the Tennessee River in Blount County. It transforms itself from a whitewater stream popular with trout fisherman and kayakers, to a waterway bordered by farms, its deeper segments populated with smallmouth bass and bluegill. This kind of change is less obvious on the Tennessee, which descends a total of 500 feet in its 652 miles, an average of only about eight inches per mile. Still, going upstream meant that I'd not only be battling current but scaling gradient as well.

On the 1998 downstream trip, the landscape ran in cycles, from wide lakes to narrow riverine sections below dams. Starting with Fort Loudoun Lake in east Tennessee, I would leave what I considered the monotony of a lake and look forward to the relaxing process of being lowered in the lock of a dam to the tailwaters below it, where the banks rose high and muddy, cut off sheer from the frequent rise and fall of the water. I could coast here without much effort as the banks slid past. On this trip, I would approach the riverine sections with some dread, at the mercy of tailwater current that fluctuated from flood control or power generation. The high banks and the muddy, narrow flats below them also made the riverine sections a challenge for camping. On this trip, instead of dreading open lakes, I looked forward to the lock gates opening up to their expansive views, in particular the gravel and sand bars that reached out to extend a surface for smooth canoe landings and flat, firm plots for my tent. Wind was the wild card in the downstream/upstream landscape esthetic; it could change my affections for a lake in an instant, no matter whether it blew at my back, across the bow, or in my face.

Now, on Kentucky Lake, the wind was working against my goal of making headway in a generally southwesterly course. Crossing my path early on that day, a fisherman foot-pedaled a kayak, leaving his hands free for vaping and for casting with one of the several rods that protruded from his boat like porcupine quills. Steam flowed from his mouth and nose like the smokestacks of sternwheelers from Mark Twain's time. His progress

We stopped for a break on the Land Between the Lakes side of Kentucky Lake, where Maggie considered some rock climbing.

against the wind seemed effortless as I struggled to inch forward alongside the jagged rocky bluffs of Land Between the Lakes.

"Like your setup," he said, blowing past me.

I would have camped in LBL another night, but my sister's place was on the west side of the lake, and I wanted to cross before the end of the day to meet my launching buddy Mel at Cherokee boat ramp, where I planned to camp. During the crossing that afternoon, the wind rose up so strongly that Maggie and I had to break through waves that bounced us up and down for two and a half miles. We would fall far short of our goal and have to improvise to find a suitable place to pitch the tent that night.

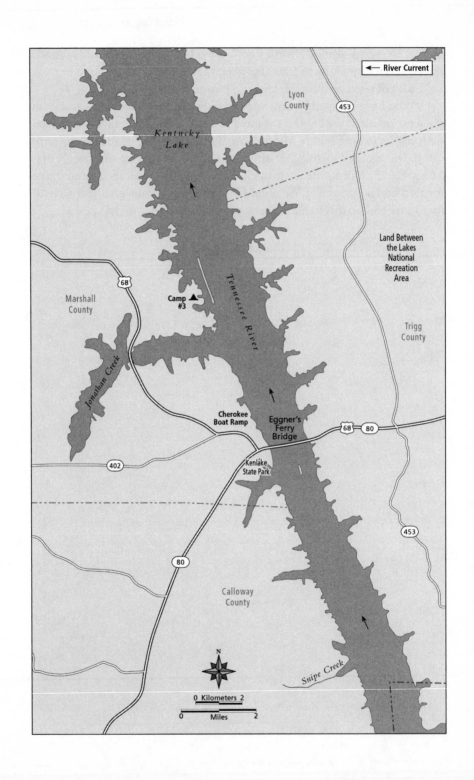

4

THE FAMILIAR MADE EXOTIC

Wilderness is good for us—we know this. Trouble is, we live in a culture that values economic growth, development, and the commodification of nature over the preservation of wilderness, making it necessary for most of us to travel a good distance to visit wild places. They are disappearing, and the ones that remain are becoming more and more remote from where we live. Remote does not equal wild, and often the definition of each is slippery and subjective.

Rebecca and Ryan Means have been on a quest to find and document the most remote places in each state. Their definition is precise: "The remotest location within a state is the point that is the farthest straight-line distance from a road or a city/town. It is a point on the landscape that is marked by a set of geographical coordinates (latitude and longitude)." The goal of what the Means call Project Remote is to show how difficult it is becoming to find the proverbial "middle of nowhere," that these places are disappearing, and that we need to preserve them. The authors acknowledge that the *feeling* of remoteness "varies with a person's experience, perspective, and comfort zone." What they're after is a quantitative, non-biased measurement, a complex task. They did not, for example, include places on the water, and they only included islands after some deliberation about whether they were "developable" or not.

On Kentucky Lake, I felt immersed in remoteness that third day, particularly as I paddled near the LBL side where roads are fewer, often unpaved, and no houses or businesses are allowed. Other circumstances added to a more subjective feeling of remoteness on both sides of the lake. After we made the bouncy crossing through the waves from the east side to the west side of the lake, we stopped on a gravel bar for a break. Other than the pedaling kayaker of early morning, the lake was empty of boats and I'd seen no one on the banks. I got the dog food bucket out of the boat to sit on and look at the Corps of Engineers charts to determine how far we were from Cherokee boat ramp. As I eased my weight onto it, the bucket sank into the shifty moist gravel, and I fell over sideways, so tired from the bouncy crossing that I was unable to extend an arm out to brace myself for impact. I lay there for a minute. Maggie, who had been exploring, came over and poked her nose into my hair.

Clouds crowded the eastern horizon as the day waned, and I thought I could paddle a bit farther to find a good campsite short of Cherokee, but the wind rose up and cut short our scouting. A twenty mile-per-hour gust drove us onto an even more narrow gravel bar only fifty yards from the previous rest stop. This place I would dub Locust Point campsite, a peninsula featuring a grove of thorny locust trees up on a knoll. The light went out of the day and the wind gusted harder. Rain splatted off and on. To call this knob of land where we settled that night a clearing would be a stretch. My first task, in the dark, was to set up a windbreak with tarp, rope, and bungee cords. Meanwhile, Maggie, whose mood fit the weather, ran wild. I'd get one corner of the tarp secured and then snatch at another corner and almost get the knot tied just as the wind gusted and jerked the fabric out of my grasp. Then followed my cursing of the wind and then of Maggie as she rampaged through camp tromping over the fallen tarp. She grabbed a piece of rope from the bag and took off running with it, leaving a trail of white nylon through the thorny darkness. At one point in the process, I shined my headlamp on the ground and caught her fondling my snorkeling gear, which she had dragged out of the rope bag. I yelled at her again, my voice faint in the roaring wind, and chided myself for bringing along gear that seemed absurd in this weather, on this lake. Though Maggie didn't feel the need for it, there was some urgency in my preparations for camp because I thought a storm was fast approaching.

Too frantic to stop and check the radar on my phone, I kept working at the tarp, and Maggie kept mocking me by barking and obstructing my path and feinting, as if to get me to chase her. As I staggered about on the uneven terrain, low hanging thorns gouged my face and hands. Rain fell off and on, big drops flung unevenly from the sky, and the temperature dropped into the forties. Stringing up the tarp as a windbreak would make it possible for me to pop up the tent and take shelter on this windblown peninsula, fifteen miles from Murray, where I was born and grew up, the gravel bar that the wind had chosen for us transformed by circumstance and weather into remote wilderness.

When I got the fourth corner of the tarp tied off, it ballooned out like a sail, creating a little calm place for the tent. Once we got inside, our weight held it in place. It never rained much that night. We were within a mile of somebody's driveway, and a bit past that was a road and a small community, but as far as what I was feeling that night among the locust trees, I may as well have been scouting for Alexander MacKenzie in the Northwest Territories of the eighteenth century. How anyone could have come to get me tonight at this place, I did not know.

I was grateful for daybreak and the passing of a night that promised storms but didn't deliver. Across the lake from the Locust Point campsite rose the rounded-off bluffs of LBL, scenery that some might find monotonous because of the absence of humanity, of houses and yards and docks, the lack of what might be termed majesty in landscape, something rocky, jagged and dangerous-looking, perhaps a violent waterfall or a pinnacle that looked impossible to scale, all features of what is known as the sublime. This landscape awaited me upriver, but just now and for the weeks to follow, I was falling in love with the more subtle esthetic of Kentucky Lake in early spring. Giant hardwoods rose on thick trunks branching into skeletal limbs, the ground beneath them crunchy on top but soft underneath, all of it a calming blend of browns and grays, with the occasional smattering of cedars and pines. On both sides of the lake, coves led up to creeks that trickled from the hillsides, clear, greenish-tinted water revealing gravel bottoms. The coves, named after tributaries that once flowed freely into the main channel—Jonathan Creek, Blood River, Ledbetter Creek—made good places for camping, boat ramps, and a few beaches, like Wildcat, a high school hangout for me. Though the landscape looked austere, especially this time of year, and though it could treat you cruelly if you were living outdoors, it also created deep calm and stillness inside me. I had grown from this soil and it still nurtured me. I looked forward to heading farther south and tracking the change of seasons, the emerging buds and blossoms, but just now the lingering winterscape of Calloway County gave me a deep sense of connection to my surroundings.

Propelling me forward that morning was the knowledge that I was only a few miles from Cherokee boat ramp and lunch catered by Mel, the friend who had kicked off my voyage with the hard nudge that almost capsized us.

"Surprise me," I said to him on the phone, "and it doesn't have to be healthy."

Three and a half days into the trip, I didn't know how much weight I had lost, though I knew from a recent doctor's visit that I could stand to lose fifteen to twenty pounds. I felt hollowed-out by the trip so far. The constant, panic-fueled paddling and the rigors of setting up campsites left me craving something besides dehydrated food packets. I fantasized about what Mel would bring. If anyone knew what Murray and Calloway County could offer a starving canoer, he would. For some reason, I longed for a cheeseburger, as I would the entire trip. Murray was not known for haute cuisine, but you could get good burgers, great barbecue, and excellent country cooking.

Rain misted off and on as Maggie and I landed near the Cherokee boat ramp, a sloped concrete driveway thirty yards long and ten wide like hundreds of others on this river, though this place had a history that went deeper than the utilitarian access point. I was waiting for my lunch at what used to be Cherokee State Park, established for African Americans in 1951, when nearby Kenlake State Park had a whites-only policy. The TVA owned Cherokee and leased it to the state. It had a dining hall/restaurant, cabins, and a beach. Billed as the "finest colored vacation site in the South," it was one of only three segregated parks in the United States. With the advent of the Civil Rights movement and desegregation, it was shut down in 1964, and the cabins were moved to Kenlake. Over the years, the park was neglected and became overgrown. But a group called Friends of Cherokee Historic State Park spearheaded a restoration effort to preserve the park for what it represented. In 2010, the park was dedicated in a ceremony where Kentucky Governor Steve Beshear said, "Places like Cherokee make sure we don't forget our history" (Lough, *Murray Ledger and Times* September 16, 2010).

Now, aside from the boat ramp, a parking lot and a couple of overlooks, the dining hall was about all that remained; it was named the Richard H. Lewis Lodge and functioned as a rental space for conferences. For Maggie and me, it was shelter from that morning's drizzle. We stood under a canopy at the entrance near the lodge's locked doors. The park was deserted except for a couple of fishermen putting in boats at the ramp.

Mel texted me that he was just pulling into "dunkn" and he'd meet me in half an hour.

"Thanks for ruining the surprise," I texted. "Dunkn," I thought, was Dunkin' Doughnuts. I was a little disappointed, but I decided not to be picky and began fantasizing about freshly brewed coffee and what Mel would bring from DD, aside from the obvious.

Mel's front passenger seat was filled with bags of food and drink. There was nothing from Dunkin' Doughnuts, no coffee, but two tall Heinekens, a tall Coors Light, a cheeseburger, a prime rib sandwich, fries, an ice–water, a Coke, a bag of chips, two pieces of cake, and some chocolate candy bars. He'd gone to Dumplin's, an upscale, locally-owned restaurant, the kind of tidy, well-lit place where my mother liked to have lunch with her friends. Mel had also stopped at Duncan's Take Me Back Café, east of Murray; the opposite of Dumplin's, in a way, it was a gas station and convenience store with a small kitchen and dining room. That's where the cheeseburger, fries, chips, and drinks came from.

I ate the cheeseburger and some of the chips, and I guzzled the Coke— something I never drink in everyday life—then ripped off the plastic lid to crunch the ice. Dumplin's fancy prime rib sandwich was very good, but I couldn't finish it, nor could I eat many of the fries. Maggie profited from this. I passed on the cake, which was fine with Mel, who said he'd stopped at Dumplin's for the desserts. We were tempted by the beer, or I was, but it was barely noon, and I needed to get back on the river in the pause between downpours. Mel had brought me a two-gallon jug of water, though I had requested one gallon. I restrained myself from commenting on this. As he was unloading more supplies for me, Maggie jumped into the backseat of his car, as if to desert me. It took some roughhousing to get her out and much coaxing to persuade her to get back into the boat, so we could continue upriver and pass under Eggner's Ferry Bridge, my landmark for the past day and a half, now within shouting distance. The experts promised real storms tonight, an organized front, and I hoped to find a better place to camp than Locust Point, perhaps something more sheltered from the wind.

The old Eggner's Ferry Bridge, which I had driven over hundreds of times on my way to LBL and beyond, had been demolished a few years back. The dynamiting of the old bridge, playing out on social media, was a highly-choreographed obliteration of a historical landmark that I could not erase from memory, despite the shiny new bridge which I was now paddling toward. My Uncle Ed, whose shotgun I was carrying, had committed suicide by jumping from the old bridge, and I had been the last one to see him the day he did it. He'd been depressed from a long strike at his workplace, and he'd come by for me to help him check something on his car. He wasn't talking much and I didn't press him. I was fifteen, not a big talker myself, and I was grumpy because he'd gotten me out of bed before noon on a cold November day. From our house, he drove straight to the lake, walked to the center span, hung up his jacket on a bolt, and leapt.

My dad and I came to the bridge the next afternoon. We sat in the car and watched the search for Ed's body. I don't remember what we said, but I think we were hoping that it was all a mistake and Ed would walk up the bank, wet and cold, an unlikely survivor of the impact and that cold, cold water. We'd both been close to Ed, who for months had wanted the strike to end, his idleness and the consternation and harassment of his co-workers a weight he could no longer bear. He might have had other reasons to despair. A Navy veteran of the South Pacific in World War II, Ed never said a word to me about his time on a tank landing ship, and I later wondered if he might also have suffered from PTSD.

Even though the old bowstring-truss bridge with its narrow two-lane highway had been replaced by a sleek new four-lane, the place still haunted me. My Aunt Robbie, Ed's wife and sister of my dad, always went silent when we drove her over the bridge, and she'd let out a big sigh when we got to the other side. In a strange way, I liked crossing the bridge in a car, passing under it by boat, or camping near it, as I did on the downstream 1998 canoe trip. I remember starting a little fire on the shoreline, the brittle river shale popping as flames rose up into the chilly October night. I meditated on the final stage of that canoe trip and the finality of Ed's act, what drove him to it, what it meant that I was the last one to talk to him, what I could have said that might have changed his course that day.

The old bridge, built in 1932, had been through a lot. It had to be raised to accommodate the higher water level that Kentucky Dam created ten years later. Then, in 2012, a cargo ship collided with it, collapsing one of the main spans. No one was hurt, though one vehicle stopped five feet from the edge of the 322-foot span that fell. I'm sure that driver will never forget the old bridge, which was repaired and used until 2016, when it was blown up, the new version, a handsome tiered-arch bridge, already in place. New Eggner's Ferry is urban and shiny, and I miss the old bridge's rusty girders. At the same time, it's a lot easier to cross the lake on a four-lane, and a multi-use lane allows you to walk or bike from one side to the other.

The closer that Maggie and I got to the new bridge, the more the wind increased, the higher the waves rose. This made it necessary to paddle harder through a threshold where I wanted to linger. Perhaps this was a sign to move on, to avoid dwelling so much on the past. Beyond the bridge, we angled toward Kenlake State Park, on the west bank, and on this side the waves calmed and the sun broke free from clouds. Trees on the rounded-off hills reached toward a deep blue sky, and a smattering of dogwood blooms popped white against the brown and gray of the slopes. I studied the houses that began to appear on the bank and thought about what I would like to live in, what I could afford and what would be low maintenance. I would have

Maggie settled in for our passage under Eggner's Ferry Bridge on Kentucky Lake.

a cabin with a huge deck and a screened porch. It would have to be on the main lake, not back in a creek, and it would have to sit on a hill with trees and a natural area, no big lawn to mow. Houses on this part of Kentucky Lake ranged from colossal mansions with intricate terraced landscaping to older houses that looked lived-in and comfortable—places where a mutt like Maggie would fit in.

For now, we were vagabonds looking for a new home each night. Though the sun warmed us now, a storm front approached, and I focused on finding some uninhabited shoreline to land the boat and set up camp. Each time we paddled into a cove in search of refuge, the houses and private lots made my spirit sink. I began to regret passing up prospects we'd seen earlier, nearer the state park, gravel bars that extended out into the lake like welcome mats, driftwood all around for building a fire, big dark woods looming above us, no roads leading down to us. Technically, TVA owned the shoreline, but who wanted to camp below someone's front lawn? I doubted that would be tolerated, no matter the legality of it. For the first time on the trip, I began to see humans puttering about in their yards and on their docks.

One guy stood at the rail of his deck and hollered, "What are you doing?"

This was the first time I had to navigate the murky waters of explaining myself to someone looking down from above. I shouted something about

The Land Between the Lakes winterscape—undeveloped bluffs populated by hardwoods and cedars—helped soothe a wind and wave-battered canoer.

canoeing the length of the river. When there was silence, I explained my immediate goal: "I'm also looking for a place to camp."

"That's great," he said. "Why don't you camp here?"

I paused to assess his property, the big house with its dominating deck, the sloping lawn and the fancy two-tiered dock. I did not see a flat place, nor a landing other than his dock.

Before I could answer, he said, "Just kidding!"

I think I was supposed to laugh. Instead I turned and kept paddling. Rain would be coming in the next couple of hours and daylight was dwindling. We were approaching Snipe Creek, a place in my home county I'd never heard of. It did not sound welcoming. But at the first bend into the creek off the main channel, I looked up to my right, and on a little rise a flat spot revealed itself in a clearing surrounded by cedars. I looked for a house nearby. Nothing. There was a decent gravel bar on which to land the canoe, then a short climb from there to the flat spot. Maggie and I disembarked and scouted before unloading gear. We found a fire ring and a half-collapsed concrete picnic table, as if this had been an officially designated camp at some point. Designated by whom? A hundred yards away, a gravel road made a deeply rutted loop that was almost impassable by car. I walked up it a half-mile and found no main road, no dwelling. I could not believe our luck.

After setting up camp I called home and assured my mother that we were in a good spot for the coming storm. Although I envied Alexander MacKenzie's exploration of blank spaces, being able to call loved ones eased my envy, and something about finding a new place in territory I knew so well made me happy. I popped open one of the Heinekens and listened to the storm roll in while warm and dry in the tent, on high ground, a border of cedars between us and the lake. Thunder murmured and lightning flickered for a little over an hour, but the worst of the rain streamed around us, and after that, the night passed cool and calm, perfect for catching up on the sleep that Locust Point stole. Something odd must have happened as I slept so soundly. The second Heineken, sitting outside the tent doorway, had suffered an invisible puncture that had left the can empty. Where it went, who drank it, I do not know. Perhaps this place was occupied by someone or something we couldn't see.

Regardless, the Snipe Creek turnaround got a five-star rating, cozy shelter when I most needed it, as good as it gets for a canoe camper.

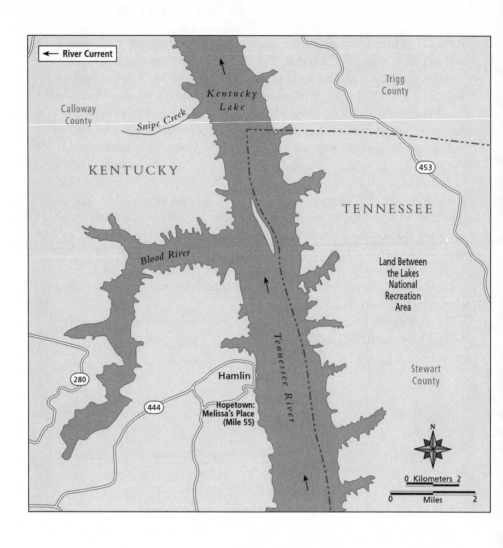

5

SHELTER

My sister's place, Hopetown, loomed seven miles away, an easy paddle, I thought, to a place where I could recover from the dings and dents of the first fifty-five miles and strategize for the remainder of Kentucky Lake, 150 miles. I avoided thinking about the other 400-odd miles that stretched out beyond Pickwick Dam.

The run from Snipe Creek to Melissa's place was a short one, but it was cold, 40 degrees starting off that morning, and the east wind kept pushing us sideways toward the bank. It was a dreary day preceded by dreary days, with more to follow. I began to note that when I crossed the mouth of a creek that the wind would pick up or shift, even if it was coming from the east and the creek mouth was on the west side. I quartered back and forth against the crosswind, trying to keep from running aground. Even though I was working hard to keep the boat straight, this was nothing compared to what awaited me on the trip. My relationship with moving air would grow more and more contentious. No matter its origin, intensity, or character, the wind would never be my friend.

When we got to Hopetown around noon, Maggie and I had the place to ourselves. Named after a resort in the Caribbean, Melissa's place has a double decker dock, where I parked my canoe, a lawn that slopes upward past a couple of 100-year old oaks to the two-story house, and the cabins and cottages where campers and staff stay in the summer. It's a cheerful place, light gray siding with white deck railings top and bottom. Melissa said she chose this site for Hopetown in 1996 because the lake is uncrowded with boat traffic here, and wildlife such as eagles, fox, turkey, raccoon, deer, geese, and ducks make frequent appearances. The proximity of the Land Between the Lakes (a lake crossing of two miles here) and two state parks enables her campers to explore nature and benefit from the therapy of being outdoors. At this point in my journey, I needed Hopetown for renewal and rest. Although I was nowhere near giving up, the first few days had been a lot harder than I thought they would be, and I didn't know how much more of a beating I could take from the outdoors I loved so much, which wasn't loving me back. I needed a bit of couch lounging therapy.

Geezer update: after three days of paddling upstream and living outdoors, I had been soaked and wrung out like an old rag. My right hip ached when I tried to sleep. My left shoulder throbbed from the fall off the dog food bucket. My eyes watered all the time, not from allergies but from exposure to my old friend, the chilly wind. My hands had turned to claws. When I made a fist and tried to open it, some of my fingers locked into place. Worst of all, the tip of each finger and thumb had broken open with tiny cuts that made any kind of chore painful. I slathered them with Neosporin, but it would take a few weeks for them to heal. The neoprene paddling gloves I'd brought seemed to make my hands even colder and didn't allow me the kind of feel I needed to power the boat upstream.

In preparation for this trip, which I didn't know whether I could complete, I looked for advice among experts about how to stay active as a geezer. They didn't reveal much that I didn't already know from experience, and some of the advice annoyed me. Dr. Andrew Weil's book, *Healthy Aging*, has a chapter titled "The Denial of Aging." He argues against the notion that you can continue to do what you always did. For me that meant playing competitive tennis (mostly singles) in ninety-plus degree heat, running through the woods with Maggie dragging me along, or paddling upstream to the point of exhaustion. Weil urges caution. Maybe you shouldn't be doing these things anymore, he suggests. Middle-aged people who have hurt themselves engaging in activities like running or basketball should abandon what they love. Weil himself says, "[I] let go of many activities as I have moved away from my youth." (Weil 2007) For example, he claims that while he still enjoys running with the bulls in Spain, he shies away from backpacking the wilderness like he used to in his thirties and forties. I don't get his logic. Why would he prefer running down a narrow alley in front of the sharp horns of a herd of large, enraged animals, elbowing drunken revelers falling over each other, rather than go backpacking in the wilderness, clearly an activity that's as good for the mind and spirit of a geezer, as it is for the body? Has he read too much Hemingway? Without going into a lot of detail, he says he spends a lot of time now with "risk assessment," presumably of the probability that taunting panicked bulls will result in a maiming or fatal goring. That is not the way I would choose to leave this world.

Though overall I found Weil's book useful, this chapter seemed sad in its resignation. At sixty, I think it's more important than ever to push the limits of what you are capable. If you get hurt and have to lay off for a while, if you puke after getting too hot, well, you went too far and you need to recuperate before attacking the trail again. I no longer dive off cliffs at rock quarries, but I think that's because my brain, since my twenties, developed to the point that enabled me to see the foolishness of such fun. On the other hand, why would a middle-aged person quit playing basketball if she loves doing it? If I took Weil's "Denial of Aging" chapter seriously, I would probably have quit this trip at Melissa's, a convenient stopping point near family and friends, most of whom would understand, some of whom would be relieved at a decision that reflected a sudden onset of common sense.

Common sense is often overrated. Ask Grandma Gatewood, who thru-hiked the 2,050-mile Appalachian Trail at the age of sixty-seven, the first woman to do so. She did it in a pair of canvas sneakers (Keds), and fueled up on a diet of Vienna sausages, berries, and meals donated by trail angels. She hiked it again in 1957, the first person to do it twice, and then at age seventy-five she completed her third and last one, becoming the first to walk the entire trail three times. Ben Montgomery, who wrote a book about Gatewood, tried to explain the toughness of this hiker who inspired so many, young and old: "She had lived a hard life," he said in a phone interview, "as many people did at that time. She survived the Great Depression, raised eleven kids, and worked on her farm alongside the men." (Trevathan 2017) And, most important of all to remember, she ventured off on these hikes on her own, without a cell phone.

I was humbled by stories like these. Not only was I younger than Gatewood and so many others who pursue adventures past retirement age, I was traversing territory near friends and family, and I'd done this trip before, in a way, though, as I'd continued to discover, the familiar could turn into

Hopetown's double-decker dock was a welcome site at Mile 55.

wilderness, and going upstream in the spring, at 59, was quite a bit more challenging than 40-year-old me floating downstream in late summer.

I think Grandma Gatewood would agree with me that pushing yourself as you get older, whether it's physically or mentally, keeps you young. Like Weil, I agree that denying age with plastic surgery or injections is a bad idea, that we should not turn to miracle drugs like growth hormones or my favorite, "Jogging in a Jug." I don't really care about aging gracefully on the outside or trying to look younger. What's more important is defying notions that people have about what's appropriate at a given age. "I don't need your rocking chair," sang George Jones. And the strongest sentiment on the subject, by Welsh poet Dylan Thomas: "Rage, rage against the dying of the light." Raging, I think, is a good preservative.

For a couple of days, I ate dinner with family and watched the rain fall, nonstop. I was in no hurry to leave this sanctuary and venture into the downpour in an open boat, but I realized that when the weather broke, I needed to embark or risk getting too soft. As I launched on a drizzly morning from the Hopetown dock and waved good-bye to my mother, Tom Petty's "Into the Great Wide Open" played in my head. Later, in the middle of vast Kentucky Lake, where no one could hear me, I would sing it loud and with feeling, under skies not so blue. Before me lay over a hundred miles of Kentucky Lake and nine more reservoirs.

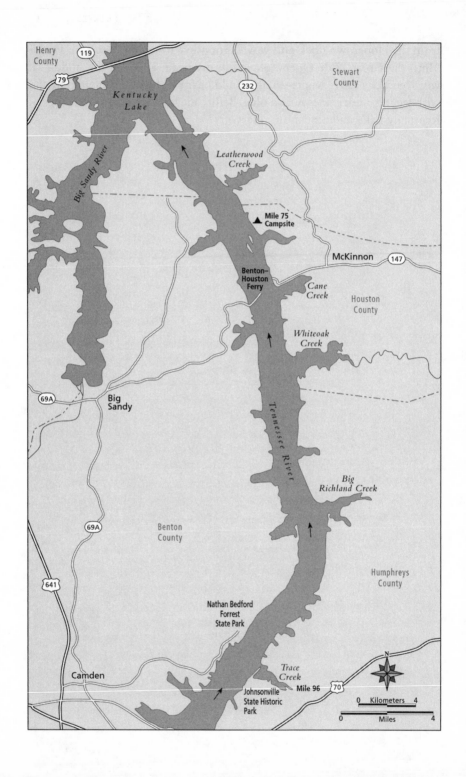

6

MAKING TIME

One thing I promised myself on this trip: not to hurry. I was not in a race. I planned on averaging ten or twelve miles a day, and I would stop when I needed to and try to pause when I saw something or someone of interest, not always easy when I had momentum, energy, and a goal in mind. I planned to make it to Knoxville, my destination, toward the end of May or the middle of June at the latest, before the heat came to stay. Maybe I'd go up some tributaries, such as the Elk or the Paint Rock off Wheeler Lake in Alabama, or the Sequatchie, off Guntersville, just below Nickajack Dam. At this point, traumatized by the harsh weather of the first fifty miles, I wasn't sure I'd make it into Alabama.

So far, my high mileage was twelve on days two and three. I was close to a ten-mile-a-day average, but the days-off at Hopetown had put me behind schedule. After I relaunched at Mile 55, I wanted to eat up some miles so I could relax and lay up when I felt like it or if the weather turned bad. Today I planned on camping at the southernmost tip of the Land Between the Lakes, somewhere in the proximity of the Highway 79 bridge. I wanted to avoid busy Paris Landing State Park and the mouth of the Big Sandy River on the west side of the lake, where I thought the wind and the waves would swirl and buck. I was seeing the full advantage of hugging one bank or the other on this upstream trip, a contrast to the downstream trip, when I'd ferry back and forth between distant points to cut mileage and stay in the channel to search for vagrant current. This trip was about avoiding current.

Crossing the lake from Hopetown to the east bank on this sunny morning turned into another passage of terror. My plan was to angle across the two-mile lake, heading in a southeasterly slant. Once I got beyond the shelter of a strip of islands that bordered the river's channel, big dark swells rose up from the east. They were pushing me so that it was difficult not to take them broadside. I got panicky because I was between the channel markers—the domain of barge traffic, heavy on Kentucky Lake—and I didn't seem to be making any forward progress. I was a flightless duck, in harm's way, and I kept checking over my shoulder in case a barge appeared. They always seemed to creep up on me, their diesels propelling them faster than you'd think. I ended up having to angle north, backtracking downstream, to get into the lee of the wind near the east bank. The crossing took over an hour.

Maggie and I disembarked on a sunny gravel bar somewhere between Panther Bay and Piney Bay. I opened a foil packet of tuna and dumped it into a tortilla. In February 1862, this area was not a good spot for lunch. Grant, moving upriver from Paducah, had debarked 15,000 troops in the area, and Confederate General Lloyd Tilghman had left 3,500 poorly equipped men at Fort Henry, moving the 12,000-man bulk of his force to defend Fort Donelson on the Cumberland. To make matters worse for Tilghman and Captain Jesse Taylor, left in charge of the fort, the river was running fourteen feet higher than normal and still rising. It threatened to rise above the barrels of the Confederate guns and their ammunition magazine, which would make the fort indefensible. After a brief but fierce battle, which included a direct hit on the Union gunboat *Essex* and the scalding-death of many of its crew, Taylor surrendered to the superior Union force, including the gunboat fleet led by Commodore Andrew Foote. In the strange circumstances of the American Civil War, the surrender took on the tone of a reunion for many of the soldiers. Taylor remembered meeting old friends and being treated with "every courtesy." Grant, Taylor wrote, "impressed me as a modest, amiable, kind-hearted but resolute man." (Groom 2012)

The Confederate loss was five dead and eleven wounded, while eleven Union were killed, thirty-one wounded, and five missing. Tilghman would die in 1863 in the Battle of Champion Hill during the Vicksburg Campaign. Directing fire for Confederate artillery, he would catch a Union shell in the chest. Upstream of Fort Henry, in Grant's future, loomed Shiloh, where the scale of misery and death and blunder would rise to epic proportions.

Now, on the new, post-TVA river, near the site of Fort Henry, the campground called Piney sat high on a hill crowded with RVs instead of 15,000-pound Columbiad cannons, and it did not allow easy access to a peaceful canoer from a border state. Since it wasn't even noon yet, I had no reason to consider it for an overnight stay, and the scalded souls which lay beneath the flooded river under a century and a half of sediment gave me more reason to move on.

Hugging the east bank allowed me to stay underneath the east wind and also placed me in a sort of funnel of northerly wind that boosted me upriver. I got to the bridge, my original destination, by one o'clock, so I kept going, my body acting like a sail, propelling me out of Kentucky and farther into Tennessee. I had no idea where I would stop, but this part of the lake, bordering Stewart County, offered plenty of good places for a canoer to pull off onto the bank. By the time we stopped, we were around Mile 75, a nineteen-mile day. I'd seen only a couple of boats that day, but one guy, who looked about my age, pulled back the throttle on his pontoon and came over to investigate us. He turned off his engine and drifted nearby without speaking. Reading his thoughts, I went ahead and told him we were paddling the entire river, upstream to Knoxville, and that we would be camping most of the way.

"You're living my dream," he said.

He had a place on Leatherwood Creek and gave me a couple of tips on where to camp. He had been part of a group that jet-skied from Knoxville to Paris Landing, so he had an idea of what was in store for us in terms of dams and the changing landscape. I imagine he could cover 200 miles a day on a jet-ski, which would reduce my trip to a week or less.

His "living the dream" sentiment was informed by a knowledge of the mileage we would cover, but maybe not such a vivid sense of how many paddle strokes it would take. I appreciated his compliment, though, because it seemed to validate my idea that what I was doing interested some people. It was flattering to hear someone say I was living their dream, while others would shake their heads and consider my project their worst nightmare. That, too, flattered me.

We found an excellent gravel bar in a cove below a wooded bluff. I let Maggie run free to explore the trashy interior while I got ready for the cold night to come, with near-freezing temperatures. So far, Maggie seemed to be living out her own dream. She roamed the banks, and waded into the water, rampaging through the woods, up and down hills, her body fully-grown and strong, but her demeanor still puppy-like. She liked most of all finding discarded items to dig out of the sand and toss around like toys: plastic bags, water bottles, ropes, and the like. I had brought her several toys—including

After a freezing night in camp, Maggie and I awoke early to see a fisherman catch a keeper from the dropoff just beyond the gravel bar.

bones with marrow-like filling and a plastic hamburger that squeaked—but she preferred salvaging on her own.

At the first hint of daylight, a fisherman entered our cove and casted a foot or so off the gravel bar where I'd pulled up the boat. From the deep water of the drop-off, he caught a largemouth bass. For the most part, bass fishermen were my only companions on the river this time of year. So far, they had been friendly but intense. This was not lazy fishing. They cast their lures with precision and speed, and they changed from one shiny, plastic fringed trinket to another so quickly that it seemed a blur of motion. This guy, in complete camo, was thrilled for us to see him catch a fish so nearby, but he didn't let on. He was curious about what we were doing and seemed to approve, in an understated way, of the project. Another bass fisherman, near the bank we hugged a few days later, cast two-handed, a quick sidearm wrist flick that landed his lure—plop—inches from his target, whether it was the bank, a stump, a bush, or a bubble that might be a feeding fish. This guy was really good, I could tell, and his intensity transcended the camo guy's, in the pace and accuracy of his casts. Like so many of these serious bad-weather anglers, he moved about the low platform of the boat with grace and quickness, always standing, sometimes leaning against the little barstool-like stand and goosing the trolling motor pedal every so often.

I drifted near him, at his back, and he glanced around at us and asked how far we were going.

"You're camping the whole way?"

"Pretty much."

"That is so cool!" he said.

It was his youth and his focus that made his reaction to my long, slow trip seem so surprising to me—after all, this kid had a 175-horsepower motor behind him.

He was prepping for a bass tournament coming up the next day, trying to figure out how dam releases, water temperature, and water clarity all factored into where and how he would catch the fish. He had to calculate how deep they were and whether they were swimming up creeks where the water was calmer. The day before, he said, he'd caught seven pounds of fish. He was semi-pro, he told me, on the verge of getting onto the Walmart-sponsored circuit called Fishing League Worldwide (FLW).

During the whole trip, when I passed near these bass anglers, even the busiest ones would pause and ask, in a friendly way, what I was doing; more than once, if they saw us on the bank or struggling against the wind, they'd motor up and ask if we were okay.

We had the river to ourselves thus far on the morning that the camo fisherman greeted us. Vapor undulated in wispy layers above the smooth warming surface of the new day. It seemed like the creek mouths were exhaling thin, morphing clouds. I thought we could make another fifteen miles at least, giving us a short paddle the following day to Johnsonville State Park, where I'd given the talk about my upcoming trip back in February. Ranger Bob Holliday had said he'd put us up in the ranger's residence if it was available, and if not, he'd let us camp in what was otherwise a day-use-only park.

Now in Houston County, I came upon some strange landmarks where the river widened: a working ferry, half a railroad bridge, and part of a building sticking up out of the lake. I think of ferries as throwbacks to the nineteenth century, but the Houston-Benton Ferry had started operating in 1988. Nobody was using it at the moment, but it was ready to go, parked near a wide boat ramp, an open-decked transport powered by a small towboat, waiting to take people and their vehicles to the other side. The *Leaf Chronicle* newspaper of Clarksville, Tennessee stated in an article that around 150,000 use the ferry each year. There had been a ferry at Saltillo, a few days upstream. In 1998, Jasper and I had been invited by the ferry operator Paul Parrish, to ride back and forth across the river. Parrish gave me a cold Dr. Pepper in a glass bottle and talked about his days as a towboat pilot on the Tennessee and the Ohio. I contacted Parrish before my 2018 trip. Retired now, he told me that the Saltillo ferry had been shut down by the county. It was a shame, he said, because even though people didn't use it all that much, it was a tourist attraction.

I angled away from the ferry landing toward what used to be a railroad bridge across the lake. Now, the channel span was gone, and only fragments of the old bridge extended from each bank. There was a beginning and an end but no middle. The Danville Railroad Bridge, I found out from the *Explore Kentucky Lake* website, had existed in some form since 1861. A replacement was built in 1932 at the same site, and during that decade Danville saw a bit of a boom. Twenty-four trains passed through each day and there was a steamboat landing, saloons, and stores. To accommodate the flood that Kentucky Dam would create by the time it was finished in 1944, the bridge was raised, with a vertical-lift span added to make room for commercial traffic that passed underneath. In 1985 the railroad line ceased operation, and the three middle spans, in addition to the vertical-lift section, were removed and used elsewhere.

As I approached the bridge fragment, the wind came up. Though I had to paddle to stay in a straight line, I noticed that a building above me seemed to straddle the railroad tracks, apparently someone's home. I could imagine the nightmares I'd have about trains if I lived in this house, though it would be hard to beat the river view and the fishing access. Just as we'd experienced under Eggner's Ferry Bridge, the waves got wilder under the Danville Bridge. As I passed a few yards from an anchored pontoon full of family members fishing, I could feel their stares, but I could not wave because I had to focus on staying upright: prying (pushing water away from the boat with the paddle) and drawing (reaching out and pulling water toward me) to stay straight and not get pushed into the wall of riprap on my left. It seemed to take forever to inch past them. Once beyond the bridge, the wind hit us head on. My goal was to angle toward the east bank and hug it in an attempt to avoid this sudden and sinister southerly wind. The ruins of an old building with large print on it was my landmark on the way to the bank. This had been a grain elevator, I'd heard, and I squinted to make the letters come into focus: Allegro. Like the marinade?

The six-level concrete grain elevator was built in 1914 on the bank of the old river. Barges could offload grain at the building for transfer to the nearby railroad line. A photograph on the *Explore Kentucky Lake* website showed more of the structure sticking out of the water, covered with graffiti, so I think "Allegro" might have been someone's creative addition to the relic, perhaps an imprecation from an Italian-speaking Tennessean for me to increase my paddling tempo. It took me an hour to go 300 yards, and the wind pushed me straight to the east into the wide mouth of Cane Creek, where several fishing boats had gathered out of the wind. I needed to keep paddling to join them there, but at this point, I was disheartened and exhausted, having worked nonstop for a couple of hours to go two miles. Then something happened, as it often would, to revive my declining spirit.

A parade of birds began to fly low from the far side of the lake. They passed close enough for me to see the intricate working of their wings. Most of them were white gulls, but every now and then a few black cormorants were mixed in, like ellipses in a long sentence. It was such a multitude that it continued for ten minutes, without a gap. I don't think I've ever seen so many birds united in purpose, at least not so low and near the water. The mix of black and white was striking on that bright day, and I was inspired by the majesty of their passage to carry on, to follow them into Cane Creek.

Wind drove us onto a barren sand bar that had sprouted one leafless cypress tree. I sat in the boat to catch my breath while Maggie jumped out to roam. Whitecaps flashed all the way across the lake. I had to wade beside the boat in the shallow water to relaunch and get farther up the creek to a smaller cove under the lee of a bluff, where we sat in the calm and waited. It was pleasant to sit on a log in the sun on a sixty-degree day. We were not so different from the turtles nearby, perched on top of a tangle of deadfall. I unrolled my Paco Pad and lay back for a nap, thinking the wind might die down in an hour or two. Maggie used her body to edge my feet off the pad and claimed the cushion's lower third. After I got up to check the wind on the main lake, she had stretched out to take up all six feet of the pad. I waited until 5:00, and struggled to paddle out of the cove to turn south into the wind. We made it about a mile and a half and pulled off at a point where I thought we could camp. Sitting there on the dog food bucket, I got an idea: we would eat, take another nap, and set out at sundown.

7

NIGHT PADDLE

After sunset, a full moon rose, and as if by plan, the wind stopped. I'd paddled after dark before, including on this trip after locking through Kentucky Dam, but this was the first time I'd planned an all-nighter as a strategy, with New Johnsonville our goal for the next day, Easter. The forecast was calling for rain the next few days, and some storms, so I wanted to land near sturdy shelter in case of a big blow.

Geezer update: some might consider fearfulness and playing it safe as qualities that intensify with age. There are logical reasons for this. If you live long enough and witness enough calamity and things that go wrong when people act rashly, it works against your confidence. You don't have to imagine doom; you've experienced or observed it over and over, and it erodes your willingness to take chances, even if it's as minor as jumping over a yard-wide stream to a slick-looking boulder on the other side. Conversely, as you get older, with your memory more or less intact, you know better what to worry about and what not to. I'd paddled at night enough to feel as if we'd be all right, and I was desperate to escape this windy stretch of the river. Maggie was up for anything.

Even on calm waters, paddling at night creates an initial uneasiness, the transformative power of darkness distorting sound and sight and the ability to identify objects, particularly the ones with which I did not want to collide. Whiteoak Creek was our first big crossing, and breezes ruffled the dark surface as I paddled hard toward lights on the southern bank of the creek mouth. No other boats troubled the water. Some dogs started barking and then a pack of coyotes called out. Maggie stood and listened but did not reply. For this I thanked her. We passed Turkey Creek and vast Richland Creek, where I thought I saw a night fisherman across the lake, with a light. And then the big beam swept across the water and lit us up, a push-boat's beacon. He was making up a load and would sweep the light across us every ten minutes. Drizzle fell. I pulled over to a muddy sloped bank four miles upstream of Trace Creek, the turn-in for Johnsonville State Historic Park. It was three in the morning, and I thought we would rest a bit before continuing. From upstream came an industrial roar not identified on the charts, though outfall and intake pipes were designated. The steam plant at New Johnsonville had been closed, but something else was emitting an odor and sounds that filled up the night. When the rain picked up, I put my sleeping bag and pad away, and we loaded up. Maggie disapproved. Until now, this had been an ideal night for travel. Not only did the rain annoy us, but I began to run aground on shoals I could not discern. Freeing our craft required some jostling and scooting and prying with the paddle that upset Maggie.

We passed what I would later find out was a paper mill, its lights and gi- ant fan-like noise an intrusion upon our peaceful night paddle. The rain fell harder when we turned into Trace Creek and the day dawned a dull gray. By the time we reached Pebble Isle Marina, next to the state park, Maggie and I were soaked and chilled. We pulled into the first vacant boat slip under the metal roof to see if Ranger Bob would answer his phone on this Easter morning. No signal. I was shushing Maggie, who was making it known to me that she wanted to get out of the boat. Despite me whispering "Stay, stay, stay!" she jumped out. I was afraid that if people were sleeping late on these big boats and we woke them up, they would alert the authorities, who would recognize that we were trespassing and order us back out into the rain. Meanwhile, Maggie was touring the different boats, lingering at the big ones as if considering a desertion. She caught the attention of an irate Chow in a houseboat. He got up on the helm and roared. He frothed at the mouth so fiercely, I was sure he'd awakened everyone. I retrieved Maggie, scolding her in my amplified whisper, and we paddled back out into the rain toward the boat ramp. We found a flickering sweet-spot for a cell phone signal under the marina walkway and left Ranger Bob a message. We waited, like trolls, under the walkway, for a callback. We'd broken our distance record with twenty-two miles that night, but there was no one to tell.

At half-past eight, over two hours after we'd arrived, Ranger Bob pulled up to the boat ramp in his big white pickup. He helped load all my gear and the canoe into the back of his truck for the drive up to the ranger residence. He allowed Maggie to ride in the back seat of the ranger truck! After he showed us around the two-bedroom house up on a hill above the river, he told us to make ourselves at home and handed me the keys to the ranger truck. I could drive it around the park, he said, and when I got ready to launch again, I could leave it near the lake, with the keys locked inside. What twilight zone had we entered? I could not believe our luck, and neither could Maggie, who curled up on the old couch in the ranger den, not far from the fireplace. I was welcome to build a fire; there was a big stack of dry wood in the car port.

Bob seemed the epitome of a park ranger, friendly and knowledgeable, serious and formal in his bearing and speech. He was a Civil War scholar, an expert not only on this site but on the war as a whole, and also on the river, particularly the old river before the dams.

The rustic ranger quarters seemed the ultimate in decadence for Maggie and me. That morning, after Bob left, I showered and fell into a deep sleep on the couch. Around mid- afternoon I lectured Maggie to be a good girl, which meant don't destroy anything, and walked the mile or so down the hill to the Gray Heron, a restaurant at the marina. Thus began my gastronomic survey of marinas, focused on food that might have come from the lake: catfish in particular, and the traditional sides—hush puppies, slaw, and French fries. This first sample of marina food I rated as excellent. The two pieces of fish, which I ate first, were light and crispy on the outside with just the right amount of salt. I polished off the slaw, my vegetable, and sampled the hush puppies and fries without finishing. My stomach had shrunk.

Next day, I laid out our gear on the carport to dry and studied the weather on my phone. Uncle Ed's shotgun had gotten a bit rusty in spite of the water-resistant case I'd put it in. I cleaned it with Civil War re-enactment supplies that Bob got out of the closet in the ranger quarters. The closet was full of uniforms, rifles, and accessories like canteens and packs. After cleaning the gun, I watched some of the rangers' DVDs because there was no cable. *American Hustle*, based on an actual FBI investigation into political corruption, was first up, because I didn't understand all of it the first time I saw it a few years back. *The Help* was sad but very good. One of Liam Neeson's revenge/rescue movies made me think that I needed some self-defense lessons, and I made it through a *Sherlock Holmes* special-effects showcase that featured Robert Downey, Jr. Then I re-watched *American Hustle*, subtitled, without sound, and found the script lacking. If the weather didn't clear and

I stayed much longer, I'd have to delve into the *Ace Ventura* pet detective series.

Bob showed up that evening to take me to a city council meeting with him. As soon as he got in the door, he told Maggie, in a gentle, firm voice, not to jump up on him. He didn't want dog hair on his uniform because he was making a report about park plans. Before the meeting started, he introduced me to a reporter for the local paper, thinking the guy might want to do a story on my trip. When Bob described my project, the reporter peered down at me, in my chair, shook his head slowly, and said, "God bless you. God bless you." I babbled a bit and he took a few notes with a pencil, but his main reaction was to shake his head.

After the meeting, people came up to Bob and thanked him for his service at the park. They pointed out changes that had been good for the community. This would happen again in Waverly, when we got out of the truck to go to a restaurant. I'd toured the park during the day and understood their praise. The park was well-groomed, with the remnants of the battle, like earthen emplacements and cannons, set up to explain the defense the Union had mounted against the attacking Confederate cavalry across the river. Bob had a history degree from Albright College in Pennsylvania. He loved talking about the battle. The fort itself was mainly a supply depot for General Sherman, who was fighting his way across Georgia. Confederate General Nathan Bedford Forrest's victory here, achieved by firing across the river with his artillery, was the first time cavalry had defeated a naval force. "That devil Forrest," as Sherman referred to him, had placed his guns strategically behind a levee so that the Union shells sailed over his emplacements. In the end, Forrest destroyed thirty-three vessels and captured 150 Union soldiers. He was also helped by the Union commander, who ordered that soldiers set fire to boats to keep them out of Confederate hands; wind blew the fire out of control and destroyed much of the depot, including supplies. The battle was noteworthy for the fact that the majority of troops who constructed the fort and defended it were African American, freed slaves who formed the Twelfth and Thirteenth Colored Troop Infantry Regiments. Ultimately, the Confederate victory ended up being of no great consequence. Bob said that the destruction of the depot actually precipitated Sherman's advance deeper into Georgia and eventually to the Atlantic. Bob called Forrest's victory "a success that failed."

We were lucky to land at Johnsonville State Park and be under a roof during high winds and severe thunderstorms, the worst of the trip so far. As soon as the weather cleared, we loaded the ranger truck and drove as

We prepared to launch from Johnsonville State Park
after staying in the ranger's quarters.

close to the lake as we could get, a 150-yard portage that began near a
"parrot gun," a cannon which was set up near our put-in as if to cover us
as we plunged ahead on our trip. It wasn't an ideal day, but it was time to
make some miles after laying up in the ranger's residence. I was recharged.
I hungered for movement up the river.

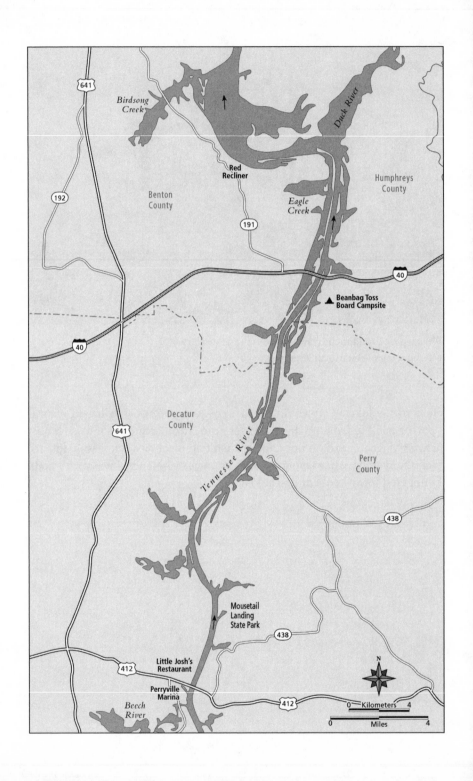

8

MY COMPANION

I hadn't planned on getting a dog so soon after my German shepherd, Norm, died, but a few months afterward, my former wife, Julie, a veterinarian, called and said there was a puppy at the Knox County Humane Society that looked just like Jasper, the dog who had accompanied me on the 1998 canoe trip. She had brought Jasper home from the Auburn Veterinary School, where he had been dropped off and abandoned. It was a fortunate adoption for all. Seeing the photo of this new orphaned puppy brought back memories of Jasper, so uncanny in his charisma and intelligence. She had the same yellow-tan coat as Jasper, the same dark shepherd mask and eye shadow. So I went to check out her behavior to see if she shared Jasper's intelligence. The first thing she did when we were alone in the visiting room was to sit and stay, looking up at me, as if to say, "What are you waiting for? Let's get out of this place." I had given her no command. A three-month old puppy was playing me, and it worked.

Not long after her adoption she was in the bow of my canoe, calm enough to lie down and nap. She also threw up the first few times. Maggie was more active in the boat than Jasper, prone to moving around and tilting us this way and that. I found myself yelling, "Get in the middle" over and over at her, until she understood. She made me yell, it is true, but she also made me laugh. In one of our training runs on Tellico Lake, she barked at

When I visited three-month-old Maggie at the Knox
County Humane Society, she conned me into adopting
her by pretending to be obedient.

something on the bank, and then cocked her head at the echo of her own
bark. What ensued was a barking exchange with her own echo that lasted
five minutes, as if she were thinking, Who is that dog that sounds just like
me, who seems to be mocking me from the pines somewhere?

When I got her, she weighed about ten pounds, and at the Humane Society they said she'd probably be around fifty pounds fully-grown, Jasper's
size. After six months, I got a little worried about the length of her legs
and the fact that she was already 45 pounds. Our spring launch date was
coming; how much more would she grow? People had theories about her
breed—Anatolian shepherd, Belgian Malinois—and I mostly ignored all
speculation, but when Catherine joked that she looked like a Great Dane,
I had her DNA tested.

What came back surprised me and everyone else: twenty-five percent German shepherd, twenty-five percent boxer, twelve percent Labrador, twelve
percent Siberian husky, twelve percent miscellaneous herding dog, and the

kicker, twelve percent beagle. I hoped this wouldn't add up to a pup who would grow much heavier than the sixty-five pounds she weighed when we began the trip.

Enthusiastic is the one quality that defines Maggie. She doesn't do anything halfway. Sometimes her enthusiasm manifests itself in disobedience. She loves people so much that she jumps on them, repeatedly, upon each meeting. She licks them until they run away. She knows how to sit, shake hands, and lie down for treats, but she has trouble with the "stay" command. Besides her fetish for disemboweling pillows, she has also destroyed other precious objects, such as a small wooden canoe that my sister had given me. I hoped this wasn't an omen. Sure seemed like one.

One of my greatest fears on this trip was that she would jump up on someone intolerant of her enthusiasm, like one of the legendary Tennessee River meth addicts that Catherine had referred to. What would a meth addict do in the Ninja-like embrace of a big puppy like Maggie? A close second in my fears related to Maggie was her getting so excited about somebody new on the bank that she might turn over the boat. I was also concerned about her playing with animals like snakes and skunks. Turns out I had no clue of the worst that awaited me on this trip. Maggie would act in ways that created adventures I'd never conceived of. She was a loving pup with a zest for life and a penchant for devilment. She knew how to have fun, whether she was digging, tossing a log into the air, or sprinting up and down a beach. What better companion for a geezer trying to make it upstream in a canoe?

Leaving Johnsonville that morning, we had the advantage of a brisk tailwind that helped us to a twenty-two mile day, past the mouth of the notorious Birdsong Creek, where the tweakers and their workshop had allegedly been spotted, and beyond the mouth of the Duck River, where the Tennessee made a strange bend that was almost a right angle east and then south. Our campsite, a little ways beyond I-40, the second interstate we'd passed underneath, was notable not only for Maggie's antics but also for the interesting refuse that had washed up on the beach. This wasn't the sort of beach you'd see near the ocean at, say, Daytona. Mixed in with the sand of a Tennessee River beach were pebbles and mud and tiny mussel shells. This one had the advantage of a sparse line of saplings that provided us some shelter from the wind. The temperature would dip into the thirties once again, so being out of the wind made it much easier to carry out the essential functions of life in camp: setting up the tent, eating dinner, getting into the tent, getting warm, and going to sleep. Maggie complicated my setup of the tent and preparation of dinner by doing her sand kicking routine a little too close to the boiling water and open tent door, both of which received grains

A beanbag board washed up near Mile 119 entertained Maggie, an example of exotic trash that we saw after the high water receded.

from her exuberance. I distracted her with the most interesting trash so far, and we'd seen quite a bit of it, the lake's descent from the high-water mark in February revealing much detritus, organic and inorganic. What lay intact on our beach site across the lake from Morgan Creek was a new-looking beanbag-toss board. How it got there, from whence it came, who knew? I got Maggie to walk up it by putting a Liv-a-Snap near the target hole. The board took top honors in the contest for most unusual litter of the day. On a pit stop at the Tennessee Wildlife Refuge, across from the mouth of the Duck River, lay a fully-upholstered red recliner on its side, this at a place where I expected to see an abundance of waterfowl, maybe a coyote or a deer. We had also seen what looked like an intact section of a house deck, overlaid with a nice rug of blue, purple, red, and yellow in a Southwestern pattern.

Having Maggie along with me might have reduced our sightings of animals, but, all the same, traveling by canoe without a motor at this time of year, we were privileged to be an object of curiosity for non-human animals. A gray fox tracked us from a sloping field near some houses, trotting out of range by the time I got the telephoto lens attached to my camera. Osprey, geese, and great blue herons were the most common waterfowl. Each of them scolded us, and while I was charmed by the heron's loud croak as it flew from its fishing perch, time after time, at our approach, the ospreys' shrill cries got old. They were like hysterical helicopter parents when we floated within the general vicinity of their nests, their reactions to us way out of proportion to our proximity. On that section of the river, one type of duck stood out; it had a swatch of white, like a crest, on the back of its otherwise black, green and purple head. Its breast and belly were brilliant white, its back jet-black: a bufflehead. There was one stuffed, on display at the Mousetail Landing State Park office where we were headed. We'd seen eagles as early as Day 3, a pair near the Cherokee boat ramp where Mel had brought me lunch. On a brief pickup-truck tour of Mousetail, Ranger John Bowen would show me an eagle nest, barely visible in the top of an oak.

The famous intruders, silver carp, had been with us the entire trip, becoming more and more commonplace the farther upriver we went. They did not leap out of the water upon the approach of my paddle strokes, as they did when a rotating propeller agitated them. Instead, they boiled up near the surface, sometimes flipping their tails to make sharp splashes that always startled me and Maggie. It was almost as if they were disappointed that we had no motor, and we only merited the tail-flip.

As of spring 2020, this species of invasive carp had been spotted as far upriver as Chickamauga. Fisheries biologist Dr. Timothy Joseph, of the Watts Bar Ecology and Fisheries Council, released a video on social media calling for action to stop the silver carp from continuing up the Tennessee River system and drastically affecting sport fishing and boating recreation. The carp, he says, outcompete the fish like bass and crappie, for food, and they can reproduce at very high rates. Boaters and water skiers risk serious injury from the leaping carp, who can weigh as much as fifty pounds, the force of colliding with one enough to break jaws and fracture skulls. Noting the devastating economic and environmental damage that the fish poses, Joseph recommends closing the lock at Watts Bar until an electric barrier can be put in place to stop the carp migration upstream.

Another non-native animal we began to see was the armadillo. We spotted three of them, at separate places, dead on the bank. When I told Bowen about this, his comment was succinct: "Good." As in good that they're dead. Like the coyote, the armadillo, not native to these parts, began migrating north and east as far as Tennessee by the 1970s. Bowen said that alligators were also moving north, one of them spotted by the Tennessee Wildlife Resources Agency (TWRA) on Wolf River, a tributary of the Mississippi.

After the beach camp near Morgan Creek, the charmingly-named Mousetail Landing would be our next stop, about fourteen miles upriver on Spring Creek. A front was bringing more rain, so we stopped at Mousetail after a fairly short paddling day. I felt it was better to be at a state park in a storm than having to find a suitable campsite in the wilderness. We had a decent landing that required a ten-foot climb up a wall of riprap to our campsite. Bowen and his colleagues gave me rides up to the bathhouse a couple of miles away, and to the office, where I could charge my devices and admire the museum-like lobby, which, in addition to the aforementioned bufflehead, included a coyote, a snarling bobcat, a gray fox, a beaver, an owl, a wild turkey, a hornet's nest, a glass case full of arrowheads, and a framed collage of historical documents and photos. Mousetail Landing, a busy commercial area in the nineteenth century, had tanneries, ironworks, and a thriving timber industry. The landing got its name during the Civil War, when a tannery burned down and an army of mice escaped. Bowen said that there were probably more rats than mice, but rattail landing didn't sound as appealing.

I told Bowen that my least favorite animal was the raccoon because it had terrorized me at so many campsites. Bowen, a hunter, said that raccoon was good to eat, and described how to prepare it. Good dark meat, he said. He would not eat a possum, he said, when I asked. Too greasy. Bridget, working the park office desk, got up and left at this point.

At Mousetail I commenced my rating of organized campgrounds, in particular the amenities such as bathhouses, landing zones for the canoe, and the sites themselves, usually situated in the "primitive area," if, like Maggie and me, you were living out of a tent. Under ordinary circumstances, I'd complain about the separation of Mousetail's primitive sites from the visitor center, and the bathouse even farther up the hill. But since I'd gotten rides there and back, and had been offered a ride about anytime I wanted one, that invalidated my observation as a complaint. The showers had good pressure, plenty of hot water, the bathroom clean throughout. Our campsite faced Spring Creek, sheltered from the main lake, and was a hundred yards from a point of land that extended out into the channel, a popular fishing spot with a bench and a billboard-sized sign that said "Mousetail Landing." We had no electricity at the site, but there was a sturdy wood and metal picnic table, a grill, and a sweetgum tree for shade. Maggie rated the tree as an amenity because she liked chomping on (not swallowing) the spiny sweetgum pods.

One of the young rangers, Michael, from Memphis, had moved to Mousetail from his previous station, at Reelfoot Lake, a dramatic swamp that had formed during the earthquakes of 1811-12, when the Mississippi River ran backwards. We discussed the strange lingering winter of 2018, and he said

At Mousetail Landing State Park, we waited out some rough weather
after a visit from my mom and sister.

that he'd begun to have success catching crappie, the unfortunately-named
fish which is among the best eating on the lake—mild, tender flesh, with
few bones. His crappie fishing tactics interested me, but thus far, I had not
tried my luck.

"This is a great part of the world," Michael said.

I agreed, though many would not put west Tennessee at the top of their
list of vacation landscapes. If you like to hunt and fish or canoe and camp
among acres and acres of undeveloped land, maintained as a refuge for
wildlife, you would have fun here any time of year. This park in particular,
with its heavily forested hills, a beach/swimming area, and extensive trail
system, made it the number one state park for me, so far; I placed Johnsonville in a special category since we didn't camp there.

The rain started at four o'clock in the morning on our first day at Mousetail, and it set in for the rest of the following day. Rather than paddle through
continual rain and take my chances on finding a soggy campsite, I opted to
stay put a second night on the nice gravel plot near civilization, just in case
the weather got crazy.

When my sister and mom came to visit me that evening, having driven a
couple hundred miles from Murray, there was some discussion of landscape

esthetics. My mom had stopped surveying her friends about my project and passing on to me their negative comments, having swung to the opposite extreme in her support. She went on and on about how beautiful the drive had been and what a nice place this Mousetail Landing was. I was sorting through supplies from the back of Melissa's vehicle, discarding a few items but keeping most. Turkey jerky and high-end chocolate were treasures. My mother had made turkey sandwiches on cinnamon bread, an innovation that made me skeptical but which turned out to be a tasty and fortifying breakfast the next morning. Melissa's handyman, who went by the name of Slick, sent me an entire reel of nylon rope that I scoffed at and then took anyway. I would end up using all fifty feet of it.

My mom praised my humble camp setup, complete with a tarp I'd strung over the tent, in an extra effort to keep my leaky shelter dry inside.

"We're so glad we found you!" she said.

"It was pretty easy," Melissa said. "Who else would be camping here now?" It was true that I was the only primitive camper, though I pointed out that there were some RVs parked up the hill, next to the bathhouse.

They took Maggie and me to Little Josh's, a restaurant across the river. A long line spilled out of the small house with a screened in porch. Melissa got us in somehow after a short wait at the end of the line, and later revealed that, when she told those in front of us what I was doing, they insisted we go to the front of the line. We left Maggie in the truck. I told her to be a good girl, and she obliged by devouring Melissa's turkey sandwich, which had been sitting on the console between the seats, wrapped in tinfoil.

In the restaurant, we sat elbow-to-elbow with the locals. My mom and sister, prone to conversing with strangers, described my trip to nearby diners, prompting me to have to explain myself further. I whispered to Melissa that I was trying to keep a low profile. She didn't see the point in this, having a sunny outlook on human nature, so I didn't bother reiterating to her the heckling I'd undergone on the 1998 trip, some of it in nearby Perryville. A gaggle of drinkers on a pontoon had motored up and asked me if Jasper was my girlfriend. I laughed with them, but the ribbing continued for longer than I thought it should, a contest of wit I had to endure because I couldn't start a motor and outrun them. Finally, I held up my ring finger to show that I was married and didn't need a girlfriend of any species. One of the female pontooners turned to the loudest heckler and said: "See, he's married! I guess he told you!" For some reason this silenced them and they moved on.

All of Little Josh's was learning of my trip and my current residence at Mousetail. We placed our orders—fish for me, to continue my survey of fried fish on the river, and a chicken sandwich for my mom. Melissa, an off-and-on-again vegetarian, ordered a fish dinner—without the fish.

After our order, my mom, who speaks as if addressing a small audience, said this: "We were wondering why you hadn't asked for more toilet paper!"

Heads swung around from neighboring tables to hear my answer. There was no acceptable answer. I switched the subject to hear about their Easter dinner, which had allegedly made my brother sick.

They would not confirm this. Melissa asked, "So, what do you do all day?"

The implication of this remark—that I did nothing—I took as a challenge. I detailed the essential chores of setting up camp, of organizing items so that I could find them, and so on. It had taken me a while to rig up the tarp, and I'd interviewed a couple of park rangers, also documenting some of my own thoughts on my microcassette recorder. I constantly checked the weather and consulted the navigational charts to make plans for the next few days. This seemed to satisfy her.

What I'd left out was this. After communing with the stuffed animals in the park office and chatting for a while with Bridget, the ranger at the desk, I got a ride back to my campsite for a nap and panicked when I couldn't find the recorder, where all of my thoughts on the trip so far were stored. I called the office and asked them to look around for it. Bridget called back and delivered the bad news: no recorder. Would someone mind bringing me back to the office, I asked, so that I can look myself?

Bowen came to get me. He was in a good mood because someone had come and taken away the park garbage, which was a bit overdue. He loaned me his flashlight, and I searched under the couches and tables in the visitor center, near the coffee machine where I'd made a couple of cups, in the bathroom and all around the dead animal displays. The owl stared down at me, glassy-eyed, in mild disparagement. The bobcat snarled with contempt. We searched the sidewalk between the truck and the visitor center door. No recorder. I resigned myself to having to take notes the old-fashioned way, to recount all the silly thoughts that had leaked out of my head for the last week and a half. Bowen let me search around in his truck, floorboards and all, and it gave me an odd feeling to be searching the vehicle of a law enforcement officer. I uncovered an impressive-looking shotgun on the back floorboard. I told him it looked in-between a sawed-off and regular length. He told me it was a 12-gauge pump-action Remington 870. It made Uncle Ed's sixteen-gauge look like a pea-shooter.

Bowen, who had grown up in the area and worked at Mousetail for twenty-seven years, had seen a lot come through, so he didn't seem surprised at a canoe-paddling professor panicking about a small recording device. He probably lit his pipe back at the office to tell Bridget about my search of his truck.

Just in case, I went through my backpack again and found the thing in a pocket I never use. I called the office and confessed to Bridget, who congratulated me.

Little Josh's fish dinner narrowly edged out the Gray Heron back at Johnsonville. I gave Josh bonus points for the jalapeno-spiked hush puppies. Plus, the ambience of the low-ceilinged, packed house with the loud waitress, who made fun of my sister saying "hold the fish" on the fish combo-plate, narrowly beat the quiet solitude of my day-after-Easter dinner at the Gray Heron.

"Where will you camp next?" asked Melissa.

"Double Island."

"Devil's Island?"

"Yes!" I was tired of repeating things, ready to get back to the simple discourse between Maggie and me, which featured the word "No!"

I lay in the tent back at Mousetail, belly full, thinking I'd get a good night's sleep. Sometime after midnight, a thirty-mile-an-hour wind kicked up, sucking and blowing at the tent walls. Something was clanging so loud it sounded as if a bear was making music with two trashcan lids. I crawled out of the tent to investigate. No bear. I had tied off one corner of the tarp onto the hinged top of the grill. The wind was strong enough to fill the tarp like a sail and lift the grill over and over so that it landed with a clanging alarm every half-minute. I tied off to something else and tried to sleep.

We awakened to a windy drizzle that blew in from the north, a provident tailwind for most of the day, but a problem at the outset because we had to launch in Spring Creek and head north for a few hundred yards to get to the main channel. I paused in my paddling to comment to a couple of fishermen in a boat: "Great day for fishing."

"Might as well," said one. "We've got it all to ourselves."

It was chilly and moist that overcast day, but the tailwind propelled us efficiently upriver to a beach on the east side of Double Island. Little white signs nailed to the trees proclaimed: "TVA Public Lands: Handle with Care." Landing here was a great relief after a couple of trials earlier that day, harbingers of challenges to come.

First, at a pit stop near a small community, Maggie leaped across a narrow creek and disappeared. So far, she'd been good about coming back from her adventures, but when she didn't appear after a half hour, I had to leap across the creek to look for her, calling and calling. I waited at the boat another half hour and then saw her slinking in my direction from a group of houses across a field. Poor Maggie, who jumped into the lake and waded around at each stop, had been shivering in the cold, so I couldn't blame her for investigating nearby houses. I was cold, too, no matter how hard I paddled. I got really concerned when, after relaunching, I spotted a cabin cruiser approaching us heading downstream. He slowed down when he got almost even with us, fifty yards away, but we had to jump his five-foot wakes and think about how it would feel to capsize on a day like this.

It had been a desolate day and a cold night, so the Double Island alarm clock the next morning set a new tone: two manic barred owls (a "who cooks for you?" rapid-fire duet), honking geese in a circular flight pattern, a cardinal with opera-level volume, a bellowing cow, a mild-mannered barking dog, and some kind of fish-monster leaping up and belly flopping over and over. It had gotten down to twenty-eight degrees that night, and a rime of frost covered the top layer of my gear, including my black paddling gloves and my camp footwear, a pair of old running shoes. We had a sixteen-mile paddle before arriving at our next refuge. A chiropractor who read my first book, Chris Alexander, found out I was paddling upstream and had offered to put Maggie and me up for a night. An avid paddler who liked to race, he lived at Martin's Landing, near Eagle's Nest Island, where I had camped on the downstream trip in 1998.

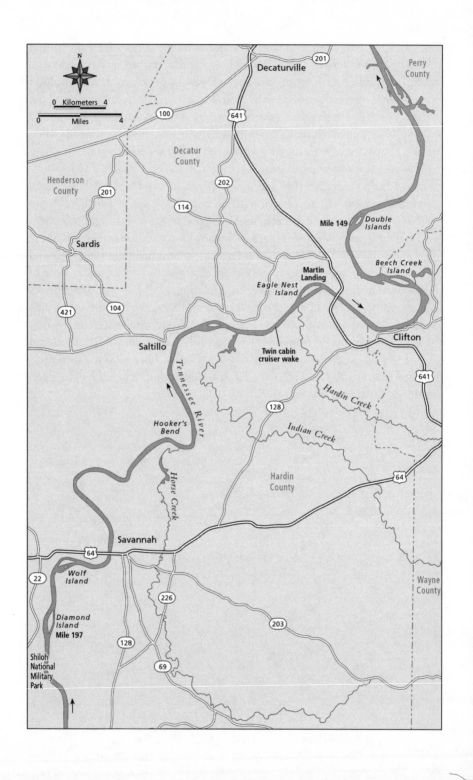

9

SHADOWING ULYSSES

For a while, it looked like I might arrive at Shiloh on April 6, the same day that Ulysses S. Grant did, but like the general, who was late for the battle, I was a few days behind arriving there on this auspicious anniversary.

Martin's Landing, where Chris and Mary Carol Alexander lived, was a community of thirty or so houses, similar in style, built up on pillars so that the main floors were raised twenty feet off the ground. The Alexander's house was off the main lake on a small creek, and when I arrived, Chris and a neighbor helped me haul my boat up next to the seawall and lock it up because they'd heard about Tennessee River pirates arriving by boat and breaking into homes. They put all my gear into a golf cart for the quarter-mile portage to Chris' place. Inside the Alexander house, Maggie harassed their good-natured dogs until they were exhausted. After I ate a bowl of homemade chili, Maggie and I retired to a guest room that overlooked the creek. The Alexanders had moved here fairly recently because they wanted to downsize and because they liked the Martin's Landing setting, with the solitude, the open fields, and the peacefulness of riverfront living. Although 200 yards from the river, they could still see the barges going past. Chris mentioned Eagle's Nest Island and the rocky bluff overhangs as two components of the landscape he looked forward to exploring in his kayak.

The next day, on our way to the boat, Maggie ripped the leash out of my hand and ran into the pasture, provoking dozens of cattle into a stampede. No cows were harmed, but she ran them the length of a football field before responding to my calls and trotting back, unrepentant.

We had a little sendoff at the riverfront, led by one of Chris' neighbors, Nada (pronounced Nayda), who held Maggie while I loaded the boat. Nada gave Maggie treats and then handed me a bottle of water and a package of peanut butter crackers. Off we went, upstream toward Shiloh on a sunny, calm day, warmer weather in the forecast. Well-rested and well-fed, with a general sense of positivity after all the support and interest from new friends, I was in love with my own trip and congratulated myself on constructing this project that was bringing me so much joy at the moment. Instead of feeling isolated, as one might expect, I was feeling connected.

I feathered the paddle softly through the water, taking my time in the warmth of the sun to examine a rock wall that rose from the water, layers of thin shale stacked on top of each other, the edges uneven and irregular, as if someone or something had been in a hurry to construct it. It loomed overhead, leaning out over the water. I wondered what it looked like underwater. I wanted to stay longer at this place, drifting and deconstructing the landscape that I'd been a part of for almost two weeks. Lost in contemplation, I happened to glance up just in time to see two northbound cabin cruisers approaching. It was odd not to hear them before I saw them, I thought, but there was no time to ponder such oddities. The river was narrow here, maybe 400 yards, and the big boats, within the channel markers, would pass within fifty yards of us. They followed each other, convoy style, two hundred feet apart, going about half-throttle. Neither slowed down. This was serious trouble, and I had to shift into action mode fast. As the big swells of the first boat's wake rolled toward us, I turned the bow and paddled hard. As far as I know, that's the only way to approach this problem, head-on, with plenty of my own momentum to crash through the walls of water. The last thing you want is to get hit broadside. Up we climbed to the top of the first wave, then down we went, roller coaster-like, water washing over the bow. We climbed four of these and then had to turn in the opposite direction to jump them again because they bounced off the rock wall. No time to relax or shake my fist at the first boat. Here came the second boat wake like an undulating monster, and away we went, back toward the middle of the channel again. After it was finished, I slumped over, shaken. How quickly the tone of the day could change.

No people were visible on these boats, their anonymity as irritating as their willful disregard for Maggie and me. How much would it hurt to pull back on the throttle when you first see a person and a dog in a small, motor-less boat next to a rock wall? Or any kind of small boat. How much malice or willful ignorance did it take to keep going, as if they hadn't seen us? Did they think about what might happen? Did they even look back? Did they think of me as I was thinking of them, wondering what I was doing on the river in a canoe, as I wondered what the hell they were doing here in a seaworthy vessel?

My brother Steve called me later that day, his birthday. I'd given him David Grann's *The Lost City of Z*, about Percy Fawcett, an Englishman who returned again and again to the remote, snake-infested Amazon jungle in search of a lost civilization, only to disappear there with his son in 1925. A procession of pilgrims had traveled there in search of him, as many as 100 of them disappearing into the jungle, like the object of their quest. A kind of explorer's cult arose around Fawcett, who explored much unmapped terri-tory, and some believe that he passed through a portal into another dimen-sion. In 2008 Grann trekked to the vicinity of Dead Horse Camp, the last place mentioned in Fawcett's diaries. His plan was to retrace the explorer's course and to discover what had happened to him. I gave my brother this book not only because it's a great story, but also because I thought it would put my little trip into perspective and ease his worries about me. Fawcett (and Grann, to a lesser extent) contended with the following: chiggers that consumed human tissue; cyanide-squirting millipedes; flies that "deposited larval eggs that hatched and burrowed under the skin"; and mosquitoes that "transmitted everything from 'bone crusher' fever to elephantiasis to yellow fever." (Grann, 2005) Oh, and also jaguars, crocodiles, anacondas, electric eels, piranhas, and vampire bats.

A former sailboat owner who took me on my first wind-powered voy-ages on Kentucky Lake, Steve said he liked to think up boat names in his spare time. He wasn't sure whether mine should be *Insanity* or the *Intrepid*. *Insanity*, if he'd seen the wake-jumping. A few freshwater swells seemed minor in comparison to the tropical torture of the Amazon. Meditating on Fawcett's obsession, I felt grateful for this chilly spring on the Tennessee.

Near the head of Wolf Island, downstream of Savannah, the site of Cherry Mansion, Grant's accommodation among Union sympathizers, I came upon Harold Howell, anchored near the shore in his flat-bottomed johnboat. He wore a tan shirt, khaki trousers, and an old straw hat. Affixed to the stern of his boat was a thirty-horsepower Johnson similar to the motor my father had on the steel-riveted utility boat he used to let me take out on my own for fishing and exploring. Harold was fishing for white bass using crawdads for bait. He wasn't having much luck, but he didn't seem to care.

Downstream of Savannah, Tennessee, Harold Howell was fishing
for bass with crawdads.

He had been retired for twenty-five years from a mirror factory in Bolivar,
Tennessee, a detail which gave me pause, not just the exotic name of the
town but the resonant image of a mirror factory. I imagined workers constantly distracting themselves with likenesses of their own making, a factory
of infinite narcissism. Harold said when they laid him off, he just decided
not to go back. I told him about the cabin cruiser convoy and he shook his
head. He said he'd turned over a boat one winter on the Hatchee River. He
and his brother had been rabbit hunting from the boat, and Harold had
reached for something that threw them off balance.

I told him I'd gone past Saltillo earlier that day and did not recognize it.
This was one of the places I remembered well from the 1998 trip because
of the free ferry ride, the heat of the day, and ferry pilot Paul Parrish giving
me a cold Dr. Pepper and inviting Jasper and me up to sit on a porch swing
in the shade. The swing had been next to a small, wood-framed house. I
knew the ferry was gone, and I could not find any other landmarks from
that day: no porch swing, no porch, no house, and no boat ramps where
the ferry had launched from. There were houses lining the bank that didn't
look newly constructed, but the town had lost everything that made up that
day's vivid memory.

Harold, who had bought some real estate in Saltillo, was not surprised when I said I didn't recognize it. He said there had been a lot of development there, that a lot had changed in twenty years. The specifics and the extent of the changes seemed too overwhelming for him to describe. As I paddled away from him, he warned me to be careful.

I kept looking back to check on him. He hadn't moved. How great it would be, I thought, to have a retirement of twenty-five plus active years, when a day of fishing was a good one whether you caught anything or not. Aside from Harold, I'd seen little human activity that day, though I paddled past Savannah, favoring the right bank away from town, on the inside of a bend, in the easy water. Around noon, a guy in a runabout sped up and down the same stretch of river, about a quarter mile, just enough to get up to top speed, before he turned around and went the other way. I counted about five laps, while Maggie and I had our lunch on the bank, and I tried to keep our beached boat steady in the constant wakes he sent our way.

Not far from where we lunched, an authentic-looking cannon was mounted next to someone's picnic table, and it was aimed at Savannah, across the river. Upstream of Clinton, two iron silhouettes of soldiers were frozen in the act of loading a cannon. This one was also pointed in an odd direction, toward a marina across the creek from it. Perhaps the proximity of Shiloh inspired this lawn art. There were other oddities: a pair of concrete hippos, male and female, frozen in contemplation above a wall of riprap, a wooden gazebo nearby; two twenty-foot long multicolored serpents arrested mid-writhe, cast in iron.

Beyond Savannah and Harold Howell, the river became more desolate, fallow flatland atop the muddy banks, almost no one out on what was a pleasant spring day. At the upstream tip of Diamond Island, our campsite, Maggie seemed more subdued than usual, prodding around and not straying far. We set up camp a couple of hours before dark, out on a narrow gravelly point where we might have lobbed artillery onto Shiloh battlefield, about a mile upstream. Everything on the island tip had been underwater in previous weeks. Driftwood and weeds clung to the base of scrubby trees that leaned downstream. I carried our gear to the highest ground, where I pitched the tent on a patch of sand among a scattering of jagged tennis-ball-sized rocks. On the west bank sat Santana Dredging, a couple of pushboats—the *Lucky D* and the *Melissa R*—moored to a platform for loading sand and gravel onto barges. It was deserted, and there would be no sign of life there the next day when I paddled past, up close.

I could find no mention of Diamond Island in any accounts of the battle I'd read, but I knew that thousands had gone past it on steamers and gunboats, many of them doomed, others destined for bravery, and still others who would panic and run to cower on the banks above Pittsburg Landing, unable to face the horrors of battle, what veterans called "seeing the elephant."

In the spring of 1862, the Confederates in this region had suffered losses at Fort Henry, on the Tennessee, and then Fort Donelson, on the Cumberland. The Union army occupied Nashville, and Grant was poised to continue up the Tennessee River into Alabama and Mississippi. General Albert Sydney Johnston, with 44,000 Confederate troops, marched on Grant's Army of the Tennessee (42,000 troops plus a fleet of gunboats) to attack before Union reinforcements arrived from Nashville. The battlefield was named for Shiloh Methodist Church, near the Union encampment. When the Confederates attacked, Grant, eight miles upstream in Savannah at Cherry Mansion, was surprised, as was Brigadier General William Tecumseh Sherman, who was in command of the forces on site. The Southerners had a chance for victory but squandered it after Johnston, who might have been saved with a tourniquet, bled to death from a leg wound, and P.T.G. Beauregard, who took over command, did not act decisively. A counterattack by the Union and reinforcements from Nashville precipitated the Confederate retreat back to Corinth, Mississippi. Tennessee River historian Donald Davidson called Shiloh "one of the bloodiest and most savage conflicts in American history," with more than 1,700 dead and 8,000 wounded on each side (Davidson 1978). Noting the close proximity of the two armies, who had little room to maneuver, Davidson said that after Shiloh everyone understood "how grim the war could be" (Ibid.). For the first time, having confronted the hard-fighting Rebels, Grant conceded that the war would not end quickly, as he had previously thought. I doubt he could have imagined what all awaited him and the others who survived Shiloh.

I'm glad now I had not done an internet search on Diamond Island. After the trip, I came across a chatroom of Hardin County yarn spinners with some tall tales about the area, some comic, and some a little chilling to somebody like me, open to the possibilities of the paranormal, especially camping with a jumpy dog in the vicinity of a place like Shiloh. The first post starts with a description of a "strange light" beneath the water near Diamond Island and then rambles through a number of mysteries, from unidentified black cars at the boat ramp to aliens in flying saucers to a bigfoot-like character with a hog under each arm. Another tale, more skill-fully told, describes a recent excursion through the woods in the vicinity of the battlefield with a "historical friend." The pair hear cannon fire and come upon a group of Confederate artillerymen preparing to shoot their cannons at a herd of deer. Thinking they are reenactors, the men call out to the soldiers, and they vanish. What follows this in the chatroom is a slew of ghost-soldier sightings, almost always focused on the Confederate side. The best one is about someone's papaw finding a small sack of gold coins near the battlefield and taking it home. He receives a visit from the owner of the coins that night: "Boy, bring me my gold!" says a voice outside the door "loud as thunder." Papaw opens the door to sixteen Confederate horsemen, who carry him away to a poker game among ghosts on the bank of the river. He lays the purse of gold coins on the table and a skeleton hand pushes it into the pot. There's some vagueness about how he returns home safely, but Papaw remembers the smell of cigars and whiskey lingering in the night air. In a later post, this same Papaw, who has a great eye for detail, reports having come upon some ghost soldiers on the bank, talking about ramming a Union gunboat. One of them takes a swig of whiskey and lets out a Rebel yell when the liquid leaks out, glowing, onto the ground. Papaw remembers the haunting thousand-yard-stare of the drummer boy, tapping out his moribund beat (Savannah Topix Forum).

The glowing stuff may have some basis in fact. Turns out that some soldiers were brought into field hospitals from the muddy battlefield with wounds that glowed. These soldiers, who tended to have been left in the field longer than others, healed faster, possessing what came to be known as the "angel's glow." The glow, it was posited in the twentieth century, came from a bacterium (P. luminescens) and the nematodes that feed on it, producing a chemical cocktail that not only glowed blue but also helped the soldiers' weakened immune systems fight off other pathogens (Soniak 2012).

In September 1998, Jasper, that amazing dog, followed me up fifty feet of rickety metal steps that I thought would come out near the battlefield. Instead, we emerged at the parking lot of a restaurant and had to hike through the woods to Shiloh. The heat of the day made the place somnolent, the battle itself remote from the air-conditioned visitor center and the tourists who surveyed the park from inside their idling cars. I thought if Maggie and I visited the battlefield about the same time of year that Grant did, during a chilly, soggy early April, that it would create a better sense of authenticity. This time, instead of coming out at the restaurant, I planned to arrive at the same old steamboat landing where Grant and his forces disembarked: Pittsburg Landing. The current was up that morning as the river followed a straightaway that later curved east toward Pickwick Dam. I paddled past the old steps that Jasper and I had climbed and began to look for a place to land the boat. Above loomed the fields of war, now mown like vast lawns, near the bank a stack of cannonballs. Alas, there was no place to land the boat, only a high wall of riprap, too steep for me. Rather than drift back downstream to the old steps, I paddled on, anxious to lock through Pickwick and find a good campsite on the lake above.

I wondered if, in 1998, Jasper and I had been among the few to arrive by boat to Shiloh National Military Park. Had we been the first since Grant? If there were a place to land one's boat and ascend from the bank, I had no doubt that visits to the battlefield would increase.

10

THE HORROR

One thing I hadn't done on 200-mile-long Kentucky Lake: fish.
Since I was mainly occupied with paddling, minding Maggie,
and trying to figure out where we were on the charts, my fishing
technique would be more passive than active. Some, like the bass anglers I'd
observed, might call it lazy. So be it. What I did was cast a Little Cleo spoon
behind me, prop my rod out the back so that it would be out of the way of
my paddling stroke, and forget about it as I propelled us toward the face
of Pickwick Dam, three miles away. The river was growing more and more
narrow, the banks sheer, crumbling mud, twenty to thirty feet high, above
narrow boggy beaches. I caught two fish, one a striped bass, the other a
white bass. If I had been starving, I would have put them on a stringer, but
I'd never consumed a striped bass and heard they were not all that great to
eat. In my preoccupation with paddling against the current, I didn't even
know the striped bass was hooked until I happened to make a pit stop and
pulled in my line. How long had I been dragging this poor guy, fighting him
as well as the ever-increasing current? The white bass swallowed the lure
and I killed him extracting it. After that, I lost the heart for fishing.

The pungent, fart-like smell of a paper mill added to the desolate tone of
the day and made it more urgent that I lock us through the dam and start
anew on another reservoir. As if resisting my efforts to be lifted free and

A mile below Pickwick Dam, Maggie jumped ship
and made fast friends with this Vietnam veteran.

clear of this landscape, the current got stronger and stronger, and because
the lock was on the outside of the river's bend, we were getting the brunt
of the flow. I stopped near the bank, in the easy water, to rest, and Maggie
jumped out and sprinted down the shoreline. A man in a small utility boat
had pulled off to check on us, and in spite of my calling her with all the
energy I had left, she jumped into the guy's boat and embraced him as if he
had arrived to rescue her from me. The man was sitting down at his motor
in the stern, and the impact of her greeting might have knocked him into
the water had he not been prepared. I slogged down there through the mud
and apologized over and over. The rescuer, who was wearing a "Vietnam
Veteran" cap, said he was all right, that he was a dog lover.

He told me about his golden retriever, who was a rescue dog like Maggie.
The retriever had brought home a kitten one day, held by the nape of his
neck in the dog's mouth. After this, the retriever tolerated giving rides to

the kitten, perched on his back. Amazing. As Maggie and I put river miles behind us, she began to do things that I thought amazing, though not quite as cute.

I coaxed her out of the Vietnam veteran's boat, and we struggled the last mile to the dam, a paper-mill-scented headwind adding to our hardships. When I could see the guide wall ahead, I pulled into a little bay out of the current and called the lock operator. Despite our success at Kentucky Dam, I still wasn't sure if the operators would lock us through each dam, going upstream in a small boat without a motor. I recited my line and hoped it didn't sound too rehearsed: "We're in a canoe going upstream, and we'd like to lock through."

The lock operator, who had identified himself as Randy, said, "Who's we? Who is in there with you?"

"Nobody," I said. "Oh, my dog, Maggie."

"That's somebody," he said.

I asked if he could turn down the current. With sudden formality, he said that he had no control over that. Uh-oh, I thought, I've annoyed the lock operator with a lame joke he's heard a million times. He said to come on up and wait behind the long guide wall. There was a barge coming through going downstream.

As we got within 100 yards of the guide wall, the dam sheltered us from the paper mill's foul breeze, and it was a great relief to glide into this sanctuary of calm, sunny slack water. On the bank, Shane Scott was catching one bluegill after another and tossing them into a five-gallon white bucket. He told me he would filet the big ones and stock his pond with the ones too small for eating. Then he began to notice that bass were pursuing the bluegill he hooked, so he switched from crickets to an artificial lure, a small white grub.

As he fished, he asked questions about our trip. He wanted to know about my boat, about where we were camping, and what it was like to lock through a dam in a canoe. Then he got quiet for a minute or so and said, "People say I'm old school, but you're on another level."

I took this as a compliment. Shane understood our project: an attempt to connect with earlier eras of river travel. He seemed to understand why I'd brought along a large, unpredictable puppy, too. After her latest adventure, I'd started to think about how much easier the trip would be without her, but then I'd be alone, and after all, I knew from experience that a dog was the best kind of companion for a trip like this. She listened to my ramblings, rallied me with relentless optimism, generally did what I asked, and never held a grudge.

Shane said he liked to travel with his mountain cur to the Big South Fork area, on the Cumberland Plateau, and hunt raccoon. He didn't kill the raccoons. He just let his dog chase them up trees, and then he let them be. He hunted squirrel also, and them he killed and ate. We talked about the different fish we caught and what lures we used. I mentioned walleye, and he started talking about how many sauger he used to catch from the lake. He called them cigar fish because of their shape.

"It's been a very long time since I've caught one," he said.

Not five minutes after that, he pulled one out of the water and declared that our conversation had brought him luck.

Randy called me back and said to come on in after the barge had gone past on the other side of the guide wall. Twenty minutes later, I was paddling through the big gates as Randy leaned over the top of the wall, looking down at us.

Locking through Pickwick Dam seemed peaceful—for a while.

"Sorry I'm so slow," I said.

"No problem. We got all day!"

So far, the process seemed so different from the first lockage at Kentucky Dam, where we had to wait so long, isolated, the communication sporadic and confusing, the lockage itself full of tension.

I tied up near the front of the lock, where Randy told us to, and as we began to rise, with hardly any turbulence, three or four guys gathered at the top of the wall and started chatting with us. They said there was some bad weather coming.

I said, "Well, maybe I can paddle out of it."

"No," said one of them. "It's going the same way you are."

This system, a long string of rain coming out of the southwest, would become the main focus of my adventure for the next few days.

I told the guys that this was sure a smooth lockage and asked if they were giving me a "slow lift."

"We ain't got but one speed," said one of the guys.

Maggie was sitting and looking around as we rose, as still as she had been inside the Kentucky Dam lock, but more relaxed. I was thinking about how much she had matured in our two-week ascent of Kentucky Lake. Her only transgression at Kentucky Dam, as I recalled, came just before the lock doors opened and she stood up to bark at the lock operator as he shouted instructions to us. Now, Randy was leaning over the wall twenty feet above us. He was telling us to paddle to the right once we got out of the lock because a barge was coming from the other direction. The lock doors in front of us had begun to swing open, the giant iron gates revealing another world, a wide reservoir with unknown possibilities for us. After the current of the past couple of days, I conceived of this as a threshold to peace and ease.

I was about to ask Randy about camping at Pickwick State Park when Maggie, wanting in on the conversation, raised up and put her paws on the wall of the lock chamber. It was as if she wanted to embrace Randy, fifteen feet above us. She pushed the boat away from the wall until she was fully extended, and then she plopped into the nasty water. It seemed to happen in slow motion. Because I was in the stern and Maggie ten feet away near the bow, I could do nothing to prevent her exit.

Aside from my greatest fear, capsizing the boat, this was a close second: my dog doing something crazy inside a lock. I never envisioned Maggie's "something crazy" as it unfolded, not in all the worried fantasies I'd concocted, but there she was, treading the nasty water where many fish and turtles had met their demise. We had a small audience for Maggie's fall, and I'd been pontificating to them, confident and self-assured, as I was getting

As the gates of Pickwick began to open, Maggie was about to try
to make friends with the lock operator in an unusual way.

through lock number two so smoothly. I had been thinking about how hard
the day had been, that now I deserved a little attention and ease. That's when
bad things happen, when you least expect them.

Maggie, treading water, put one paw on the gunnel near the bow and
nearly turned the boat over. Then she did something else I could never have
predicted. She began to swim out the lock doors onto Pickwick Lake. Randy
had to stop the mechanical process of the doors, for fear, I think, that Maggie
might get caught in the big hinges. I yelled and yelled at her, and she must
have finally realized the vastness of what was in front of her, the nothingness
beyond, in contrast to the confines of my canoe. She turned and swam back
to the side of the boat, nearer to me, and I grabbed her by the two handles
on top of her life jacket, lifted her dead weight into the canoe, and rolled
her over the gear into her position up front. She must have been exhausted
from her swim because it felt like lifting a limp chicken, a sixty-five-pound
one. She lay on her Thermarest pad, and Randy finished opening the doors.

I wish I'd had something witty to say as we paddled out of Pickwick, the
workers still at the top watching us, but all I could think of was, "I sure
didn't expect that to happen."

The guys laughed. I'm sure that we gave them a story to tell, and I wondered if they would alert the other dams upriver. Maggie slept as we headed to the right, and then back to the left, three miles across the lake to our next campsite, Bruton Branch, part of Pickwick State Park. We'd finished almost a third of the river, and even though much of it hadn't been graceful, including our grand exit of Kentucky reservoir, I felt that surviving and continuing onward had been an accomplishment. Having completed this much of the voyage, we had the momentum to do the whole thing. Short of catastrophe, I thought we might just make it.

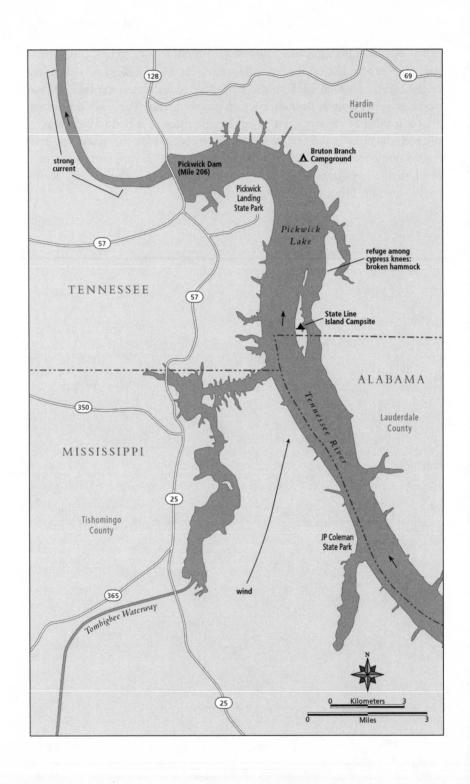

strong
current

128

69

Hardin
County

Bruton Branch
Campground

Pickwick Dam
(Mile 206)

Pickwick
Landing
State Park

Pickwick
Lake

refuge among
cypress knees:
broken hammock

57

State Line
Island Campsite

TENNESSEE

57

Tennessee River

ALABAMA

350

Lauderdale
County

MISSISSIPPI

Tishomingo
County

25

JP Coleman
State Park

365

wind

Tombigbee Waterway

N

25

0   Kilometers   3

0   Miles   3

11

PEOPLE WHO NEED PEOPLE

As requested by Randy, the lock operator we'd just entertained, I angled to the right, away from the oncoming barge, toward Yellow Creek, where a waterfall had served as backdrop for a Darryl Worley ditty called "Tennessee River Run." This is a song about people who wait for warm, dry summer weather to bust out of the workaday world and "party" on the river. Here's what the river party looks like in the music video: pontoons, basically a deck and canopy mounted on metal tubes, virtually unsinkable, are the party-barge of choice, though among the fleet gathered around Worley's floating stage are also sleek speedboats rearing up high out of the water and more conventional runabouts dragging people around on wakeboards. There is prodigious beer drinking; swinging from a rope, Tarzan-style, into the water; and catfishing, which consists of throwing out a hooked worm or chicken liver and letting it sit, while you wait for the bottom feeders to strike. If you're lucky, and Worley undoubtedly is, there are "honeys baking in the sun." (Leslie, Worley 2003) In fact, in the video, there are hundreds of these honeys swarming the floating stage and the party barges. The outlier is a geezer in a white cowboy hat fishing alone in a tippy old utility boat. He shakes his fist at the floating party, and a speedboat brushes past him, rocking him with its wake. Comic relief. After a wakeboarder jumps over his bow, a supersized cabin cruiser appears to run over the poor guy. Why such malice toward the uninvited geezer? In the end, it's all harmless fun. Worley pulls the old guy up onstage, and he's grinning like the star's long-lost papaw.

I'm the geezer, in my own video, "just about a mile above Pickwick Dam," as Worley's song goes. Was this my idea of fun? At the moment, it was. I was having a blast, in no way feeling left out of a party somewhere. The lake was empty except for me, my dog, and the crew of an oncoming barge, who would no doubt be regaled, upon arriving at the lock, by the story of poor Maggie's mishap. She remained on her Thermarest pad, sleeping off her ordeal, as I paddled with ease through the flat water, grateful not to be struggling against dam-generated current. When Maggie roused and lay her chin on the gunnel, I decided it was time for a talk.

"That was a very bad thing you did. You know that? Bad girl." I hadn't raised my voice, but I was aware of overstating the obvious.

She cut her eyes at me and then turned her head to stare back out at the lake, her nose quivering, feigning disinterest in my lecture.

"Let's not jump out in the lock. Ever again. Okay?"

She turned and looked at me straight on, as if I were an idiot. How much dogs understand is a mystery to me. I choose to talk to them as if they understand a good bit, in their own way. I decided, at the time, to think that Maggie got it now, that there would be no more shenanigans inside the lock of a dam, but I felt the need to explain a bit more. There were seven more of these things to pass through, I told her, and if we're lucky the lock operators will be friendly, like Randy back there. But that doesn't mean you have to try to jump on them for your version of a hug. That doesn't mean you should test them.

Our progress was steady across the wide lake in the sunshine, a complete shift in tone from the strenuous battle against the tailwater current that morning. We coasted onto the gravel flat that fronted Bruton Branch campground, where Pam, a retired nurse, greeted us. She was walking along the shore collecting driftwood, tiny rocks, and shells. I restrained the suddenly revived Maggie and warned Pam that she would jump on her, but she insisted I let her go. Maggie sailed out of the boat, almost knocked Pam over, and began licking her hands and arms and face.

For the third time that day, I apologized for the actions of my dog and tied her off to a picnic table with a twenty-foot lead. The table and a fire ring stood under a stand of pines just a few paces from where we pulled up the boat. This was rare, this proximity of official campsite to the boat, and it made the process of setting up camp so much easier. I didn't have to unload everything at once; I could do it piecemeal, as needed, without worrying about the boat getting swamped or pirates stealing what I'd left in the boat at some takeout remote from where we camped.

The campground manager, Alan, pulled up in a pickup as I was depositing my garbage near the bathhouse quadrant. He told me that the bathrooms were brand-new, brought in prefabricated the previous month. With faux stone walls and sheet metal roofs, they seemed the epitome of prefab. Alan, in his twenties, with a thick mop of black hair that he combed to the side, was proud of the bathhouse quadrant. Each of the four rooms had a shower, a toilet, and a sink, he told me, so that campers had a module to themselves. I refrained from wondering aloud what would happen during the busier summer months, when demand for the bathrooms exceeded the quadrant's capacity. Just now, Maggie and I had the campground to ourselves, except for a woman with a couple of small kids down the way.

Alan sold me a bundle of wood, and I gathered up extra pine and driftwood for a fire that I got roaring by early evening. My plan was to sit and stare at the fire for hours, but I was distracted now and then by the landscape that surrounded us. A great blue heron lifted off from the gravel bar just a few yards away. Pickwick Dam, which from this side looked like a

Bruton Branch campground, a mile or so above Pickwick Dam, welcomed Maggie and me with a luxurious gravel bar landing, a brand-new quadrant of bathrooms, and a dazzling sunset.

low bridge decorated with lights, marked the horizon below a sunset that streaked the sky in shades of pink and lavender.

If I'd known what we had in store for us the next few days, I might have stayed longer at Bruton Branch, within walking distance of the pristine bathroom quadrant. As was so often the case, I had no idea how good we had it, nor what awaited us upriver, toward the Alabama state line and a sliver of Mississippi. I'd been warned about the weather, and I had become an obsessive devotee of my weather radio and weather.com, but paddling to J.P. Coleman State Park, my next stop, and living in a tent through a "weather event" would, unbeknownst to my fire-poking Bruton Branch self, surpass all the cold and wind that we had endured so far. High winds, with thunder and lightning, would sweep across the area. Rain would linger. I was in prime tornado territory, but I tried not to think too much about that. For now, the calamity that awaited me was merely a long stripe of reds, yellows, and greens on the radar screen, a benign and painterly representation, remote from the reality of our near future.

Coming onto Pickwick, we had made our second transition from riverine section to reservoir, and although I'd met some great people and seen some memorable sights on upper Kentucky Lake impoundment, the spread-out, wide-open Pickwick and the fine gravel and pine needle carpet under my feet made me grateful, in the moment, for the artificial landscape and recreation areas that TVA had created when it built the dams. Here, on the tamed reservoir nearest the upper face of the dam, you could get out of your boat without sinking in a half-foot of mud. There seemed to be fewer animals—aquatic or otherwise—rotting on the banks. You could see the landscape and the oncoming weather, spread out before you, for long distances. You could stroll along the lakeshore collecting driftwood, as Pam was, or lollygag with a camper and talk about your vacation in Jamaica, as Alan did. There was an unhurried sort of lonely-hearts community that I became a part of at Bruton Branch, on the opposite side of the river from Worley's Yellow Creek and the big marina. In the glow of the spectacular sunset, the great blue heron reappeared, swooping down and perching on a dead tree branch just a few yards away, as if he were getting used to me. The Beatles' "Eleanor Rigby" began playing in my head.

Earlier that afternoon, Pam showed me the red scratch that Maggie had scored from her shoulder to her elbow. She kept saying it was all right, and after I tied Maggie up, Pam stayed and rubbed Maggie's ears. I mentioned to her that I'd gotten the pup just three months after my German shepherd Norm had died, on his own, out in the yard under the shade of a dogwood, and Pam told me about a pet pig she'd had. Not one of those pot-bellied kinds, she said. A real pig, nine feet long! She was devastated when he died, and her sadness deepened when the crane operator couldn't lift the hog to put him in his grave. Instead, he had to drag him there.

"I've heard pigs are really smart," I said.

"Pigs are really smart," she said. "He would come when I called him."

We discussed Arnold, from the sitcom "Green Acres," who seemed to smart off at his owners with expressive grunts. To simply be a pig who communicated was one thing; to be able to act in the character of a pig quite another.

For a while, Pam said, she'd thought of becoming a veterinarian. She kneeled down and petted crazy Maggie some more. Maggie strained at the leash and boxed the air. Veterinarians in her future quailed at her hyperactivity.

Alan, the campground manager, was trying to quit smoking. He thought he might take up vaping. Once, on a vacation in Jamaica, a policewoman shook her finger at him and told him he could not smoke outside on the street. He said he was very polite to her, emphasizing that he traveled to learn about customs with which he was unfamiliar.

"Why is it," he asked the policewoman, "that you allow all these people to smoke marijuana and I can't enjoy a cigarette?"

She did not have an answer.

Alan told me the worst crime at the campground was a stolen picnic table.

"I could have made one of those in a couple of hours," said an acquaintance of Alan's who had dropped by in his truck and talked to us from the cab, engine idling. His point was that stealing the heavy table took more effort than making one.

Alan started in talking about the bathrooms again. They made him happy. But he dreaded a visit from the Cub Scouts. "When I hear they're coming, I break down and cry," he said.

Why? For starters, he said, they put everything imaginable in the toilets. Alan dreaded the damage these boys would inflict upon the new bathrooms. I think he secretly wished he could lock up the quadrants and not let anyone use them. In a weird way, having seen some nasty campground bathhouses and having some appalling ones in my future, I understood his angst, his dread. Almost as an afterthought, he mentioned that "young people" used to park down at the end of the campground road and cook meth. The park had to put a chain across the road to discourage that.

Back at camp, I stayed up past eleven o'clock feeding the fire, and Maggie sat under the picnic table, fifteen feet away. She'd been barking at two women in a van who let out a gaggle of kids that whooped and hollered and slammed Alan's new bathroom doors. They used all four quadrants and used them hard, and I don't think they were campers. I felt bad for Alan. Maggie would not sit next to me beside the fire. She always kept her distance, as if there remained in her something untamed and wild, like coyote. Perhaps the enjoyment of feeding a fire with dry sticks and logs, watching it grow and smolder, of staring into one's creation, a work in progress, and speculating about the nighttime sounds rising from the lake and the trees, was exclusively a human pleasure. I hoped Maggie wasn't staying apart because she blamed me for the Pickwick Dam incident; I didn't see how she could.

Next morning, waves washed in from the southwest. Coincidentally, this was the direction we wanted to go. I thought about crossing the mile-wide channel right away, before it widened, and to hug the west bank in an attempt to avoid the brunt of the wind. A park ranger who came by in his pickup suggested a different strategy. He said he would hug the east shore and get in behind State Line Island until I could cross over to camp in Mississippi. The island would block the wind, he thought.

For a while, it was brilliant strategy, and I was grateful for having met this wise ranger, who had driven up right as we were about to launch. State Line Island was a couple of miles long and between it and the east shore, a wildlife management area, I paddled a channel of calm water. We pulled over at a narrow beach on the island and had lunch. A couple of fishermen trolled by; they had camped the night before at the head of the island. Good for them, I thought, but tonight I'll be at a state park, in a much better place for this weather event. I was looking forward to J.P. Coleman because I had great memories of it from the 1998 trip. I'd pulled right up to the bank and camped in soft, cushiony pine needles right where we landed. A park ranger warned us about rattlesnakes, which was nice of him, I thought. And then, the next morning, after a good night's sleep and no visiting rattlers, Jasper had refused to get into the boat. I paddled away, leaving him there on the shore, just to see what he would do. When I'd backpaddled about fifty feet, facing him the whole time, he took a great leap and swam out to the boat. That dog could swim. He had a big deep chest like Maggie, and like her, he was longer than he was tall. I wasn't sure if the fake launch would work on Maggie. So far, she seemed less committed to our mission of getting upriver, less disciplined about staying put in the boat and on shore than Jasper had been.

After lunch, we crossed the narrow channel to the east bank and experienced the paddling treadmill. The wind blew with such force between State Line Island and the shoreline, which was still Hardin County, Tennessee, that no matter how hard and fast I paddled, I could not move the boat for-

Near the Tennessee-Alabama state line, cypress knees emerged
in a swampy area where the wind pinned us for most of an afternoon.

ward an inch. It was all I could do to keep from being pushed backward.
Finally, I quit. I let the wind blow me backward around a little point where
we found calm refuge. Although we were technically in Tennessee, I like to
think of this as our first landfall in Alabama because sprouting all around
us, in this little swamp, were strange stake-like plants from six inches to a
foot-and-a-half tall. They looked like little tree trunks with knobs on top. I
sent a picture of them to Catherine, and then to Charles Rose, the Tennessee
Riverkeeper vice president who was going to meet me in Florence. Those
are cypress knees, Charles texted.

I launched a couple more times, but the treadmill started up again, so
we found a little clearing among the phallic plants to wait out the wind.
I set up the hammock that I had borrowed from my sister, having left my
own somewhere at her lake house. This one seemed to work pretty well,
to do what it was supposed to, and in five minutes, I was asleep. When I
woke up, Maggie was on the ground asleep too, and as I sat up to ask her
what she thought we should do, I suddenly found myself on the ground,
the hammock in shreds. I had broken a borrowed hammock but managed
not to have broken any of my own parts, the swampy refuge providing a
spongy landing in between the lethal cypress knees.

Because high winds pinned us to the bank for much of the day, we only made it as far as State Line Island (background) after our cushy stay at Bruton Branch campground.

Late afternoon, we tried again to make progress toward the point of the canal where we could attempt to cross the main channel or at least find a decent place to camp. We made a little progress, but dense forest right up to the shoreline afforded no takeout, much less a place to pitch a tent. In desperation, I crossed the secondary channel to State Line Island and got a camp set up in a trashy area just before dark. This would be one of my least favorite sites of the trip, and not just because of the bottles and cans and plastic bags. It had a weird vibe, the woods thick and dark at our backs. Perhaps the loneliness of the place, along with the dreary weather and our lack of progress that day, contributed to the spooky feeling. Maggie stayed on alert for much of the night, and sleep was scarce. The wind stayed constant through the night. I feared having to stay here at this place for the duration of the storm front moving in that evening, forecasted to linger for a couple of days.

I hadn't really thought about it since the first few hours of the trip, after launching from Paducah that first terrifying day, but if I were so inclined, this would have been a good place to quit. The only trip I'd quit on, with conviction, was my attempt to canoe 70-mile long Clarks River, its headwaters in Calloway County, near Murray, Kentucky. I quit on Day 3, after the cold weather and the shallow water and the constant portaging through tangles of deadfall defeated me. I had been told that the river would only get worse after I left Calloway County. "Intolerable" was the word an experienced paddler had used to describe what lay ahead of me in Clarks River National Wildlife Refuge. It was easy to call Mel Purcell, fifteen minutes away by car, to come pick me up. I could laugh about it. Now, marooned by the wind at this dark place, it made sense to measure the meaning of what I was doing against the obstacles rising up against me. There would be no dishonor in quitting now, after over 200 miles. Contemplating this for a few minutes, I decided I was too far into the trip. And anyway, nobody would be able to find me here.

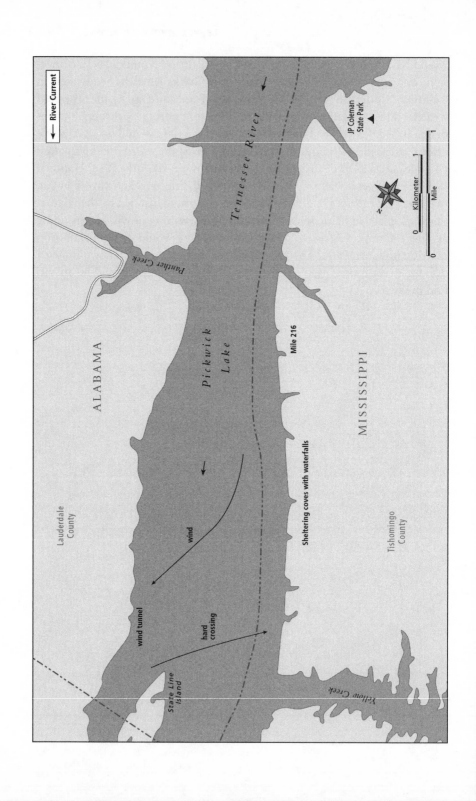

12

LONG RAIN

That morning, early, the air was moving at about the same speed, no letup from the day before. I loaded the boat and launched, determined to give the lake crossing a try. The State Line Island vibe hadn't improved with the breaking of a new day, so I gritted my teeth and made up my mind to venture out into the wide water ahead for a crossing. By the time we got to the tip of the island, the wind hadn't let up, but I found that I could quarter against it, angling to the south, and make progress toward the far bank about two miles away. Somehow, I thought, looking back over my shoulder at the channel between State Line Island and the Alabama shoreline, I had been pinned down in a wind tunnel, where the land masses had formed a corridor of inertia just for me.

The crossing was just south of the Tennessee-Tombigbee Waterway, a 237-mile canal that enables boats to get from the Tennessee River to the Gulf of Mexico. I didn't have time to contemplate the mouth of this man-made wonder. Waves washed over the gunnels of my little boat, and I shifted into accelerated paddle mode. The farther out I got, the less it scared me. It took about an hour to get within the lee of the western shore, a couple of stone throws away from the rocky sheer bluffs of Mississippi and more hospitable inlets. A bass fisherman said he had been watching me the whole time.

"Did you think I was gonna make it or not?"

"You looked like you knew what you were doing."

His statement took me aback. The events of the last two days, including the comic lockage through Pickwick and breaking through the borrowed hammock, made me feel as if I had no idea what I was doing. It's strange how your self-perception can be so at odds with what observers see and assume about you. Of course, he might have said that to be nice, suspecting that I needed a little confidence boost.

I told him we were making toward J.P. Coleman State Park, about six miles upstream, and he suggested we head downstream instead, into the Tombigbee, which had a lot of little coves and good places to camp. I didn't say this aloud, but there was no way I was going downstream. I could not backtrack after having fought the wind for every inch of upstream locomotion.

The fight continued all that morning, but unlike the day before, I was making progress. What helped more than anything on this western shore were the inlets that we could turn into and rest after each sprint against a wind that was gusting up to twenty miles an hour. I was becoming a student of wind. The little coves were narrow, no more than fifty yards across, and they went inland about 300 yards before ending at steep bluffs with waterfalls. Here the air was completely calm except for breezes that ruffled the treetops in the opposite direction of the wind in the main channel. Could wind bounce off of things?

On the 1998 trip, it was in one of these coves where I met Bob and Ruthie, the captain and crew of the *Mallard*, a sailboat that Bob, an engineer, had built out of concrete. That's right: concrete. And it floated just fine, he told me. He and Ruthie, his companion, were anchored in the cove waiting for hurricane season to play out before heading down the Tenn-Tom to the Gulf. They looked the part of people who lived on a boat. Bob had a long gray beard and flowing white hair. Lean and weathered, he sat at the helm with his long legs crossed, no shoes and no shirt. Ruthie's blonde hair fell about her face, and she had a natural beauty and serenity about her, as she gazed down at me and Jasper in the boat and told us that she and Bob had saved each other's lives many times. Once, she said, in a horrific storm that she thought would sink the boat, an angel appeared and hovered near the top of the main mast. The image seemed hokey, but I believed that she had seen it. They invited me onboard for a real visit, but since cats were a part of their crew, I declined. Bob and Ruthie were typical of a few couples I met on the 1998 trip, living out of their boats, most of them retirement age. I knew it couldn't be an easy life on the fairly modest boats they tended to favor, but all of them seemed at peace and happy, having simplified their lives by limiting their possessions and discarding their preoccupations with making money and rising in status. I envied the floating existence of Bob and Ruthie and often wonder what became of them. The phrase Bob uttered, "waiting out hurricane season before we sail to the Gulf," stuck with me. It evoked grandiose visions of romantic adventure. I still wonder if they felt the same way about my voyage.

This was Friday, the thirteenth of April, and I was going to make it to J.P. Coleman even if it killed me. When the wind gusted, I paddled hard to maintain my position, and when it slackened, I paddled even harder and faster, knowing it was my best chance to gain ground. When I entered the inlets for rest, I was breathing as hard as I would after a series of sprints. I wasn't in the best shape of my life—cholesterol high and carrying about twenty spare pounds—so the canoe sprints were taking their toll. To motivate myself, I envisioned the state park campsite as a kind of paradise, unchanged from my memories of it in 1998: a short hop and skip from boat to flat, pine-needle plush campsite, no snakes, no bugs, no noisy neighbors, perhaps a vending machine with cold drinks nearby.

I texted my mother a sanitized description of my predicament on the lake the last couple of days. I mentioned how hard I'd been paddling.

She had this to say: "Be careful of your heart rate with all that exertion."

Geezer update: I hadn't even considered this a concern, a heart attack, more ominous somehow from the perspective of my ninety-two-year-old mother, whose main secret to longevity was the trivialization of health issues to the point of denial.

Early afternoon, I began to search around each bend in the landscape for the familiar point where I remembered the J.P. Coleman campground. I yearned for it. And I knew better; my memory had a romanticizing filter. Eventually, a cove opened up to a marina and a hotel, the upscale 2018 version of J.P. Coleman. We paddled a half-mile to the primitive tent area, which, unlike the rest of the park, had been downscaled and relocated to a swampy inlet. I had to moor the boat at a steep muddy bank among the branches of a fallen tree and carry my gear 300 yards up a steep slope— another workout—to the nearest campsite. I leashed Maggie near the boat while I unloaded, and she managed to knock over the infamous white dog food bucket. The lid, its seal compromised because I'd been sitting on it, popped off and half her kibble spilled out into the dead leaves. From then on, Maggie had twigs and leaves mixed in with her dinner.

My dream of the 1998 paradisiacal camping experience was shattered by the reality of the brutal uphill gear-humping and the bare-bones campsite near a road that led to the boat ramp. In the process of preparing my favorite dinner, I set the dehydrated beef stroganoff pouch on the picnic table bench, and a gust of wind toppled it onto the ground. Unsalvageable. This was my Friday the thirteenth, a day of food spillage. Maggie had a look of smug satisfaction, as if to remind me of reprimanding her a few minutes earlier. She didn't touch the powdered stroganoff on the ground.

The tent walls would become familiar to us for the next two days. In one stretch, starting early the first morning, it would rain for twenty-four hours straight, with one two-hour break. The park ranger there, John, went to the store for me and got another tarp, as well as a bag of apples. When he delivered our goods in the pouring rain, John mentioned another guy who had passed through paddling a kayak. He was headed downstream, John said. In front of the weather, I thought. I wondered if this guy, my doppelganger, was out ahead of the storm front, whether he would get far enough north to miss it completely.

I now had a ground tarp and a canopy tarp, a big improvement in the long rain. The afternoon of the second day there, when the rain held off for a couple of hours, I made the half-mile trek to the RV sites and the laundromat. Somebody had pasted a page from a magazine section called "Points to Ponder." Next to a photo of comedian Dave Chappelle was this quote: "It's OK to be afraid, because you can't be brave or courageous without fear."

There had been a tornado early that first morning, not far south of us. I'd panicked about seven a.m., hearing warnings on my weather radio about severe thunderstorms and high winds. With Maggie, I trotted the 500 yards uphill to the bathhouse, where you're supposed to go if you're living outdoors during tornado season. The only other primitive campers—middle-aged guys in sleek cycling outfits—were getting ready to ride their bikes to Shiloh. In the driving rain and lightning!

"Shiloh?" I said. "It just took me three days to paddle here from Shiloh!"

They gave me a look, a guy in a raincoat, with the hood up, his dog dripping wet.

Shiloh, one of them said slowly, as if I were daft, is about a twenty-mile ride from here. He named the campground where they would stay, which gave me another twinge of regret. I'd missed a campground near Shiloh in favor of haunted Diamond Island? From Oxford, Mississippi, they were in the middle of a three-day ride that would end near the battlefield. I mentioned the severe thunderstorm warning I'd heard on my staticky radio, and one guy said, yeah, his wife had called, all worried, but that was east of here, and he thought the whole thing would blow through fairly quickly. They joked around as they put on their scanty rain gear and their helmets. Maggie and I trooped back to the tent when the thunder stopped.

My main occupation that day in the tent was listening to the weather radio, which was powered by a solar panel and a plastic crank on the side. I used the plastic crank a lot. At some point that day, on my back staring at the tent ceiling, I was folding the antenna down and broke it off at the base. Now, to get weather reports from the robot man, the computerized voice of the National Weather Service who delivered information in the same monotone whether he described sunny days or a warning about hundred-mile-per-hour winds, I had to hold the antenna to the metal base where I'd broken it off. It would have been funny had I not relied on the radio so much.

The second night was rainy, too, but not stormy. Next morning, I bailed a few gallons of water out of the canoe, and we were off, focused on Kogers Island, fifteen miles upstream. This was an archeological site where, in the late 1930s, TVA did a dig before finishing Pickwick Dam and creating the lake. They found remnants of the ancient Shell Mound People, who made their camps on mounds built up from mussel shells, and of a later culture known as "Round Heads," named for their practice of using binding to flatten infants' heads, resulting in a cranial deformation common among many cultures. I thought it might be interesting to camp there and see what I dreamed.

A north wind kicked us out of Mississippi toward Colbert Ferry and Florence. At a rest stop on a gravel shoreline that dropped off steeply, waves crashed into the side of the boat so that I had to pull it up onto the shore. Relaunching after our break was a challenge. I persuaded Maggie to get onboard and pushed off the gravel into the oncoming waves, but when they hit us broadside and splashed into the boat, Maggie jumped out and sat on the shore. Relaunching again, I had to wade out into the lake a few feet and make a jumping/pushing off entry into the canoe. This time Maggie stayed in the boat. Water had poured over both of my rubber boots, and my socks were soaked. About a gallon of water sloshed around in the bottom of the canoe that I'd just bailed out on that chilly morning, the temperature in the mid-forties.

It was a Sunday, and bass anglers sped from cove to cove, their heads and necks and faces all wrapped up, as if they were on some secret mission. Later, as we pulled over for lunch and I was changing into dry socks, a pair of guys tooled over and asked if we were okay. It looked bad, a barefoot geezer sitting on a downed tree on a forty-degree day, but I assured them that we were fine and they carried on in their quest for largemouth.

At Colbert Ferry Park, just downstream of the Natchez Trace Parkway, a guy on the bank bent over and pulled something big and swaying out of the water. He straightened up with it so that I could see the stringer of catfish that had to weigh sixty or seventy pounds.

"That's a nice stringer," I said. I think I might have startled him, floating up so quietly in the canoe.

"Did you ask me what kind of fish they are?"

"No, I can see they are catfish. I just said that's a nice stringer."

"Thank you."

He went back to his business of adding to the stringer, in no mood for conversation. He may have thought I was going to hone in on his territory, a common practice among less scrupulous fishermen. Just a few yards downstream, a group of four were bank fishing.

"Having any luck?" I asked.

"Sporadic," said the elder.

I mentioned the guy down the way with the loaded stringer.

"He's got the spot," said the elder.

Kogers Island was about three miles away. TVA owned it now, and it was protected from development. I hoped it was wild and empty, but not so wild that I couldn't find a place to land and a flat dry place to pitch a tent. But like so many islands that looked like good camping on the charts—isolated, government-owned, undeveloped—Kogers Island was dense with vegetation and low-lying areas, with no good gravel bar for landing. It was probably for the best. Archeologists had found four mass graves on the island, with indications that the occupants died from trauma, probably inflicted in battle. Sleep might have been scarce at such a place.

Where I ended up that evening, near dark, after a twenty-mile day, was on a narrow shelf of shore backed up to a gravel wall. It was cluttered with undergrowth and overhanging branches, but I hadn't seen anything better. I stomped around on the brush and set up camp, about fourteen miles away from Florence and the McFarland Bottoms campground where I'd arrived in 1998 during the Trail of Tears Motorcycle Ride, a commemoration of the Indian Removal Act of the 1830s.

We had this place to ourselves. I pulled the boat up onto the rocks as far as I could and tied it off. Waves slapped against the hull. I hung some gear on branches to dry. The tent was about ten feet from the water, not ideal for a campsite this close to the face of our next dam, Wilson. Sometime after midnight, I awoke with a strange sensation. It wasn't a sound that alerted me, but the absence of a sound that had lulled me earlier into an uneasy doze: waves no longer slapped against the canoe. With the beam of my head lamp, I discerned the reason for this new silence. The lake had risen so that the boat was floating free. So was my cookware, which I'd left on the ground. I estimated that the water had risen a foot. I got everything out of the water and pulled the boat up farther. I had to rouse Maggie and pull the tent back from the lake the few more feet that the narrow shore allowed. Then I tried to sleep again. I woke up about every half-hour to check the lake level. Yep, still rising. Around four-thirty, when the water was only a couple of feet from the tent door, I packed everything up and left. TVA had flooded me out. I'd always suspected this might happen, and now it had, at a poor place for it, on a narrow strip fifteen miles downstream of Wilson Dam, built before World War I, the oldest on the Tennessee. The rising waters may have been a byproduct of power demand on a night that dipped below forty degrees. Had they not considered a canoer and his dog camping on the edge of the lake with nowhere else to go?

I often consulted a TVA web page that listed dam releases and lake levels, but most of that data was after the fact. There was "predicted data," an estimated average for an entire day of releases, but this really didn't help a guy concerned about pitching a tent near the water's edge. I'd had nightmares about this, and now it was a dream come true.

I hoped for a better reception in Florence than Jasper and I had twenty years previous. Arriving near nightfall amid the chaos of the Trail of Tears Motorcycle Ride, surrounded by revving motors and roving headlights, we searched over an hour for a person in charge. We found the manager who, beset by requests with the campground filling up, refused to give us permission to camp near our boat in the picnic area, requiring a half-mile portage of gear. This time, the Tennessee Riverkeeper vice president, Charles Rose, said he'd pick me up and take me to dinner. Charles, who grew up in nearby Sheffield, would do far more than feed me during my stay in Florence.

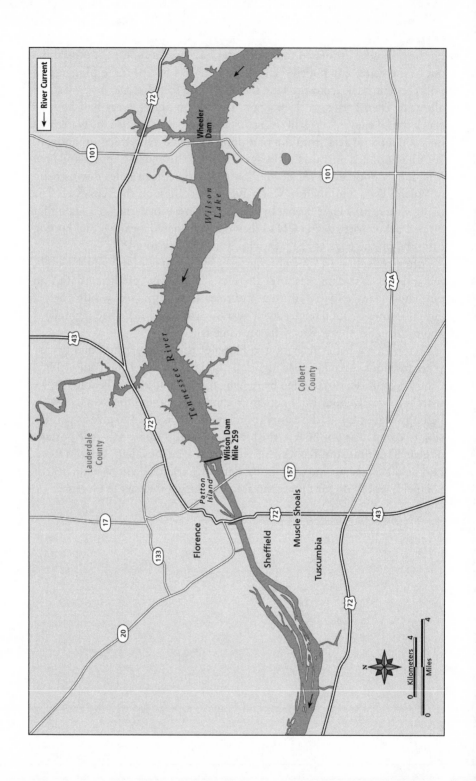

13

HIGHS AND LOWS

Having started out that morning long before daybreak, we made our way on an inside passage favoring the north bank alongside Seven Mile Island, out of the main channel. The current pushed against us as the day progressed, but we made the thirteen miles to McFarland Bottoms by mid-afternoon, mooring the canoe at a flat spot below a steep bank reinforced with the chunky limestone rocks known as riprap. This was the same spot where I'd pulled up the boat in 1998, and just like last time, I figured out that the mown grass with the tables and grills directly above us was not for campers but for picnickers only. This time, a Florence policeman came by and confirmed, with sympathy, that I could not camp near my landing spot, but that I was welcome to leave my canoe where it was. He didn't think anyone would bother it. Meanwhile, I faced another epic portage of dog and gear. Having somehow lost her lead, I tied Maggie off to the long braided yellow bow rope, and she was not happy about it. She was creating an elaborate network of tangles among the riprap stones when Charles Rose showed up in his old truck with a camper top.

Quiet-spoken Charles suggested that it might be a good idea to take my gear, boat and all, to the campsite a half-mile up the road. Charles, a tall, thin fellow about my age, started picking up big loads of my stuff and hauling it up the slope. Maggie, meanwhile, was fussing because she had tangled the bow rope so thoroughly in the riprap that she could barely move. I got frustrated trying to get the rope loose because I wanted to get it done in a hurry and help Charles, who was having to load all of my gear by himself. I jerked hard on the rope, not expecting it to come free so suddenly, lost my balance, went airborne, and tumbled down fifteen feet of riprap. It's a wonder I didn't break my arm. Or neck. I had jammed my left wrist and sustained gravel punctures in the palm of that hand. Other than that, nothing. I wished Charles had seen it. I wanted a slow-motion replay. This was Fall III, much more spectacular than toppling off the plastic dog food bucket on Day 3, even more comical than shredding the borrowed hammock.

This new injury, to the wrist, gave me cause for worry, but I could still lift with it and, though stiff, it still rotated, so I thought it would be fine for paddling. Perhaps the fall hadn't been as dramatic as it seemed, but I felt lucky, and I told myself that it would be best for a geezer like me to avoid losing his temper on steep rocky slopes, probably best to keep my cool in general.

The campsite at McFarland Bottoms was glorious. We were high on a bank overlooking a channel about 300 yards wide. Toward the dam, upstream, traffic crossed on O'Neal Highway Bridge and beyond this was the

At McFarland Bottoms in Florence, Maggie surveyed a barge heading downriver after it locked through Wilson Dam.

defunct Southern Railway Bridge. Wilson Dam was a couple of miles farther upriver, the lock on the left bank, my side, up a canal. It was great to have all my gear and my boat at the campsite, knowing that Charles would help me with it again in the morning.

The upscale Mexican restaurant where Charles took me was fancier than Little Josh's, 200 miles downstream. Instead of fried fish, I gorged on shrimp tacos, a cold beer, and plenty of chips dipped in salsas green and red.

Charles, a musician, toured with Lyle Lovett's band as a trombonist. He also played keyboard with a trio at mostly local gigs. Between cramming my face with chips and gulping the wonderful beer, I coaxed Charles into revealing that he'd met three of the four Beatles (not Ringo) and Bob Dylan. He'd walked into a studio in Muscle Shoals when Paul Simon was recording "Graceland." We talked mostly about the river and the work that Riverkeeper was doing to protect the Tennessee from pollution. Charles said that David Whiteside, the president, wanted me to come to a fundraiser in Huntsville the day after tomorrow. I didn't see how this would be possible. After locking through Wilson the next day, I did not know where I would be, exactly, and it was difficult, paddling a canoe, to fulfill promises to be somewhere at a certain time.

Before the trip, I had agreed to help raise money for the Tennessee River-keeper, a nonprofit group headquartered in Decatur, by using my canoe trip for publicity on social media. I hesitated at first to seek publicity while a trip was ongoing, but I thought why not help out an organization that was caring for a waterscape that I loved.

At the same time, I hesitated to interrupt the momentum of my trip to go to a fundraising event miles off the river. Charles said he understood, no problem. Then he revealed that Robert Kennedy, Jr. would be the speaker there. This gave me pause. Just now, filling my gut at a Mexican restaurant, it seemed important to get back onto the river and stay on it, but this was a chance to meet Robert Kennedy, Jr., not only a celebrity, but a major protector of rivers, the founder of the Riverkeeper organization. Later that night, I called Catherine about it and she said I should definitely go. I didn't know how we'd pull it off, but I texted Charles, and he seemed confident about the logistics of picking Maggie and me up in his truck somewhere upriver.

Charles came back to my campsite the next morning with breakfast. While we ate, the biggest vessel we would see on the Tennessee chugged into view and idled: the *Delta Mariner*, a 312-foot-long, fifty-foot-high cargo ship, waited its turn to lock through Wilson Dam. It shuttled between Cape Canaveral and Decatur shipping rocket parts. I was a little antsy to leave, but I didn't think it wise to cut line in front of this behemoth, so I took my

Charles Rose, vice president of the Tennessee Riverkeeper, brought us breakfast the morning that the Delta Mariner, the cargo ship that took out a section of Eggner's Ferry Bridge in 2012, waited to lock through Wilson Dam.

time with breakfast. Turns out that the *Delta Mariner* was the same vessel that ran into Eggner's Ferry Bridge on Kentucky Lake in 2012, knocking out its 322-foot center section. I hoped that the piloting of the *Mariner* had improved since then.

My goal that day was to lock through Wilson, make some progress up Wilson Lake, which was fifteen miles long, and find someplace to camp before locking through Wheeler the following morning.

Before I launched from Florence, Charles reminded me that Wilson Dam had been built before TVA existed, so all of the property on the lake above the dam was developed and privately owned. For a canoer and a dog, this would make pit stops and camping more complicated than usual.

Locking through Wilson, after the disaster at Pickwick, was suspenseful. We had to wait an hour, but where we waited, in the shade, on a little creek, near a forest just beginning to leaf out, was pleasant and calm. The approach to Wilson going upstream was superior to all the other dams because of the prepared channel that separated us from the main face of the dam. Patton Island, where I was moored, lay between us and the wind and current of the main channel. Wilson was the oldest dam on the Tennessee, and at one time, the highest lock lift in the country, at around ninety feet. Inside this monstrous barrier, wet gray walls rose up and shut out all but a small section of sunshine. Maggie, in her first-mate position, did not whine or make one sudden movement. She had listened to my lecture after the debacle at Pickwick.

After leaving the lock, we hugged the left bank of the lake and got jostled pretty well by the waves, driven by crosswinds that crashed into concrete sea walls and bounced back to create a chaotic chop that we had to power through. Coves without houses were very rare, and when we found one, it was so clogged with driftwood and trash that we couldn't land the boat to get out. I thought about paddling up to Muscle Shoals Sailing Club and begging someone to let us camp there, but there wasn't much real estate for camping, and no one was around on this Monday except a guy in overalls who was busy with chores. We kept on going until six o'clock, when we were within sight of Wheeler Dam. I could either paddle up Mill Creek and gamble on finding a place to camp, or lock through Wheeler—two dams in one day—and keep going, trusting myself to find Wheeler State Park campground after dark.

I called the lock operator and told him we were on our way. I was ready to leave Wilson, and I had fond memories of Wheeler State Park from the 1998 trip. As I remember it, landing at Wheeler twenty years ago was all the sweeter because of how much trouble we'd had finding places in the days leading up to it. We'd been turned away at Lucy's Branch, a big marina/resort that had a campground but didn't allow tent campers. We had to camp on a slanted bank near the mouth of the Elk River. Wheeler's good landing spot, just a few feet from campsites under a grove of pines, had been a big relief for Jasper and me. Now, in the twilight, I could not find any indication of the campground on the three maps I consulted: the navigational charts, the *Alabama Atlas and Gazetteer*, and Googlemaps on my phone. Soon, I was paddling through the darkness searching for the perfect cove, which was vivid in my memory of it, formed twenty years earlier. Cove after cove passed, with no tall pine trees, no flat landing spot. On a sloping wooded landscape clear of underbrush, some small structures became visible under security lights. I turned in. Bathrooms! Picnic tables! Across the cove from the picnic area twinkled tiny lights, but not enough of them to convince me that it was a campground. I squinted for a landing spot below the picnic area. A branch reached out and scored a deep scratch across the back of my hand. When I collided with a floating log, Maggie jumped out into a pile of flotsam that she thought was solid ground. She pulled herself up onto the bank, shook hard, and disappeared up the slope toward the bathrooms. I found a small strip of mud to land the boat and started throwing gear over the high bank toward a picnic table, which was crumbling at its base, the ground beneath it uneven, as if roots had burst through to destroy it over time. No matter that this was not an officially designated camping spot. After a twenty-three-mile day (a distance record so far) and locking through two dams, I was finished blundering through the dark looking for Valhalla. I set up the tent illegally and let Maggie wander until she came back on her own.

To avoid getting caught camping in a picnic area, I got up before dawn, broke camp, and launched. As soon as the dim first-light filtered into the cove, I saw it, 300 yards across the water from our crumbling table: the pine grove, unchanged from my memory of it. We set up at the site nearest the water and lay down inside the tent for a long morning nap.

Charles was coming to get us sometime that evening to attend the $500-a-plate fundraiser. Maggie and I occupied the day in the way that mystified my sister. We walked the mile to the guardhouse to pay for the site and chatted with the ranger, who was curious about a tent camper checking in so early. He kept asking if we were there the night before and I assured him we weren't at the campground. After that, I organized gear. I smeared Neosporin on various cuts, the new one on the back of my hand, the gouges in the palm of my hand and numerous tiny cuts on my fingertips, some healed, others still open. I showered. Wheeler's bathhouse, which I had to myself, ranked higher than the brand-new facilities at Bruton Branch. It was very clean and the showers let loose a torrent of hot water. So far, only the McFarland Bottoms bathhouse received a failing grade. There, the lukewarm water shut off every twenty seconds, and you had to push a button to restart it.

Wheeler, unlike J.P. Coleman, remained true to my idyllic recall of it. In many ways the upstream trip was becoming more about memory and perspective than about how the river itself had changed. So far, going upstream instead of down—in spring instead of late summer—had made this a completely different river, a different journey, and when I found links that lined up with the 1998 trip and with my younger self, it grounded me in a way that made all my blundering through the darkness the night before, feel worth it. I was filling in my own blank spaces. Instead of retracing the journey of some historical figure, as travel writers sometimes do, I was retracing the journey of my former self, the forty-year-old experiencing the river for the first time.

I spent a lot of that day looking around and sliding pieces of the memory puzzle back into place. Twenty years ago, just a few yards from where we now camped, a guy was putting in a canoe. He had a trolling motor on it and was having a difficult time launching and deploying the motor in such shallow water. A woman stood on the bank, waiting. I'd offered to help, which made it worse, I think, but they finally launched and stirred up clouds of bottom mud when they got the motor running just before sunset. Today, my fellow primitives were a mother-daughter team. They arrived that afternoon, and with military-like efficiency, set up a big tent, went for a hike, came back and started a bonfire. Later that afternoon, I went over and introduced myself to make sure they didn't think I was a creep. I told them that we'd be going to Huntsville to a fundraiser and getting back late. I started to explain what sounded like an unlikely scenario, but the mom cut it short.

"So you were scared we'd steal your stuff?" She was smiling.

"No, I wanted to ask you to keep an eye on it."

She nodded: "No problem."

I left them assured that no one would mess with these two, that any would-be thieves would stay clear of them.

I greeted Charles in my cleanest long pants, thick canvas trousers with a million pockets and loops, a blue short-sleeved button-up shirt I'd worn on the 1998 trip, and over that my fairly clean, mostly snag-free gray fleece jacket. The event would be at Huntsville Botanical Garden, a swanky venue about an hour's drive away. It felt strange to ride shotgun in a vehicle. Maggie curled up among blankets in the back with the camper windows cracked.

14

FISH OUT OF WATER

In the cab of his truck at the parking lot, Charles changed into his tux. Inside, everyone was dressed as if for a wedding or an adult prom. I got a cold beer from the cash bar and Charles introduced me around. People had quite a few questions about my trip and seemed happy that I'd come, so I lost my self-consciousness about my outdoor apparel and the fact that my face was tomato red from the sun and wind. David Whiteside, the president of the Tennessee Riverkeeper, flitted about the room with high energy. He seemed anxious for the event to go smoothly, but he took time tell me that he was glad I'd worn my best clothes for the event.

I didn't mind that the caterer ran out of chicken. The vegetarian plate, featuring two large mushrooms, was excellent, and the people at my table seemed to know all about what I was doing, well-informed about the river's geography and the threats to its well-being. David went to the front of the room and spoke about how he came to be the leader of the Tennessee Riverkeeper, what it meant to him, what the organization was doing, and what he wanted to accomplish. And then, his voice a little shaky with nervousness, he introduced his godfather, Robert Kennedy, Jr. Tall and elegant, commanding in presence, he seemed strangely familiar to me, as if I already knew him. When I started this trip, the last thing I expected was to be sitting at a fundraiser eating mushrooms and listening to a speech; nor was I expecting that speech to articulate and affirm what I'd be trying my whole life to understand: why I feel such an attachment and loyalty and passion for the land—the rivers and fields and woods of my region in particular.

Kennedy started out by saying that clean water is not a Democrat or Republican issue, that everybody has the right to be able to eat clean fish from a public waterway, that rivers are a part of our environmental infrastructure, and that we should protect them and keep them clean for our children and their children. The water, the woods, the wildlife, and the fisheries are public-trust assets, part of what's called "the commons."

He told the story of the Hudson River cleanup, the project that launched the Riverkeeper organization, first called the Hudson River Fisherman's Association. In 1966, the Hudson, which he called "America's first river," was the butt of Johnny Carson jokes on *The Tonight Show*. The river turned different colors every day. It could burst into flames. It had been a valuable

Before Charles Rose came to take us to a swanky Tennessee Riverkeeper fundraiser at Huntsville Botanical Garden, Maggie and I spent a restful day at Joe Wheeler State Park campground.

resource for those who lived near it, and they had practiced sustainable fishing there since colonial times. Polluters had all but destroyed the fisheries with industrial waste, including PCB's and daily oil spillage. In 1966, the community mobilized itself to rehabilitate the river. What people discovered was that the most effective means of fighting polluters was not to break the law by stuffing their outflow pipe with blankets or the like, but to enforce a legal principle that dates back to the ancient Romans. "It's illegal to pollute," Kennedy said more than once. The founding of the Hudson River Fisherman's Association helped to enforce the laws that make polluting corporations accountable. Now, said Kennedy, the waterway is an international model for ecosystem protection, and the Hudson River story has inspired the formation of more than 350 other Riverkeeper organizations.

"The public owns the waterways," Kennedy said. "Everybody has the right to use them, but nobody has the right to pollute them" (Kennedy, 2018).

At the Tennessee Riverkeeper fundraiser at the Huntsville Botanical Garden, from left to right, David Whiteside, president of the Tennessee Riverkeeper; Robert Kennedy, Jr., president of Waterkeeper Alliance; Kim Trevathan; and Charles Rose, vice president of the Tennessee Riverkeeper. Photo credit: Nancy Muse.

He provided a larger context for the Riverkeeper philosophy, a history of the battle over the commons that included Rome's Code of Justinian and England's Magna Carta. What it meant to be American, as distinct from European, at first emerged from our identification with ancient Greece and Athens, the cradle of democracy. Then in the 1830s and 1840s, Thoreau and Emerson, among others, began to assert that our connection to nature and the wilderness was what made us distinctly American.

"Our relationship to the land was the source of our values and virtues," Kennedy said. "American democracy came out of the landscape, and it defines us spiritually as well," he added, noting that in every religious tradition, the central epiphanies come from the wilderness.

The Tennessee River gives historical, biological, cultural, and spiritual context to the communities that live here, he said. It's an important resource to protect for the health and prosperity of generations to come. Long-term economic prosperity is dependent upon a clean infrastructure, not short-term gains free of the regulation that protects rivers.

I was fired up after this speech, and also humbled that my adventure was part of something larger. My crazy little trip was helping in some way to draw attention to the mission of the Riverkeeper as a watchdog for the Tennessee.

Kennedy stayed around afterward and posed for all of the photos that people requested. He was approachable and comfortable with his celebrity status, able to be himself among strangers. After such a rousing speech, he seemed to have reserve energy to interact with people for another hour. Charles told him what I was doing, and he looked me in the eye, shook my hand, and said, "Good luck." It was fine that he didn't have a lot to say; he'd already said plenty that would sustain me the rest of the trip.

Charles drove us back to camp, and I lay in the tent and mulled over the evening, letting the speech, like a good book, resonate in my mind. I had embarked upon a reservoir—Wheeler—where development would be prominent in some areas, but public land would be widespread, designated areas like Wheeler National Wildlife Refuge a model of Kennedy's idea of the commons. Brown's Ferry Nuclear Plant, heavy industry at Decatur, and the expanse of riverside land owned by the army, Redstone Arsenal, would also punctuate this stretch of the river.

It's easy to forget on such a working river that waterways belong to the public, that, in essence, I owned the water I was paddling. When I worry about locking through a dam or finding a clean, safe place to camp, the concept of public ownership arises. We have the right to be able to navigate an entire river, and if somebody blocks it with a dam, they should be obliged to let you through the structure that altered the river. We not only have the right to clean water where the fish we catch should be edible, but we should also be able to access the river and be able to enjoy the sacred pleasures of waterways. The prevalence of private property on Wilson Lake, the reservoir I'd just left, made the ideal of the commons more of a challenge. But the speech had emboldened me to see what the commons meant, in practice, as a canoer going up a working river in search of public lands to inhabit as a wayfaring experiment in democracy.

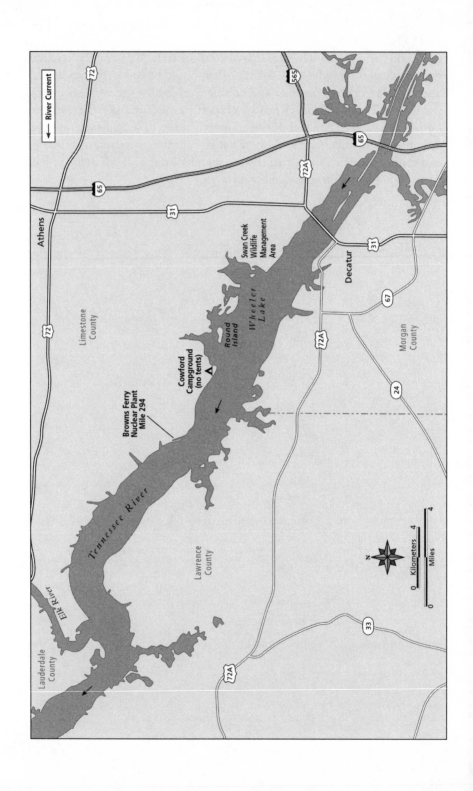

15

COWFORD OR BUST

My next planned overnight stop—a private campground called Cowford—said on its website that it did not allow tent camping. To me, a tent camper traveling by canoe, this seemed the ultimate affront, an undemocratic policy that I wanted to test. I had no backup plan for that night's lodgings. It was Cowford or bust.

I tied the canoe off at the fishing pier at Cowford Campground and found what I needed: the campsite nearest the boat ramp was unoccupied. But the camp office was locked, so I had to call the manager.

"I just arrived by canoe," I said, "and I'd like to rent this campsite next to the boat ramp."

"I can't rent you a site," said the manager, Wade. "We don't allow tent camping."

"Look," I said, trying to sound reasonable but also emphatic. "I just paddled nineteen miles to camp here, and I've got the twenty-four dollars to pay you for a site that's unoccupied. Why does it matter that I'm in a tent?"

"That's just our policy. It's above me."

"I'm just curious. Can you explain the reasoning behind this?"

"It's our policy. I don't have to explain it to you."

As if realizing how this sounded, his tone softened. "We've had some trouble with tent campers." He mentioned tent people getting too wild for the sedate RV folks nearby.

This, then, was a business decision, a policy intended to protect one kind of client—more affluent and more mobile—at the expense of another—less numerous, prone to being loud and drunk.

"I'm going to help you out," he said. "Meet me down the bank a ways and I'll show you a good place near the campground where you can stay."

I untied from the pier and paddled down the riprap, where Maggie and I floated below a group of RVs and waited for Wade, who, to his credit, either understood the injustice of his employers' policy or felt like his code of ethics as a human made finding me a campsite more important than doing his job by the book.

Waves crashed against the shore, and I had to sweep back and forth with the paddle to keep from being dashed against the rocks, which afforded no place to land. Maggie, untied from the thwart, took the opportunity to make a great leap out of the boat and onto the riprap. She climbed up it like a goat and then jumped up to hug a guy on the bank. The RV camper, at my request from the boat, tied her off to a tree with the lead she was dragging behind her. So far, we were fitting the stereotype of the disruptive tent camper, and we were lucky to have come into contact with another dog lover tolerant of my pup's lack of boundaries.

Wade drove up in a golf cart. "Just paddle down to them cedars," he said, "and I'll come meet you and show you some good spots."

Leaving Maggie behind in the care of the generous stranger, I paddled toward the cedars and pulled out at a swampy spot beside the last RV in the row of designated Cowford sites. Out in front of the vehicle, on a flagpole, fluttered the Stars N' Bars above Old Glory. A gruff country song blared across the landscape, so loud that no one at the campground could escape it. A short guy in a flannel shirt was splitting wood. He buried the axe head into the end of a log and stood staring at me, breathing hard.

"It won't bother you guys if I camp over here, will it?" I asked the axe man. I gestured a few yards away at a patch of stunted weeds. "The campground manager, Wade, won't rent me a regular site, but he said I could camp here."

The other Confederate sat in a folding chair, his eyes closed, chin drooping onto his chest, a beer can clutched in one hand. Axe Man, with his own beer, walked toward me a few steps and stopped.

"I don't know. I'll have to ask Tracy. He owns this site."

"I won't bother you guys and I'll be gone early in the morning." It helped my case, I thought, not to have Maggie along at the moment.

"I guess I don't mind, but I'll have to ask Tracy. He'll be back in a little bit."

It was odd, I thought, that Tracy claimed ownership of a campsite that he was clearly renting, and I started to say as much, to add that I was asking permission just to be polite and neighborly. I didn't think about it at the time, but Tracy's claim of ownership aligned him, in a way, with the ideal of the commons, a patch of land next to a lake that made up part of a river that extended across the Southeast. Was it right to dam a river, create an entirely new landscape, and then sell parcels of land to people who could then rent it out and make a profit? Philosophically, he had a point. On a practical level, from my perspective, the fact that Tracy (and his spokesman, the Axe Man) felt his ownership entitled him to dictate where I could camp seemed petty, paranoid, and exclusive.

Wade drove up in his golf cart and took me back to pick up Maggie.

"I don't think those guys want me to camp there," I said. We were rocketing up the campground road so fast that I hung onto the bar beside the seat. Wade clearly had other things to do besides finding us a campsite.

"What did they say to you?" asked Wade. One of his eyes was swollen.

"The one guy said it was all right with him but he'd have to ask the owner, Tracy." I shrugged. "Not a big deal."

"I'll have a talk with them," Wade said. "Tracy doesn't own anything. They are a-holes. Besides, I meant for you to go farther down the bank. I'll show you where."

With Maggie, I walked the quarter mile back to the rebel flag site and waited for Wade next to my boat. He had gone to load up some firewood in his golf cart to bring to us. Tracy had arrived, fresh beer in hand. Maggie, seeing Tracy's black Labrador, jerked the lead out of my hand and started wrestling with him. I retrieved her and introduced myself.

"Wade's going to show me a campsite farther up the bank," I said.

I corralled Maggie and got her back into the boat. We met Wade about 200 yards from Tracy's site, a little clearing in the woods that had been used by people unfamiliar with the Leave No Trace concept. I considered paddling on toward Round Island, a lump of land looming in the twilight a mile away, but Wade assured me I would not find a good campsite there.

I didn't have a bathhouse or a picnic table or electricity, but this place was free and it was flat. Cans and bottles lay about in considerable profusion, and poison ivy crawled along the ground and up the trees at the borders of the clearing. The dirt path Wade had driven in on was closer to the tent site than I would have liked, but across the lake from me industrial landings twinkled like small cities on the horizon, picturesque at this safe distance.

The lights of Decatur, Alabama, glittered across the river from
our campsite near Cowford Campground.

Wade helped me unload the wood, no charge, more than enough to burn
all night. And then he apologized for the no-tent camping policy.

"If those a-holes bother you, just call me," he said.

Wade's amenities made it seem like an outdoor bed and breakfast, but
the place gave me a feeling that stealth and laying low would be important
to getting a good night's sleep. The ideal of the commons becomes more
complicated when it involves an overnight stay, in particular when somebody
is charging people to camp on a parcel of land they've purchased near the
water, and somebody like me is freeloading nearby.

I'd boiled my water and poured it into the pouch of one of my favorite
dehydrated dinners—Mexican rice and chicken—and I was just about to dig
in with a green plastic spork when Tracy's friend (the Axe Man) and Tracy
himself showed up in their own golf cart. They had the black Labrador with
them, unleashed, and Maggie, tied on her long lead, was jumping around
trying to get him to play.

"Is your dog mean?" asked Tracy.

I said something about her licking people to death. They wanted to know
all about our trip and expressed some doubt about my goal for the day
after tomorrow: Guntersville Dam. Axe Man said it would take them two

days in Tracy's motorboat, a "Hot Shot" that would go fifty miles an hour. By my math, that put the dam about a thousand miles away.

I looked at Axe Man's cap with the scarlet "A" on it and asked if he was an Atlanta Braves fan. I wasn't joking on purpose, but later on it seemed hilarious, especially since I wore a camo cap with the "Power T" on it, for the Tennessee Volunteers, and it may have seemed like I was trying to get a rise out of him.

"Alabama," said the Axe Man. He did not smile.

"How long have y'all been camping here?" I asked. I was wondering if they were taking an extended vacation in the RV or maybe just partying over a long weekend. It was Thursday.

"All my life," said Tracy. Each word staked out its own space. There was a menacing silence, a pause that gave me time to contemplate my status as an outsider, the infiltrator occupying a spot they'd frequented for decades. Even if it was public land, it belonged to them by virtue of their history here.

"What did Wade say? Did he say anything about us?" asked the Axe Man.

"Not at all! He just thought I'd like to camp farther down the bank, where it was less swampy."

They didn't believe me, but they didn't press the issue. I guess I could have revealed that he'd called them "a-holes," which seemed school-marm-ish in its restraint. These guys were a little rough in their manner and they were beer drunk, but they hadn't done anything explicitly a-hole-ish. Yet. I just wanted to eat my Mexican dinner, start a fire, and nod off like the old guy back at their RV site. Their interest in me and Maggie seemed to fade.

"We'll let you get back to your, uh, dinner," Tracy said. He was looking slantwise at the dehydrated dinner packaging. "We like to run up and down these trails in the cart all night. Hope that won't be a problem."

What was I going to say? I really would like to sleep, and your golf-cart racetrack is two feet from my tent? Is it really necessary to ride around in that thing all night? I wondered if I should call Wade and tattle. What good would he do? This was TVA land, he said, out of his jurisdiction as the campground manager. Tracy's proposal to drunk-drive through the woods all night seemed an infringement of our sharing of the commons. It would deprive me and Maggie of sleep and possibly put us in danger of what might be a historic precedent of drunken golf cart manslaughter on a dirt trail.

I bid Tracy and the Axe Man a good night and they sputtered off. I lit a big fire and sat on the dog food bucket to eat dinner. After a while, with a full stomach and the heat of the fire making me sleepy, I stopped worrying about a confrontation. They must have passed out about the same time I dropped off to sleep. There was no golf cart racing that night. I felt a little badly for Wade, who had gone far out of his way to help me. I wondered if my testing of the no-tent policy at Cowford had inflamed a festering feud. I wondered if a punch from one of Tracy's gang had caused his eye to swell.

I'm convinced that the Cowford policy is discriminatory, but being a canoer camping along the length of the Tennessee made me an exotic minority. Not one of a kind, as I would find out, but rare. Wade's generosity made the policy a moot issue. He wasn't getting paid to spend his time finding ways around his employer's rules. The policy itself, meant to keep noise down, based on assumptions about the behavior of campers in tents, seemed absurd, since Tracy's site was the loudest, drinkingest campsite I'd see along the entire river. I was just a guy in a tent who wanted to get to sleep around nine o'clock.

To Tracy and the Axe Man, I was an interloper, a nonconformist living in a tent, traveling by canoe, camping for free near where they had to pay. Should the right to share public resources depend on your conformity, to the proximity of your upbringing? I thought not.

In the morning, I batted the trash and driftwood away with my paddle and exited Cowford with little fanfare. I had received a message from a Maryville College colleague, poet Christina Seymour, and Maggie and I stopped within Swan Creek Wildlife Management Area off the main channel to return the call. As I talked with Christina about advising one of our writing majors, the brilliance of the day and the beauty of the swampy peninsula struck me, particularly since the conversation reminded me of my office at the college, which was, by most standards, a very nice third floor office with a view, though it lacked the transcendent qualities of our current parking place next to blooming golden ragwort splashed yellow like clusters of paint across cropped grass so bright green in the slanting sun that it hurt to look at for too long. Something catastrophic had lifted one large cottonwood, massive roots and all, fifteen feet into the air, to lodge itself in another tree, as if cradled there. As Maggie roamed the small clearing and sniffed the yellow flowers, I tried to tell Christina about my night at Cowford and meeting the Axe Man and Tracy. It was too much for a short phone conversation with spotty service, but I think she got the gist of my geographical and spiritual distance from academia and the usual spring semester drama. She wished me luck and said it was good to hear from me. I was grateful then, for supportive friends and for the opportunities that my professor job afforded me, to be sitting here warming my neck and arms in the sun at a calm and empty wild spot dominated by flowers and grass and greening trees, no trash in sight. I could phone in some actual work, and then have no problem forgetting it as I back paddled and headed upstream.

After paddling through industry-heavy Decatur, we shadowed the long, narrow islands that bordered Wheeler National Wildlife Refuge. Several fishermen were working the channel-side banks of these islands.

One of them paused in his casting and said, "You know you're going the wrong way, don't you?" Meaning upstream.

I did know that. What I didn't know was that "wrong way" would have a significance on this lake beyond what I'd experienced so far in terms of current. On Wheeler and Guntersville, going upstream would be "wrong" in so many ways.

"What are you doing, just going upstream a ways and camping? Somebody going to pick you up tomorrow?"

I went ahead and told him what we were doing.

"Oh lord," he said. Then he told me about a good campsite near the right bank next to the dam.

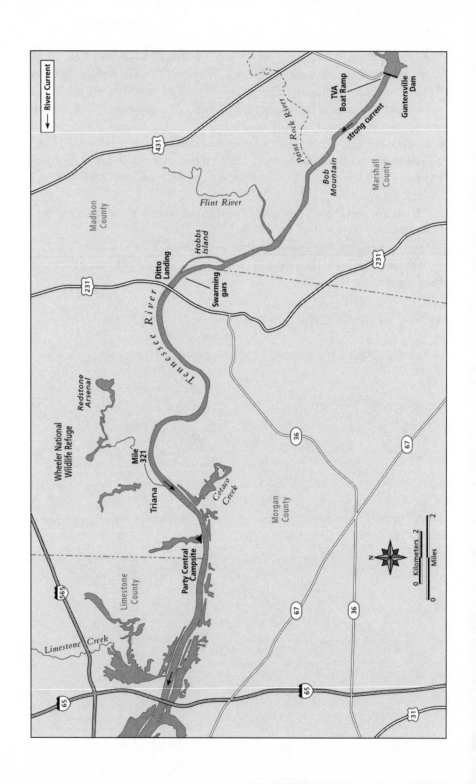

16

SPIRITUAL FISHING

After a twenty-mile day got us deeper into Wheeler National Wildlife Refuge, we pulled up into a creek, narrow and clogged with underbrush, and I hauled the gear down a gravel road to a clearing under a tree on a high bank overlooking the river. This unofficial campsite had been used hard and trashed, but since I'd found a good hiding place for the boat down in the creek, and I liked the idea of camping in a wildlife refuge, an officially designated public domain, we stuck it out. Never mind that our tent was just a few feet from a road, that people would cruise this gravel road like Main Street in a small town, and that I had to sweep aside bottles and cans and mysterious black plastic gloves to spread the ground tarp. A fish head stared up at me from the base of a tree. This was all fine with Maggie, who sniffed around with great interest, and it didn't bother me so much because the view of the river and the sunset beyond calmed me down as the cars, one every ten minutes or so, cruised by slowly, as if in a parade. Surely, I thought, the traffic would cease by dark.

That night, upstream of Decatur, the procession of vehicles on that gravel road made me wonder how the locals perceived this wildlife refuge, how they used it on Friday nights. It seemed that I had arrived at Party Central, and it wouldn't have surprised me had Tracy and the Axe Man screeched to a stop here in their golf cart.

The first to stop was a big guy alone in a four-door 1990s-era Ford with squeaky suspension. He lowered his dark window and asked me this: "Do you mind if I sit here a few minutes?"

I said that I didn't.

Silence for a few seconds as he texted.

"What's your dog's name?"

I took a few steps closer and almost asked for an autograph he so closely resembled the actor Bernie Mac.

I had to repeat Maggie's name three times before he understood. He nodded and raised his window. He poked at his cell phone, his engine idling. Then he continued on at a walking pace without saying goodbye. Came back again a half-hour later, going in the opposite direction just as slowly. He stopped again. I tried not to stare. Maybe he was getting a cell phone signal at that spot, or I was camping at a rendezvous location for some kind of transaction. Perhaps he was merely one of those people who enjoyed the natural world from inside a car.

Others came by so fast they raised a plume of dust that lingered after they were long gone. About dark somebody in a pickup slowed down, then floored it in an attempt to spray gravel on us. A hatchback went by and some guy said in a stoned drawl: "Looks like a spaceship," referring to my dome tent. I had the feeling that my camping here had disrupted many plans, that I was residing in a parking space.

Once the traffic thinned out, cows bellowed, dogs barked, two barred owls hooted, and a beaver splashed in the creek near my boat. On a gravel road across the river, a car ran full throttle, at intervals, as if practicing for a drag race. In fact, I came up with a new nickname for Alabama: the full-throttle state. Drivers and boaters were in the habit of pushing the throttle all the way, starting out, and keeping it there, as if they were in a constant state of emergency. Nobody really took the time to stop and harass me in the noisy wildlife refuge; it was, after all, Friday night, and people had better ways to celebrate the weekend.

I looked forward to paying for a campsite at our next stop, Ditto Landing, a marina with a campground where I'd camped in 1998 and met a couple, Dale and Joanne Haubenriser, who were living out of a sailboat, like Bob and Ruthie, back on Pickwick, and also, like Bob and Ruthie, on their way to the Gulf of Mexico, via the Tenn-Tom. The difference was the boat, not concrete like Bob's, but a beautiful teakwood-trimmed 1970s model. They had quit their jobs and sold their house, but Joanne said she had signed on for three years and couldn't imagine never owning a home again. Heading downstream, I would shadow Dale and Joanne for a few days, and chat with them on my marine radio. That night, twenty years ago, I remember camping on a knoll alone, within sight of the marina, and feeling blessed by the trip and the opportunity to meet such remarkable people. This time, Ditto Landing, roughly the halfway point of my trip, would be the second-worst camping experience so far, close behind the shoreline downstream of Florence, where TVA flooded me out.

We paddled under Heart of Dixie Highway Bridge about sundown, after eighteen hard-fought miles, much of it alongside Redstone Arsenal. The marina store at Ditto Landing was locked, but I got the manager on the phone, and he said it was okay to tie up my boat at the fuel dock. He said it would be right under a security camera, and it wouldn't be in the way because no one would be buying gas the next day, a Sunday, with storms rolling in. This was nice, letting me tie up for free at the dock, but what followed was one of the worse portages of the trip, a quarter-mile walk to a swampy campsite close enough to a race track that the roaring of the engines and the announcer's excited voice penetrated the pine woods that stood between the campground and the track.

I needed four trips to get Maggie and all my gear to the site, and by then it was dark. I took a shower in what would rank at the absolute bottom of my bathhouse experiences. Hot water trickled out of a shower head onto my shoulders. One toilet was stopped up and the other stall's door had been ripped off. The floor was so slimy I avoided walking on it barefoot. I peeked into the laundry room. There would be no washing here at Ditto. It looked as if someone had tried to destroy the machines with a sledgehammer, my best guess was for the treasure of quarters inside. A cop car, lights flashing, was down the way at a campsite where 1980s metal had been cranked up earlier. Our site had a good pine needle carpet that I spread the tarp over. I tied off the overhead tarp and felt as if we were ready for the coming storms. Sometime that night, a couple arrived at the site next to us, and set up camp in a panic just before the rain began. The woman talked in sorrowful tones, and the guy didn't have much to say in reply. They had a pit bull who came over to visit Maggie, whose collar I grabbed just in time. I asked my new neighbors please to come over and get their dog, and they did, with profuse apologies. The first night wasn't so bad, and the next day, one of the Riverkeeper guys who lived in Huntsville—Charles Lee—brought the towels and water I requested, and surprised me with homemade banana bread and a six-pack of locally brewed IPA called Blue Pants: "unreasonably good beer," it said on the can. I agreed. Charles' son got a tongue bath from Maggie that he seemed to enjoy, to a point. I managed to corral her and keep her from knocking the kid over. After Charles left, the rain started up again, and I visited the marina store, where I filled my five-gallon water container. A worker there said he'd help me portage from camp the next day, using his pickup truck.

As the hard rains fell that second night, I kept eyeing the asphalt parking strip of my site as a new home for my tent. I didn't move for two reasons: number one, I couldn't stake the tent down, and I knew big winds were coming; and number two, I didn't want to sleep on asphalt. Big mistake. That night, the big blow hit, reds and yellows blinking across the radar on my phone. The wind roared up to forty miles an hour, and rain fell heavily for eleven hours straight. At one point, around eleven o'clock, I noted that all the towels I'd arranged as dams around the edges of the tent, were soaking wet. Our pine needle campsite was turning into a pond, so I turned Maggie loose in the rain, and she promptly disappeared while I repositioned the overhead tarp and dragged the tent and all of its contents onto the asphalt pad. I used what dry clothes I had left to swab out the tent, rounded up Maggie, and we got back inside, both of us dripping. Next morning, the whole campground had been transformed into a swamp, with standing water, fallen leaves, and branches everywhere. I had to wade ankle deep in some places to get to the marina. While I was there, bailing out my canoe, a guy with a camo head rag and a cigar stub in his mouth came and stood over me.

"Old Town?" he said. "That's the first boat I paddled in."

We rehashed our weather experiences of the previous night, and he said that one of his boat slips had come unmoored, and he had to get some guys to help him secure it. He didn't introduce himself as the marina owner, but I started to get the feeling that he might be. The last thing he said disturbed me: the river's probably going to come up about five feet in all this rain, he said, and they usually open the floodgates after something like this.

This news gave new urgency to my portage and got me worried about where I could camp next. Guntersville Dam was fourteen miles away, and I planned on camping one more night below it before locking through. If that much water was coming through, I might have trouble even approaching it.

The kid who said he would help me portage never showed up. I suspect he got recruited to help with the runaway boat slip. I was exhausted after hauling all my gear, and I'd worn a blister on my heel from the underwater hiking I'd done in river sandals. This would fester for the next couple of weeks.

We launched around noon, and after a mile of paddling, a thunderstorm commenced, a medium-gauge pour that lasted about an hour. In my rain gear, I paddled on through it, no place to pull off anyway. Maggie didn't seem to mind it either. When it cleared, I began to appreciate this wild and undeveloped part of the river, upper Wheeler Lake. A swarm of gars swirled to the surface of a deep eddy near a rock wall; gars had followed German distance swimmer Andreas Fath "like dolphins," on his journey down the Tennessee, said Martin Knoll, a geology professor at Sewanee, who accompanied Fath down the length of the river in the summer of 2017. (Knoll, Trevathan, 2018) I'd never thought of them as sociable and intelligent like dolphins, but I was happy to see them cruising near the surface, as if to welcome us back to the river after the big storm hiatus at Ditto.

The landscape took on a demeanor of desolation, no other boats out, the foothills of the lower end of the Cumberland Plateau rising up around us. Bob Mountain's slope, too steep to be developed, was covered in the light green foliage of early spring mixed with the darker hues of the cedars. The big rain fueled waterfalls that roared down steep slopes, some of them narrow cascades we could see, others hidden in the trees. No houses rose from the peak of this flat-top mountain that I could see, and I began to wonder what was up there. I passed the mouth of the Flint River and then the mouth of the Paint River without knowing it. I had intended to paddle up the Paint a ways, but the charts didn't have it labeled, and I thought it was another big creek mouth.

The Project Remote researchers found the most remote place in Alabama on Dauphin Island, in the Gulf of Mexico, eight miles from a road. I went through a stretch on this day where I did not see or hear evidence of a road, and I think that may have added to my emotional reaction to this place I call desolate, a term that to me, is not completely negative. It was lonely, this place, empty of houses, marinas, and boats. I saw very few signs that humans had even been here. A yellow fiberglass canoe lay on its side, half swamped on the bank, no paddles in sight. The land rose in rugged expanses above the lake, the banks less accessible and steeper the closer we got to the dam. After all my complaints about Tracy's gang at Cowford and the laundromat destroyers at Ditto Landing, a melancholy arose from being the only human around. I was on my own as far as a place to stay, no campgrounds, private or public, no wildlife refuge or officially designated public land.

About three miles downstream of the dam, there was one place where it looked like we could land the boat, but the towering wooden cross planted in the ground discouraged me. If there had been a congregation gathered around it singing hymns, I might have stopped, but under the desolate circumstances, the place had a creepy, southern gothic feel to it; a super-sized commemoration of the crucifixion did not reassure me about an overnight stay. I paddled beneath a sheer, tan bluff, mottled with gray, that towered

Downstream of Guntersville Dam, Painted Bluff, an archaeological site that includes drawings dating back to around 1400 A.D., loomed above us as we waited for a barge to get underway.

above us a few hundred feet. I didn't know it at the time, but this was Painted Bluff, an important archeological site with more than a hundred cliff drawings from the Mississippian period, around 1400 A.D. Near the top in pigments of red, orange, and yellow are human figures, some with hands raised as if dancing, and animals such as a serpent and a catfish. In 2013, the Alabama Historical Commission placed the site on its "Places in Peril" list. TVA has worked to preserve the images, which are threatened by weather and vandalism. I paddled on past Painted Bluff and approached a moored barge that angled out from the left bank. I wanted to shadow this bank because the lock was on this side and because I had resigned myself to stealth camping at TVA's boat ramp, about a half mile below the dam, where signs would be posted prohibiting camping. I paddled up close and asked one of the deck hands if I could slide past the prow of the barge where it was moored. I knew better. He said no, I could not, that they were tied off "on the hill." I had the choice of going back around the towboat to the right side of the river and then back across to the left, or of waiting for the big boat to continue on its way to lock through the dam. When the deck hand told me they would be leaving "in just a minute," I backed into a creek next to them and waited. After an hour, when they left, darkness had fallen.

Guntersville Dam was spilling from its floodgates, the current strong and getting stronger. That day, its outflow had increased from 45,000 to 60,000 cubic feet per second, significant for a paddler in the dark. Hugging the left bank meant we were on the outside of a bend, where the current ran strongest. I stayed close to the bank and struggled to keep the boat straight and away from deadfall and stickups, which appeared suddenly out of the dark, as if reaching up from the depths. Being near the bank offered false security because there were no landings in case the current got too strong and turned us back. Maggie, sensing my anxiety, fidgeted in the bow.

After an hour of this, we approached the ramp. In the parking lot above the ramp, a rotating strobe-like beacon turned everything surreal and alarmist. Already, I felt as if I'd done something wrong. Maggie and I, struggling against the dark current, came in for a hard landing sideways. I scraped my paddle against the concrete for purchase and Maggie cleared the gunnel with a graceful leap and disappeared. A guy fishing at the ramp looked a little uneasy. A canoe emerging out of the darkness into the blinking strobe of the TVA boat ramp was not what you'd expect as you stood there searching for peace and maybe some fresh fish for dinner.

I'd run over his lines in my dash for a landing, but he didn't let on until he got concerned that we might get hooked. I babbled an apology and stumbled out of the canoe, my rubber boots splashing in a half foot of water. I was looking around for a place to hide my boat.

"Catching any?" I asked. There were no cars parked at the top of the ramp, no evidence that this was some kind of hot spot, even though the current below a dam stirs up food sources for fish, some of them monstrous.

"No physical fish," he said. "I'm here for the spiritual ones."

That was a new one on me, but as an inept fisherman, I understood that the benefits of pursuit were sometimes as important as the harvest. I stood there beside my boat, shading my eyes against the blinking white light, and asked this man, this transcendental fisher, why the heck they were trying to blind us.

"It's for the barges," he said. Then he jerked the rod and started reeling something in. A physical fish. I was glad of it because I thought Maggie and I might have ruined his spot.

"Drum," he said in a neutral tone. "I am thankful for whatever comes to me." He unhooked the bony fish and released it.

"Let him go back for his daddy," I said.

The man chuckled and I peppered him with questions about TVA, the dam, and the fishing here, hoping he'd stick around to ease my loneliness and possibly to validate my imminent lawbreaking. Perhaps sensing my desperation, he walked up to his car, without any fish, and drove away. Our only companion now was the dam, lit up like a factory a few hundred yards away; the hum of electricity and the low moan of moving water flooded the blinking night.

I pulled the canoe into a tree-clogged inlet to moor it outside the current, and to hide it from the law and the lawless. In there arose a smell something like death, unclean and dank, with a hint of chemicals. I managed to snag my fishing lure in some branches, and the line tangled itself into a weaving that seemed impossible to achieve even if I'd had all day. In my attempt to break the line, I yanked too hard and broke off the tip of the rod. I had Maggie tied up above on a flat spot next to the sign that said keep off the grass. I shouldered a load that included my tent, sleeping bag, Maggie's food bucket, and the sleeping pad. On the first step up the uneven riprap slope, I slipped and stumbled into the water, deep enough for it to pour over my rubber boot top.

By the time I fed Maggie and had the tent set up as close to the woods as I could get, it was after ten o'clock, and I was shaking from exhaustion and hunger. I opened a warm beer and ate a package of dehydrated biscuits and gravy, which sounds like an impossible recipe, I know, but was surprisingly good, especially if you haven't eaten in eight hours. I lay awake much of the night, dreading the glare of official headlights. Where they would send us, I did not know. I wasn't about to lock through the dam in the dark, and I would rather have gone to jail than to float downstream, look for the high-cross clearing and then have to fight the current again the next day.

I understood the reasoning behind the prohibition of camping at a boat ramp. No one was here to manage people, to enforce rules about trash and noise, and there were no facilities for human waste. For me, it was a campsite of necessity.

Up before dawn after an hour or two of sleep, part of my routine stealth-camping getaway, I disassembled my camping gear before anyone could accuse us of breaking the law. Just after first light, Maggie and I were locking through Guntersville, heading toward a state park for our next overnight stop. The luxuries of drink machines, indoor plumbing, showers, a laundry, and the privilege of renting an official plot of land awaited us there. If we were lucky, we'd get a fire ring and a table. Being lifted up in the lock of the dam and then emerging on the next lake above buoyed me with optimism, a sense of salvation, a sort of a reverse baptismal immersion. It made me glad to leave Wheeler, even though it was one of my favorite lakes on the

Tennessee. It carried whiffs of tragedy and desolation. In a couple of days, I would find out that a thirty-year-old barge deckhand had lost his legs from below the knee in the same lock that I passed through, perhaps on the same night that we had stealth camped at the ramp. He was completing a task he'd done many times, but something with the mooring lines had gone horribly wrong.

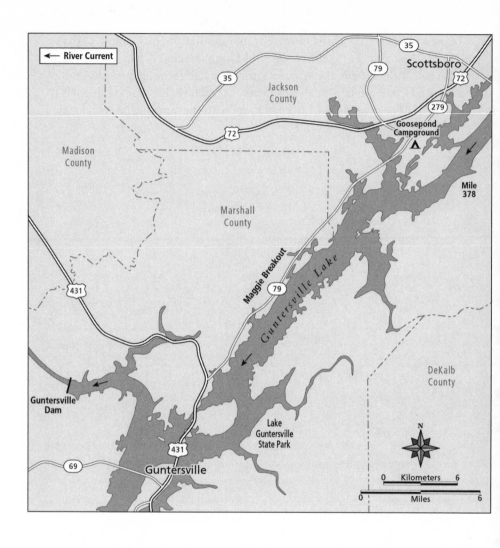

17

A FACE IN THE CROWD

The Guntersville Dam lock operator chatted me up about my trip so far, and after a pause said this: "Oh, you're not that guy."

I was not that guy. This was the kayaker that Ranger John, back at J.P. Coleman in Mississippi, had referred to. From the lock operator I learned that this kayaker makes my twenty-year anniversary paddle seem pedestrian. In his green kayak he paddles down and up the length of the Tennessee River every spring. Every spring. What was an epic, trip-of-a-lifetime for me was an annual pilgrimage for him, a routine. When I asked the lock operator if the kayaker was a young guy, he said, "mid-fifties." Not young at all.

Throughout my trip, people who worked on the river—at dams and marinas and campgrounds—would tell me about journeys that surpassed mine in mileage and difficulty. At Hales Bar Marina, about a week away, upstream from Nickajack Dam, the marina manager told me about a Californian who paddleboarded the river from Chattanooga to Paducah, including locking through the dams. Once he made it to Paducah, he took off running for California. A couple of other guys had passed through in kayaks, having started out at the headwaters of the Holston, on their way to New Orleans.

Before my trip, I'd corresponded with the only other person I knew about who had paddled the Tennessee going upstream, Bill Nederman, whose trip up the river was an extension of his retracing the return route of Lewis and Clark, from the Pacific coast. Also a veteran thru hiker, Bill—or One Gallon, his trail name—said he portaged around a couple of dams, including Kentucky, where he said locking through would have taken too long. Hard core. He paddled an Old Town canoe similar to mine.

Legendary paddler Verlen Kruger, from Wisconsin, started canoeing at the age of forty-two and logged in over 100,000 miles, including repeated trips up and down the Mississippi, and expeditions that took him to South America, some down the Pacific coastline. He also ventured on long voyages into Canada and the Yukon. Kruger designed his own decked canoes and loved to race. The trip he called the "Ultimate Canoe Challenge" was a three-year expedition of 28,000 miles, paddling and portaging in North America. He paddled and portaged up the Colorado River—a feat most didn't think possible. Kruger, who was usually accompanied by another paddler in a separate boat, resembled the seventeenth- and eighteenth-century voyageurs more than anyone I knew about. Incredibly tough and focused, he had this to say about fear and hardship: "It depends on how you look at hardship. . . . It toughens some and weakens others. The same experience that will make one person stronger and positive, will almost destroy someone else. I find that extreme effort seems to make me grow. Toughen up" (Kruger, Peterson 2006).

Thank you, Verlen. Thank you, green kayak doppelganger, going up and down the Tennessee each year. It's good to be humbled, to put your aspirations and accomplishments into the proper perspective.

Geezer update: Now, just past the halfway point of my trip, I felt stronger as I paddled, as if I were getting more out of each stroke. I still had some cuts and bruises, including the nasty blister on my heel from the Ditto Landing portage, and my left shoulder ached after long periods of windmill paddling such as the approach to Guntersville Dam, but I was much leaner now, more flexible, and much more tolerant of hardships involving weather, lack of sleep, and the routine chores of propelling and parking the boat and portaging gear. I felt fairly confident that I would finish the trip, barring a catastrophe. Having made it this far, with the feats of expeditionists like Kruger and Alexander MacKenzie in mind, I became convinced that you could get used to about anything that didn't kill you. And I began to realize that many of those undertaking long motorless journeys, much longer and more arduous than mine, were either approaching geezerdom or well beyond it.

As usual, after locking through a dam, I felt a general sense of wonderment about the beauty of the artificial lake, spread out before me as the big doors opened up. We paddled along the right bank, where saplings grew out of the shelves of gray rock walls, which trickled with runoff from the rains. Gravel bars reached out from paddler-friendly coves, not all of them filled up with houses. We were about as far south as the Great Bend of the river reached, and spring seemed to have fully bloomed overnight, the trees leafed-out and the banks thick with lush undergrowth. From cracks in the rocky gray bluffs sprouted ferns so green they seemed iridescent in the bright sun. Our goal that day was Guntersville State Park, another stop that I remembered vividly from the 1998 trip. It was—with J.P. Coleman and Wheeler state parks—among the top five campsites of that trip, all of them shaded by groves of pines, all with sites right next to the water and easy canoe landings. The difference at Guntersville on that visit was that I camped at the nearest flat spot next to the water, not an official site, and I sat around a campfire with my neighbors, RV people who shared food and drink. They didn't think anyone would bother me in my unofficial site. I probably could have left the next morning without paying, but I made the short walk up to the store, paid my ten dollars, and bought some potato chips.

Maggie and I passed under Veterans Memorial Highway Bridge and began to paddle past what looked like parts of the state park: a marina, cabins, a boat ramp. It seemed to go on forever. Finally, we reached an area that resembled tent sites, fire rings on a mown slope, a few small trees here and there. Not even recognizing the tent area I remembered from twenty years ago, I knew to discard any hopes of reliving my memory of that stay. As at J.P. Coleman, the park itself had expanded, particularly the RV section, which was like a small town now, in a grove of mature trees, separate from the tent sites that were down a slope, near the water. The primitive area had been downgraded to a fire ring and a flat spot, with no immediate access to drinking water or electricity, and no table—all of these primitive features costing twenty-five dollars. I got lucky, though. I met campground workers Fred and Sherry. These two were in a golf cart on their way to complete an errand when they saw me trudging along with my soggy backpack over my shoulder, sleep-deprived from stealth camping the night before. Fred got out of the cart and let me take his seat as Sherry drove me to the camp store, over a mile away from the tent sites, where I could pay for my stay. She lit a cigarette, blew out a long, satisfying plume, and said she hoped I didn't mind her smoking. She had to have one when she got to work.

"I got married last year, and I really don't know why," she said.

She didn't give me time to speculate on possible reasons. She and Fred, she told me, had traveled to Guntersville from Florida to live in the VIP area of the campground and to work part-time, about twenty hours a week.

"I'm fifty-nine years old. I guess it was about time," she said about getting married. "I do what I want anyway."

I wasn't sure what had prompted these confessions, and I felt a bit uncomfortable with it, glad that she didn't expand on what it meant to do what she wanted. I muttered something about that being a good plan for a solid marriage, that I'd been divorced a few years myself.

At the store, I leaped out of the cart, rescued from further conversation. Later, Fred came to cart me back to the campsite with my candy bars and a roll of paper towels. I had devoured a bag of potato chips and guzzled a Coke before he got there.

I mentioned feeling like a vagabond, and Fred seized on the word. That's exactly what he and Sherry were, he said: "Vagabonds!" The state park people had tried to get them to stay the whole year, but that wouldn't be happening, he said. He and Sherry would be going someplace warmer come winter.

"We got married last July," he said. I braced myself for a confession of some sort, but it didn't come. He was a Navy veteran, he said, living off a pretty good pension.

I took Maggie with me to do laundry because I didn't want to leave her tied to that one scraggly tree at our campsite. The shade it provided was scarce, though now the sky was clouding up and threatening to shower. While washing my clothes, I met an RV camper who was waiting for his wife to finish in the bathhouse, which was across a foyer from the laundromat. She wanted a fifth wheeler to replace their pull-behind camper, and he was upset about it.

"You lose the bed of your pickup," he said, referring to the hitch for the camper that would have to be mounted in his truck. The one his wife picked out would cost eighty-thousand dollars.

"That's a lot of money," I said.

"You're damn right it's a lot of money!"

I seemed to have wandered into a zone of marital strife. On our walk back to the campsite, with Maggie jerking me along on her leash, a woman glared at us from the open door of her RV. A little dog yapped in the background. I said something about having washed my clothes just now, just to be friendly, and she continued glaring. Perhaps we had passed too close to her rented domain, primitives disturbing the peace. It was a relief to return to the tent area, where our neighbors, set up in the only shaded primitive site, were a young man and woman with a toddler, all of them cheerful and active. They had a spacious, new-looking tent and a spiffy little car, making me think that they had chosen to camp rather than staying in a hotel. More than Maggie and me, they countered the rowdy tent-camper stereotype from which Cowford had formulated its discriminatory policy.

The young man walked by our site on his way to fish from the bank. They were from the northwest, he said. He had friends who had canoed the length of the Columbia, he told me. This was a river twice the length of the Tennessee. He waded knee-deep into the lake to cast his line, a technique not often practiced by locals.

I popped open one of the two remaining cans of Blue Pants beer and started the water boiling for dinner when Fred and Sherry pulled up in their cart. I was just about to open a pouch of dehydrated beef and peppers, one of my favorites.

Sherry held out an aluminum pan full of chicken wings and pepperoncinis. "We grilled too much," she said.

"Take all you want," Fred added. "I know what it's like living outdoors like you are." He said he'd run a trap line in Minnesota, where he grew up.

I took five or six, plus some peppers. I could have eaten thirty wings, but it looked like Fred and Sherry were making the rounds with the pan, and I would have regretted eating more than what I'd taken. My stomach had shrunk.

I had little to trade in return, but I offered up my last beer. Fred refused for both of them. He'd had a string of serious health issues, including cancer and a heart bypass, so he said he didn't drink much anymore. "I do like a cold beer every now and then," he admitted.

I think he may have put subtle emphasis on the word "cold." As I devoured the wings, a breeze came up and rain sprinkled down, nothing new about this. Intent on the wings, I didn't move, and the rain stopped after a few minutes. Best wings I'd ever had, big and meaty, with a little crunch, just the right combination of spicy and sweet. That night I dropped into a deep sleep and dreamed that the water came up. Fred, looking out for me even in dreamland, drove by in his cart and said, "You might want to move your tent."

Next morning, we headed north away from Guntersville, another fond memory from the first trip obliterated, but overall a more than tolerable camping experience, mainly because of Fred and Sherry's generosity.

The first otter of the trip swam in front of us off the bank of a small island, and Maggie, who had taken to putting her front paws up on the gunnel, standing tall like a masthead, observed intently without barking, just as she did with about every other animal, including cats and dogs. I started to think that she might become one of the greatest-ever boat dogs, starting so young and growing up on this long trip. We'd been through a lot together, and we were becoming more comfortable and skilled in the boat. Today would test our patience with each other on land.

We paddled about ten miles along a shore lined with houses, no great places to stop, so I did what I'd been doing most of the trip. I let Maggie out to pee at a place where I didn't want to get out. With the warmer weather, I'd gone from rubber boots to river sandals, and I didn't want to wade out to this brushy steep shoreline from the boat. Maggie leaped out over the water and climbed the bank with ease to take care of business. She disappeared into the dense forest. After about ten minutes, I began to call her. No response. I could not hear her rustling around in the brush. I blew on a whistle and yelled. Finally, after about a half hour, I got out of the boat, waded to shore, and climbed the mud slippery bank to retrieve my runaway dog. I might have cussed a bit as I trudged through the ivy and the thorns and the sinkholes a quarter-mile up to a paved road. I looked both ways. No sign of Maggie. Across the road was a house up on a hill. The gravel driveway was posted with multiple signs: "No Trespassing!" If she'd gone up there, the nearest dwelling, I might not see her ever again. I'd left my cell phone in the boat, so I had to trudge back to get it and fight my way back to the road once more, before I could get a signal. I had a message from HomeAgain, the lost dog service that the Humane Society had included in the Maggie-package. She wore a yellow tag with a phone number on it. Maggie had been found, the message told me, giving me the number of her rescuers. I was relieved and angry at the same time. I'd begun to think that she might be gone for good, and I doubted I would be able to complete the trip alone, without my companion. How would I have explained her disappearance? It made me look like a negligent dog owner. At the same time, I was angry at the utter lack of loyalty in Maggie. How dare she attempt to escape from me, the one who rescued her from doggie prison? Had she no sense of gratitude?

A man came walking toward me from a mile down the road, Maggie on a leash that was not hers. This was Cliff. His wife Caroline had found Maggie on the road, surveying swankier houses than the one with the No Trespassing signs. Caroline took Maggie home with her because she was trotting toward a busy highway. I thanked Cliff and put Maggie's own leash on her. I did not scold her. What good would that do? I was weak in the knees with relief, and I didn't want to give her a reason to run off again. I waited a bit to calm down, and then I had some questions for her. I may have raised my voice a bit when I inquired about where she thought she was going and how was I supposed to find her in the Alabama wilderness.

United by the leash now, we had trouble getting back to the boat through the rugged undergrowth and overhanging limbs of the forest. I stumbled in multiple sinkholes. Thorns tore my flesh. I tried to coax Maggie to follow my path so that her leash didn't get hung. From this point forward, after Maggie's Guntersville Breakout, she became my prisoner, always wearing the twenty-foot lead. Sometimes I attached the end of it to the thwart of the canoe, and other times I'd wrap it around a tree. When we landed, the thwart attachment worked well because in her exuberance to explore, she would pull the boat up onto the shore and enable me to get out with dry feet. Maggie had a job now.

We approached Goosepond Colony Resort that evening. Near Scottsboro, Alabama, Goosepond combines marina, golf course, cottages, a lodge, meeting rooms, cabins, a restaurant, and a campground, all into one sprawling location. It is vast. Arriving by boat, I ducked under the low bridge of a narrow road to enter a large, protected cove. At one of the marina's boat slips, a portly man sitting on a yacht with an iced drink in his hand noticed us and said to his companions, "Now, he's got the right idea!"

Having heard a comment like this more than once, I was never sure exactly what people meant, but instead of inquiring, which might have seemed rude, I said thanks for the compliment and asked if they knew where the campground was.

"Bear to the left," he said, making a grand gesture without rising from his seat. "About a half-mile that way, beyond the golf course."

So far, I recognized nothing about Goosepond from my stay here in 1998, certainly not the long paddle to the campground nor the golf course. Not until I got to the deepest part of the cove, past the sites occupied by RVs, did I think I had located a primitive site fairly close to the water. With yet another big rain coming, I laid claim to it and began to set up my tarp, which took a while because the trees I tied off to were far apart. The site was clearly meant for an RV, with electricity, water, picnic table, and a gravel pad for parking. Across the way, watching me, was a lean, tough-looking guy, Robert, who was living in a small, pull-behind camper. He wondered aloud why I was canoeing the Tennessee. He was a paddler, too, he said, and he liked to fish the Flint River in his kayak.

"This river is trashed," he said, "especially at Stevenson." This was a few miles upstream.

Where I'd made camp was 300 yards from the nearest RV, and on the other side of me, farther up the cove, was a low-lying area in a grove of pines where somebody had set up a big tent. This, I found out later, was the tent area: no picnic table, no water, no gravel pad and no electric. The nearest bathhouse was 200 yards away, but the store where I had to pay for my site was a mile away. I secured Maggie, asked Robert to keep an eye on her, and hiked to pay up.

Celina, the cashier, did not charge me the full price—thirty-seven dollars—when she found out I was in a tent. She said sixteen dollars would be fine, but not to tell anybody. Her husband, Cliff, allegedly retired from working at the campground and just hanging out at the store, brought us a bundle of wood in his golf cart. Maggie and I stayed a couple of nights at hospitable Goosepond. We waited out a twelve-hour rain that started the next morning, and this time we stayed dry because we were camped on the gravel parking pad and I'd also done a better job with the overhead tarp. To pass the time in my dry tent, I caught up on sleep and reading. I happened upon a *New York Times* article about Polish kayaker Aleksander Doba, who crossed the Atlantic three times, the third trip after he'd turned 70. He paddled solo, without support, from New Jersey to France. Spending 110 days at sea, he slept in his kayak's small cabin and carried on with the functions of life somehow, without the respite of dry land. He was the first person to kayak from continent to continent across the Atlantic, under muscle power only. Elizabeth Weil, who wrote the article, captured one key characteristic that motivated him to finish these incredible journeys: "What most of us experience as suffering he repurposes as contrarian self-determination, and that gives him an existential thrill" (Weil, *New York Times Magazine*. March 22, 2018). Doba loved depriving himself and submitting his body and spirit to painful tests of endurance. On his first crossing, from Senegal to Brazil, he lost forty-five pounds.

In Doba's own words, here's what drives him: "You can be made small by life or rage against it. I do not want to be the little gray man" (Doba, Weil. *New York Times Magazine*, March 22, 2018).

Words to live by. I was cozy at Goosepond in the long rain, but I would face more challenges, on my own modest scale, and right or wrong, raging would once again become part of my way of reacting to challenge. Anything to avoid becoming the little gray man.

18

SLEEPING IN A CANOE

Aside from the obvious motivation to progress toward my final destination, I had other diversions that occupied my time with something
other than paddling or conversing with Maggie. One goal was to
take photos of animals, two in particular, wily companions whose presence
was constant along the river but whose unwillingness to linger for my lens
created a playful challenge. Since I was nearing Mile 400, I needed to sharpen
my senses for these two spirit animals, one a bird, the other an amphibian.
Fifty-odd years ago, my first pet was a small turtle who lived in a bowl of
water and pea gravel. His name was Yurtle, and he depended upon me to
feed him and to change his water daily. I'd take him out of the bowl, hold
him up close to my face, and talk to him. I can still remember his beady
eyes and the musty wet turtle smell. One day I forgot to change his water.
Who knows why? I was five or six years old. By the time I remembered, he
was belly up on the surface. I still remember the intensity of my grief, and
I've felt guilty about it ever since.

Alongside Bridgeport Island near the Alabama/Tennessee border, I paddled with stealth toward a row of five turtles perched on a log in the sun. I
would see this over and over, so many times that I would try to predict when
they would drop off the log at my approach, as they always did, without fail.
I tried to discern a pattern based on size or age because they never jumped

off together. You'd think the big ones, who were older, I assumed, would maybe wait until I got close to fall off the log, having experienced intrusions like mine many times, without harm. No obvious patterns emerged. Only this could I count on. By the time I got my camera out of the dry bag and had it up to my face ready to shoot, each turtle would have disappeared. Oddly enough, turtles refused to cooperate with my desire to have the iconic shot of them dropping off a log. At the five-turtle log near Bridgeport, something unusual happened. Instead of dropping off into the water with a plop-splash, Turtle Number Five, a big one about the size of a dinner plate, ran up the bank, lost his balance, and cartwheeled to the shoreline, where he landed on his back. This was twelve miles from Nickajack Dam, so I was paddling hard against the current to gain territory. Still, I couldn't just keep paddling past Turtle Number Five, helpless on his back. So I drifted backwards, slipped my paddle under him, and flipped him like a fried egg. Off he went into the water. I thought he might reward me by poking his head out of the water to let me take a picture, but no, he was gone, and the turtle quest continued.

My spirit animal—as I decree it—is the great blue heron. I've seen hundreds of these birds—giant, pterodactyl-like, with yellow beaks and yellow eyes—their wings so powerful you can hear the air being displaced as they work their way across the water. I do not think that they reciprocate my admiration. Over and over, I disturbed them from their fishing spots: on the bank, perched on a prong of deadfall; in the uppermost reaches of a dead tree; or on a rock within the camouflage of the bank, almost invisible. They didn't seem to begrudge my incursions, though the best ones would grace me with their gravelly squawk-squawk-squawk as they lifted off, a parting shot approximating human-like annoyance, but far more majestic. I always apologized and wanted to explain that I didn't disturb them on purpose. And I'd always try to photograph one of the liftoffs, but the timing of it seemed impossible. They were like jumping fish: repeated events that were like photos in my mind, which would make great shots if only I knew when they would happen.

After we left Goosepond, the river narrowed and the current increased at the same time as a tailwind kicked up, creating a sort of détente that felt like paddling a placid and pristine natural lake. Except it wasn't. Robert, my neighbor back at Goosepond, was at least partly correct in calling the river trashy. It was a bit reductive in its negativity, Robert's description, but more accurate on this stretch than anywhere else; the section from Goosepond to Nickajack Dam won the prize for most large-scale exotic trash. Next to a beautiful island, unnamed on the charts, just upstream from a tree full

A great blue heron, my spirit animal, tried to get some fishing done before Maggie and I disturbed him.

of heron nests, a full-sized refrigerator lay tilted, half-submerged, its door removed. This was a fairly recent deposit, the shelves intact, even the little light bulb. How did a refrigerator arrive here to despoil this beautiful place? What was its story? Not far from that, near Bellefont Nuclear Generating Station, floated a giant tractor tire. There was more to come: natural beauty, household trash, and large industry comingling.

That evening, after paddling twenty miles from Goosepond, we skirted the left bank, Mud Creek Wildlife Management Area, and looked for a place to lay our heads for the night. The land on this side of the river had flattened out, but there were no places to park the canoe; the banks were low, but steep and covered with thick brush. I could see the flat terrain and the clearings above, but we could not land the boat to get to them. With a half-hour of daylight left, I spotted a ditch cut into the heavily vegetated bank. I rammed the bow of the canoe as far up that ditch as I could, and first mate Maggie, tethered to the boat, jumped out and dragged us a bit farther up the mud-slick corridor. I was able to disembark, traverse a few yards of mud-sucking bottom, and pull the canoe up far enough to unload and set up camp. The portage to the clearing wasn't the longest—about fifty yards—but it bristled with brush and branches that hung low over swampy areas with standing water. Caught in one of the bushes that grew out of the ditch bottom was a toilet seat and lid. Maggie conducted a thorough investigation of it and ignored my commands to let it be. Up above, I stomped down knee-high yellow-blooming weeds on a patch of dry ground just big enough for the tent, in this, the land of croaking frogs, mud, and pools of smelly water. A camping pattern was beginning to emerge. Every cushy campsite was followed by a horrendous one. Soggy Bottoms, as I named it, landed near the bottom of the rankings.

Maggie, who could nap as much as she wanted during the day, stayed up most of the night, on alert. She growled and emitted small, grumbling barks at something that bristled in the hedgerows all night. I guessed raccoon or possum. I was too tired to care much, but every time I dropped off to sleep, she'd wake me up and ignore my reassurances about whatever was stalking us. I also worried that some full-throttle Alabamian would race through here on his four-wheeler because we looked to be camped on some kind of track. Next morning, I couldn't wait to leave; I didn't even make coffee. Maggie, enamored of the toilet seat, wanted to linger. I convinced her to jump into the boat and got us going early. I was looking forward to some island camping on this day, my sixtieth birthday. A mile after launching and crossing to the other side, I met only the second group who had been camping on the river outside an established campground. They were on the point of a peninsula in Raccoon Creek Wildlife Management Area, a family of three: mom, dad, and a grown son. They had parked their vehicle at a campsite that featured a beach and a nice, big clearing. Another camping pattern was emerging: we'd spend the night at a substandard place and, the next day, see a bunch of good ones a short paddle away.

Bridgeport Island (also known as Long Island) was my target for the day. As always on this part of a reservoir, near the face of a dam, one challenge was to find a place to pull off because the stronger currents had cut away the banks to sheer mud walls.

For lunch we stopped at a boat ramp near Stevenson just past Crow Creek Wildlife Refuge and the Captain John Snodgrass Highway Bridge. Snodgrass left Shiloh with a head wound and went on to fight out the rest of the war, working his way up to the rank of colonel. He was in the thick of it at places like Corinth, Baton Rouge, and Franklin, having performed with enough courage on the side of the Confederacy to get a bridge named after him.

At the ramp, a young man and his girlfriend sat in a bass boat that wouldn't start. The girl was trying not to look bored, and her friend cranked the engine over and over, white fragrant smoke tainting the fresh air of the glorious spring day. A barge idled out in the main channel, and two men launched a small outboard from it and headed downstream. I wondered if this was the barge where the accident had occurred at Guntersville Dam. I hadn't seen many barges in the last week. Watching the young man get more and more frustrated with the engine, surely flooded now, I felt grateful not to have a motor to worry about. A paddle was pretty dependable, even one as fancy as I'd invested in before this trip. A sleek two-bladed tool, the graphite shaft weighed half that of my old single-blade paddle, and it was adjustable for feathering against the wind. I could break it in half for storage, but I hadn't done so since the beginning of the trip. Why would I? Turns out I should have been breaking it apart every night. Leaving it attached had made the seal swell and by now, I couldn't adjust or dismantle it even if I wanted to. Back at Goosepond, I found out my error after I took it apart and had a devil of a time getting it back together. I had to wedge the blade between the legs of a picnic table and wrench and screw it back into place, tearing the hard plastic blade in the process. So, while I was grateful for not having to fool with a stinky motor, I was not immune to equipment breakdowns.

A man and his wife backed down the ramp and put in a runabout with their granddaughter aboard. She was on her first boat ride, she announced, jumping around with rapid-fire questions that the old man was trying to answer one at a time. When I left, the kid in the bass boat had stopped cranking the motor and sat there talking to his girl. I paddled to the other side of the river and felt so sleepy after the restless night at Mud Creek that I rammed the canoe between a couple of stumps and reclined as best I could to take a nap in the shade. This was the first time I'd tried sleeping in the boat, on the water, a practice that many, including my girlfriend Catherine's son, Sam, assumed I was doing every night. The thwart, yoke, seats, and all my gear made it impossible to stretch all the way out, but I put enough soft packs under my back and head to lie back and settle in, my legs up on the thwart. I dropped off immediately. Fifteen minutes later, I started to come out of a deep sleep in fits and starts, uneasy because I had no idea where I was, though something told me I was in a precarious position. I could not seem to come fully awake, even though I was willing myself to, as if emerging from a dark place, held there by the threads of a dream, paralyzed. I don't know how much time passed in this struggle to come fully awake, but when my memory reset and I was able to sit up, aware of my floating circumstances, I promised myself never to sleep in the boat again.

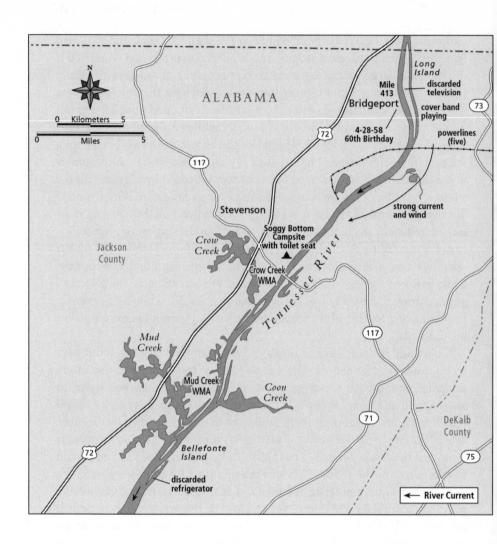

19

MOCKINGBIRD PEOPLE

An unholy April headwind rose up against me within a mile of Bridge-port Island, my destination for the day. On that wind floated the sounds of a live band. As if rehearsing, they would begin a song suddenly and end in the middle of it, though part of this might have been the effect of the variable wind and my distance from the band. As I got closer, I recognized Townes Van Zandt's "Pancho and Lefty," which I had on my phone and played from time to time on the trip. It told two stories, one of a criminal on the run, the other of the lawman on the hunt for him, a good song to travel by. The band, somewhere upstream, was doing a passable cover of it. It helped me work hard to make progress toward the island. If there was some kind of music festival, I hoped I would be allowed to camp among them. Their playing one of my favorite songs made me think we might be kindred spirits.

Between me and the island, five power lines crossed above the river, the farthest one close to the tip of the island. These were my progress markers. As I gazed up at power line number one, the band started in on Marshall Tucker's "Can't You See," got about halfway through it, and then it sounded like someone opened fire. The music stopped and the pop-pop continued for five minutes or so. I feared the worst, imagining a scorned groupie or a recently fired drummer. But what could I do about it? I was struggling to reach that first power line, and the sun was beginning to sink below the horizon. The concert seemed to be on the right bank of the island, and because of the current's push, I had to favor the left side, which faced the town of Bridgeport.

After an hour, I realized that I was on the dreaded treadmill, paddling hard and getting nowhere. I could tell because I was no closer to wire number one. Then I got mad because I was turning sixty on this day and stuck on the water when I should be taking it easy on the bank with a nice dehydrated dinner. I paddled faster. The band started up again, and even though I was glad they hadn't all been shot dead, I discovered that the closer I got, the worse they sounded. Distance had been their friend. The air began to chill as the day dimmed, and I gave up overtaking the wires and angled toward the left bank, a ferrying move that allowed me to make some progress upstream. The shoreline looked awful, no place to land, only steep muddy banks, even where the power lines crossed. Hugging the left bank, I resigned myself to trying for a boat ramp about two more miles upstream.

Then I saw a light up ahead, out from the bank, as if on a pier. I suspected it was a private dock, but the closer I got, the more people I could see milling about. It was almost dark, but as I inched closer, the place resolved itself into not one, but two piers that could only be intended for public use, with two boat ramps right there. I had struck gold on this, my sixtieth birthday!

After a seventeen-mile day, the last two on the speedy treadmill, I was exhausted. In the easy water near the piers, I floated up without paddling, not sure I had the strength to get out of the boat right away. I was trying to pull up without disturbing the anglers standing along the pier casting lines. The band started up again, a song I couldn't recognize, the lead singer's voice was so screechy and distorted.

"Where are you coming from?" asked a voice from the pier.

I shielded my eyes against the glare of the security light and found the source of this young but authoritative drawl, a boy in muddy rubber boots. He had reeled in his line when he saw Maggie and me emerge from obscurity.

"You mean today?" I asked.

When he didn't respond, I said I'd come from Mud Creek Wildlife Management Area today but that I'd paddled from Paducah starting March 21, and I was a little more than halfway through my trip up the whole river.

"How old are you?"

"I turned sixty today."

"Well, happy birthday."

I was ready to unload the boat and set up another stealth camp, in no mood for an interview, but something about this kid, Canyon was his name, slowed me down. His intonation reminded me of the kids in the movie version of *To Kill a Mockingbird*. I was, after all, still in Alabama. Barely.

His parents, he said, were sitting in their car. He gestured vaguely up the hill at a parking area.

I told him what the thwart and the yoke were on the canoe, and he asked me what I'd been eating, so I told him about dehydrated foods as well.

"I wish they would stop," he said. He looked across the river where the invisible band was playing.

"What is this place?" I asked. It was clearly a public park of some sort, but it wasn't on the charts.

Canyon paused for a minute to consider this question. "It's the river!"

I realized that's probably what his folks called this place when they brought him here. Canyon, a slim kid, was wearing a pair of shorts and a white shirt splattered with mud. He couldn't remember how he'd gotten muddy.

I spotted a dozen or so RVs up at the top of a hill behind a fence.

"Is that a campground up there?" I was still sitting in the boat, looking up at Canyon. I hadn't decided yet where I was going to camp or where I'd tie up the boat.

"No," he said. "People live there."

The kid was speaking in riddles, and there were hidden truths in all that he said. It was as if he'd been planted there to entertain me on my birthday, to help me recover from my enraged paddling on the Bridgeport Island treadmill, to help me celebrate a milestone birthday that I was destined to spend alone with my dog.

"If I was you," he said, "I'd tie up over yonder." He pointed at the second fishing pier, where several people were standing, their lines in the water.

No way was I tying up over there and causing a ruckus with restless Maggie, who had been straining to leap out of the boat and accost strangers with her aggressive affability. So far, she'd been good with just Canyon there.

"You think I could get away with camping here?" I asked him.

As was his habit, he turned the question over in his mind before answering.

"Yeah, I think you could. I've seen people do it before. I think I'd try up there." He pointed toward an old-school metal swing set that stood on the crown of a rise next to the bathrooms. A barbed wire fence marked the border of the park and the beginning of someone's pasture.

I tied the boat off on the pier and led Maggie to the swing set, where I secured her on her long lead. Back at the boat, Canyon asked if he could help me unload. I gave him a couple of light dry bags to carry.

Just before dark, I was ecstatic to see this pier reaching out from a public park in Bridgeport, Alabama, a refuge that was not marked on the navigational charts.

"There's the owner of the park up there," he said, pointing at a pickup truck with its lights on. "I mean manager," he added.

The park manager drove away. Either he hadn't noticed my clear intent to camp illegally, without much pretense of stealth, or he chose to ignore me. When we deposited the first load near the swing set, Canyon asked if I was going to worry about my boat getting stolen.

"I'll be right here," I said. I gestured at my illegal campsite, which offered a commanding view of the pier below, where the canoe was moored. "I'll be able to watch it all night."

"Sometimes I don't like people," he said. "There's some druggies around here."

"Do they come to the park?"

"Yeah."

On the next load, he said that something had spilled out of the green kitchen bag he had slung over his shoulder. "It smells kinda good. Minty."

It was my dishwashing liquid; the cap had come open and leaked onto the kid's muddy shirt. His parents tooted their car horn, a signal to leave, and he walked down to the riverside to get his fishing pole, in no hurry. I thought it a bit strange that the parents didn't get out and watch Canyon fish, even if they didn't want to fish themselves.

Canyon wished me luck with the trip and left. I imagined him in the backseat of the car trying to tell his parents about the canoer camping in the park on his birthday, crazy old guy who said he was paddling the whole river.

It would be an unusual milestone birthday, but I counted myself as fortunate, having made it to this place that I didn't know existed, just when I thought I was doomed to paddle onward through the night in this current, against the wind. There were some kind of geezer lessons to be learned from my enraged treadmill paddling. Perhaps, knowing when to alter plans. Or not to be so stubborn in adhering to an unreachable goal, the island where the bad music emanated. To be flexible, maybe?

Our campsite was half-hidden in the shadow of the bathrooms on a luxurious patch of grass and blooming clover. I asked Maggie not to bark at people coming and going from the boat ramp and fishing piers, and she seemed to understand. People would come and go all night, and the concert across the way had started up again, loud and clear. I felt like I was part of a community here at Bridgeport, a place I'd sailed past, without noticing, in 1998.

An hour after Canyon left, a young couple arrived to fish from the pier. From a weighted rig on a twenty-foot long rod, the husband was slinging baitfish (skipjack) far into the night. His wife was catching the skipjack with worms. I went down to make sure my boat was secure and not in their way.

"That's the longest fishing pole I've ever seen," I said.

"Don't tell me you come from Stevenson in that thing," he said. That was where we'd stopped for lunch.

I told him where I'd come from that day and where I'd started my voyage, in Paducah. When he didn't react, I began to explain the location of Paducah, at the river's mouth.

"I know where it is." He shook his head at the absurdity of such a trip. I went ahead and explained to him what I was doing and why, covering the twenty-year anniversary, my desire to see how the river had changed, and my having grown up on one end of the river. He reeled in his bait and gave it another long throw out into the middle of the river.

His wife took up for me. "We can always use more information," she said. "To each his own."

Exactly. But to each his own what? Obsessions? Long journeys that made no practical sense in these days of motors and information easily accessible online? Night fishing with baitfish your wife was catching for you? I didn't ask.

Maggie got comfortable at our campsite in the park at Bridgeport, where we celebrated my sixtieth birthday and interacted with some colorful locals.

I asked them if they knew what was going on across the water, if they knew the band.

"I wish they would stop," said the woman.

I said, "I like what they're playing, but they're not doing a great job of it. I think that guy was trying to sound like Neil Young."

"That was a girl singing," said the woman. "And she's either drunk or crazy."

The next song, Tom Petty's "Last Dance for Mary Jane," I could almost sing along with, but not quite. At least I could recognize it, progress for the island band.

My birthday—official confirmation of my entrance into geezerdom—came and went without incident, and having found this makeshift campsite in a city park allowed me to catch up on precious sleep, a great gift from the adventure gods.

The next morning, as I skirted Bridgeport Island, next to the bank, underneath the east wind roaring through the tree tops far above me, I spotted no campsites, but I did see a full-sized television, the last of the exotic Guntersville Lake trash. If I'd had a boat with a motor, I would have missed a lot of what enriched my time on Guntersville: the turtles, the people, the free music that I wouldn't have been able to hear with an outboard roaring behind me. With a motor, I could have sped up at the sight of the exotic trash, averting my head from such unpleasantries. I could have backtracked to good camping sites when faced with the necessity of stopping at the Soggy Bottom toilet-lid ditch. A motor would have given me choices and flexibility that would have made things easier, but it would have hidden some truths that the river wanted to show me.

Despite my affection for the eccentricities of upper Guntersville Lake, it wasn't quite finished with me. I had one more night to spend here before locking through Nickajack Dam and re-entering Tennessee.

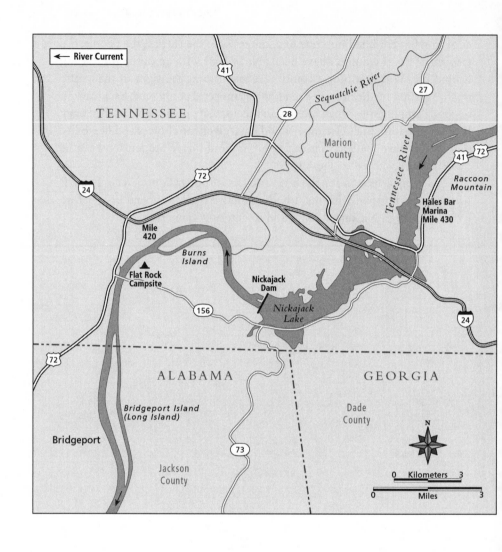

20

DRAMA IN SCENERY

As I got nearer Nickajack Dam, I began to think of Guntersville as a frenemy, a reservoir that evoked fond feelings but at the same time could not be trusted. I liked hanging out with Guntersville, but I couldn't let my guard down. I could not relax. This was most evident on my last morning there, as I left what might have been my most picturesque and unique campsite on the river, a precarious spot on a flat rock about the same size as my tent, right down next to the water, in full view of anyone who wanted to see me, except I hadn't seen anyone, not one person, since Bridgeport.

A cliff and a dark woods rose up behind us that night, full moon glaring off the water and turning the pale rock translucent. Because of the steep terrain above the flat rock, we couldn't really move the campsite back from the water, so all night I worried about releases from Nickajack raising the water level a couple of feet to flood us out. Having this actually happen to us on Wheeler made this more than an idle worry. I was thrilled to awaken the next morning to see that the lake had fallen a bit, but there would be no celebratory dancing. It was crucial, here, to break down camp with caution, to step nimbly around the flat rock because there was little room to spare. One false move, one slip, and I'd be in the water, a deep eddy that swirled dark and cold. One would be advised against partaking of strong drink at

Our final campsite on Guntersville Lake, a couple of miles below Nickajack Dam, was a flat rock just a few feet above river.

a campsite like this, where a stumble could land you in the river without a life jacket.

To load the boat, I had to climb up and down a craggy decline to the calm place among small sharp outcroppings where I had moored the boat. When I was loaded up and about ready to launch that morning, I looked across the channel at Burns Island, where I had planned to camp the night before. Three fishermen sat hunched in a boat, anchored against the current. After I got under way, the current pushed me toward them, and maybe thirty yards away, I waved at them. I held the wave to make sure they'd seen me, ten seconds at least. Nothing, just icy stares. My first snubbing.

I would have preferred that they had flipped me the bird or snarled something at me, like "Stay the hell away from our spot!" The more I thought about the snubbing, the more it puzzled me. How long had they been there watching me break camp? I hadn't noticed them until I launched. Had I been talking to myself or Maggie in an overly loud or off-kilter voice? What had I been saying? Had I become the mad canoe hermit without knowing it? Not waving back at another person on the water or on the road sent a serious message, especially in the South. In 1998, I was heckled and ridiculed, sometimes not so good-naturedly, all the way down the river. In Clifton, Tennessee, near the end of the downstream voyage, a couple of boys stood at the top of a cliff above Jasper and me. One of them shouted, "I hope you turn that thing over!" For some reason I was feeling cranky, in no mood to tolerate such hostility. I yelled back: "You're awful brave up there!" And then this guy motored over in a fishing boat and asked me what I'd said to the kids on the cliff. I told him and he motored off without another word. Welcome to Clifton, I'd thought. I was the crazy canoer then and now. Near the same point of the voyage going the other way, maybe I was scaring people again.

Drunkenness on the river, which often but not always, fueled the hostility toward me, was more common on the 1998 trip, mainly because I went at the end of the summer when more people were on or near the water. I was in the way of their speedboating sometimes, or I was convenient for comic relief, a slow-moving target. So far on this trip, river people had been generous, sane, and affable beyond my expectations. Perhaps they were saving their dark side for the last third of the trip. The tweaker, or meth user, had not surfaced, as far as I knew, but I was approaching a heavily populated area, Chattanooga, which might increase my chances of confronting depraved behavior.

Onward we went, away from the silent fishermen, happy to be leaving Guntersville, the frenemy lake, and wondering what provoked these guys to snub us, particularly stinging after the sociability at Bridgeport, my new favorite town on the Tennessee River. Oh well, perhaps Maggie and I had entered a version of Rod Serling's *The Twilight Zone*, where nothing was as it seemed, a place where the usual rules of the universe—in this case the world of the river—did not apply. It was "another dimension," as Serling said when each show opened, where, in my version, people in boats didn't return the wave of a friendly canoer professor and his mutt. In the river miles that lay ahead, plenty of events and phenomenon remained that seemed inexplicable, unworldly, even surreal, occurrences that made the fishermen's snub seem trivial in retrospect.

The day before, my intended destination had been Burns Island, but like most islands for the past 300 miles, its steep banks and brushy shoreline repelled a canoe camper. As the sun began to set and my left shoulder commenced to ache from paddling against the burgeoning current, I gave up and coasted downstream looking for some place, any place, to spend the night. It killed me to float downstream, to backtrack two river miles I'd worked so hard to earn. I couldn't help but think how easy the 1998 trip had been at times like these, when I could just sit back and drift, idle, while the river carried me. Now, it was a different story for sixty-year-old me. I'd only managed seven miles the whole day, the current had been so strong. The flat rock campsite, which I'd passed up previously because it was so low to the water, with no easy escape if the lake did rise, would end up giving me some consolation on that brutal paddling day. It felt clean to camp on rock instead of in the weeds and mud. Maggie liked it, too. She seemed to accept our limited space, her movements calm and deliberate.

I'd had a revelatory moment earlier in that seven-mile day, before exhaustion had set in. Inching past five-mile-long Bridgeport Island, I passed under the Seaboard System Railroad Bridge at the same moment a train was crossing. The whole world shook, and I couldn't help being fearful of the mechanized power passing above me. I felt dwarfed and vulnerable. It dominated the landscape in its thunderous passage—but not like thunder truly because of its metallic screeching and the bumpity friction of metal on metal. What was revelatory came afterward, in the wake of the train: a profound, blessed silence descended upon Maggie and me. And there we sat, unharmed, just a few feet below all of that moving tonnage.

Guntersville had been the lake where the southern end of the Cumberland Plateau began to rise in flattop ridges alongside the river. This kind of relief in the landscape put us in our place, tiny below the natural grandeur, as I speculated about the mysteries that the steep, wooded ridges kept secret. The shimmering lake surface reflected the hills, different shades of green rising up to a blue sky. Heading toward Nickajack Lake and the Tennessee River Gorge, I expected a healthier dose of this kind of landscape, a more narrow lake, with higher, steeper, more dramatic bluffs. I looked forward to meeting Catherine in Chattanooga, near the end of Nickajack Lake. She would be taking me to a fundraiser for her nonprofit healing center, Focus Healthcare. Unlike the Riverkeeper benefit, where I had stood out in my ragged fleece sweater and cargo pants, I'd be wearing a suit and tie to this one.

No water spilled from the Nickajack Dam gates as I approached that day after the flat rock camp, but current from power generation created plenty of resistance in my efforts to escape the clutches of Guntersville. I angled toward the mouth of the Sequatchie River after passing the tip of Burns Island. At one point, I had intended to paddle up some tributaries, and while I wouldn't say I'd been in a hurry on this trip, exploring tributaries no longer appealed to me as much as it had, during my planning of the trip. It seemed that fighting the current of the main river and maintaining progress toward my ultimate goal was more important than lingering on a tributary that could expose me to bad weather in an unprotected place.

Though I had just left Alabama—known for its frequent tornadoes—it was still the season of the funnel cloud.

Retired Maryville College chemistry professor Terry Bunde kayaked a portion of the Sequatchie with me a few years previous. We had paddled upstream four or five miles, then floated back down, fishing the whole way. I'd brought some canned Perrier water to drink, and Bunde ribbed me about it. He said that my fizzy French water would arouse suspicion in this isolated valley, that the locals might be inclined to waylay a tippler of exotic substances in a bright yellow kayak. We didn't see anyone, local or not, until we were back near our takeout. A kid fishing from the bank exchanged pleasantries with us and then launched into a description of the "fish-eating spiders" he had seen downstream of the milldam where we had put in. We laughed about it at the time, but when we got home and looked it up, we found out that such spiders do exist. This is a big part of what I like about rivers: they will always surprise you.

Now, as I struggled to make it to the dam, the Sequatchie ran high, disgorging its earthy, dark brown into the deep metallic gray of the Tennessee. Fiendish eddies arose at this confluence, and monster fish I could not identify kept swirling to the surface. The lock was within my sights, but it was difficult to look away from these monsters, who rolled and writhed and exposed a long dorsal fin each time they surfaced. They would not raise their heads to look at me, which would have helped me identify them. I estimated them to be three feet long at least, maybe longer. When I got nearer the dam, I told a fisherman about them, and he guessed they were carp. These were not carp.

Once inside the dankness of the Nickajack lock, I shouted up to the lock operator my description of the serpent-like fish.

"Spookville catfish!" he said.

"Spookville?"

"Spoonbill! Spoonbill! That or maybe gar."

I didn't think these were gar, either, because of their girth. What people called spoonbill catfish (paddlefish) was more likely. The paddlefish is one of those prehistoric giants that have survived over 300 million years, according to fossil records. Now, the International Union for Conservation of Nature and Natural Resources has them classified as "vulnerable," partly because they have been overfished for their roe to make caviar. Distantly related to the sturgeon, they are filter feeders, the spoonbill or rostrum a long snout that they use to help them navigate in their search for zooplankton. Their skeleton is mainly composed of cartilage, making them resemble sharks, though they are not related. They can grow up to seven feet long and live up to sixty years. I liked to think that one of them I'd seen shared a birthday with me.

Martin Knoll, the geologist at the University of the South in Sewanee who partnered with German speed swimmer Andreas Fath in his swim down the length of the river, said that one of the biggest concerns that emerged from their testing of the river in 2017 was the presence of microplastics, which range in size from a sand grain to medium silt, the edge of what you can see. While the Tennessee River looked reasonably clean when Fath and Knoll tested for other contaminants, the level of plasticity was way out of whack, at 16,000 particles for every cubic meter. In comparison, the Rhine River, which Fath also swam and tested, has 200 particles per cubic meter, and the Rhine watershed has a population of fifty million, versus five million in the Tennessee River watershed. Knoll said he didn't know what caused this disproportionate level of plasticity, nor does he know how it is affecting the river and its inhabitants, but invertebrates and populations like paddlefish who swim with their mouths open, ingesting plankton, might be the most vulnerable.

I'm pretty sure these were spawning paddlefish that I encountered. In *The Fishes of Tennessee*, David A. Etnier and Wayne C. Starnes note that paddlefish in the Tennessee River may frequent the tailwaters of dams for spawning, usually in April and May. The fishermen below Nickajack weren't that interested in my sighting, I think, because the only way to catch paddlefish is by snagging them with a large treble hook, and if successful, you've got a battle on your hands that, as Etnier and Starnes say, the fish most often win. In any case, I had seen something rare and wondrous rolling to the surface just a few feet away from me.

The friendly lock operator was a welcome change after the silent fishermen that morning. I'd just happened to read in the navigational charts that I was not supposed to be calling the locks on my cell phone. It was in all caps: "PLEASE REFRAIN FROM CONTACTING BY CELL PHONE." So I had pulled the cord at the lock guide wall at Nickajack, and that worked fine; the big doors opened five minutes after my pull. Still, I liked being able to talk to someone on the phone before locking through because I felt as if the operators would want to know that they were dealing with a guy in a canoe. With a dog. And not just any dog: my rambunctious Maggie. The Nickajack operator said there were four ways to contact him: marine radio, pulling the cord, cell phone, and a sequence of horn blasts, which he said no one uses. He said it was just fine to use the cell phone.

It turned bright and warm when I entered Nickajack Lake, a wondrous spring day that filled me with energy and optimism. Just after locking through, we stopped on a gravel bar with an expansive view of the open lake. On the other side, a railroad ran between sheer gray cliffs and the lush green of the treeline that grew along the water's edge. I took a quick swim, changed clothes, and paddled with vigor toward my next stop, Hales Bar Marina, about five miles away. I was going to treat myself to a bit of civilization there, to pay for an overnight stay in something called a floating cabin. A shower, a bed, and air conditioning would help fuel me for my invasion of Chattanooga, thirty-odd miles upriver.

As we paddled that last five miles toward Hales Bar, a train of multi-colored boxcars chugged along the base of the cliff and followed the bend of the river, going toward the dam and then on to Bridgeport and Stevenson. This was the same track I had paddled under at Bridgeport Island, where we sat under the bridge and felt the thunderous crossing of the freight just a few feet above us. Now, the train was far enough away that its passage was silent and picturesque next to the blue lake, the gray-streaked cliffs, and the vibrant newborn green of spring. We cruised under Interstate 24 for the second time on our trip and power-paddled toward shelter, Maggie posed like a masthead in the bow.

21

FLOATING IN A CABIN

I tied off the canoe to the railing of our floating cabin's little deck, which was about the size of the flat rock campsite, and I opened the door to a room that included a TV, a couch (Maggie's first stop), and a decent-sized kitchen. Farther back was a tiny bathroom and a bedroom. It was paradise. In 1998, I'd set up at the Hales Bar campground in a wind that blew all day and night. At one point, just after I'd assembled the tent, the wind caught it and rolled it across the campground toward the lake. I had to run fifty yards to catch it, much to the amusement of the few RV campers nearby. Aside from the wind, the whole place had a haunted quality, marina and campground dominated by the remnants of old Hales Bar Dam, which had been removed except for its powerhouse, a weathered, prison-like structure, three stories tall with rows and rows of broken windows. Built in 1913 from private funding to help provide power to Chattanooga and to improve river navigation, the dam began to leak. TVA demolished it in 1968 and built Nickajack to replace it.

Paranormal groups such as East Tennessee Ghost Seekers led haunted tours of the old powerhouse. When I camped there in 1998, marina manager Robert Terry and I talked about what a great restaurant you could put in there. He thought there was no way it could go wrong because people would come for the historic and novelty value alone. Alas, the restaurant had not come to pass in twenty years, but the current marina manager, Tony, told me that a restaurant on site would be opening soon. Shopping in the marina store, I was unable to find much in the way of fishing tackle. I was ready to start fishing again, but I'd broken my rod back on Wheeler. Tony said he didn't have much tackle in stock yet, but he offered me a rod that someone had left behind. Tony was one of the river veterans who, upon hearing of my trip, had story after story of other voyageurs who had visited Hales Bar, including the long-haul paddleboarder. When I told Tony that part of the reason I was paddling the Tennessee again was my sixtieth birthday, he described his bucket list item for his fiftieth, a couple of years before. He had traveled to the set of the TV show *Dallas* for the show's fortieth reunion. Everyone from the cast was there except for Larry Hagman (J.R.), who had died the year before. The country singer Neil McCoy performed. Tony took a friend because he said his wife hated *Dallas*. I thought this was a sad bucket list item, but I didn't say so. He probably thought my little trip was absurd, but he was kind enough to withhold his opinion one way or the other. So far, civilized river etiquette ruled on Nickajack.

Maggie and I had neighbors next to our floating cabin, their deck just a few feet away from ours, though the cabin on the other side of us was empty. As I sorted through gear and dried things out on the deck, three women and one man on the neighboring deck fished nonstop, day and night. The women sat in chairs and the man roamed to different parts of the little platform. After a woman pulled in a tiny bream, I said something about it being a state record, and the man said, "You can't make fun of us if you're not fishing."

"Fair enough," I said.

That night, the neighbor's electric knife whirred for an hour, so they must have harvested some fish large enough to filet and fry.

Late that afternoon, in the mood to explore, I took a big chance and left Maggie in the floating cabin while I walked a mile and a half to a Mexican restaurant in the town of Guild. Cars sped down the narrow road I walked, one of them feinting as if to run over me. Dying or getting maimed in a hit-and-run would have been the ultimate irony on a long canoe trip. Guild was little more than a crossroads with working-class houses and mobile homes spreading out from its center, where the restaurant and a convenience store were the focal points. I was the only person at the restaurant, where the food was, at best, mediocre. Tony had already said it was "ok," and that the salsa was "strange."

A young waitress with a nose ring was talkative and eager to please. I asked her if she went to school in Guild.

"We ain't got no school in Guild."

She went to school in Jasper, where she lived. Guild had problems, she said, most prominently that there was no cell phone service. Somebody called in an order on the landline that sent her into a near panic, it was so complex. I drank a beer and ate some of my meal before walking back to the floating cabin. I regretted not using its kitchen to cook up some bacon and eggs, which the marina had for sale.

I was relieved to find that Maggie had not destroyed anything in the cabin, though I found clear evidence that she had disobeyed my command to stay off the couch. Her hair coat had betrayed her. We watched the last two innings of a Chicago Cubs baseball game, and then I retired to the bedroom, warning Maggie to stay off the couch, but spreading my sleeping bag on it because I knew that she would disobey. As grateful as I was for sleeping in a bed for the first time in many miles, I was unable to drop off because right outside my door, somebody was blasting music. It was like an infomercial for the forgotten music of the seventies and eighties. I peeked out the window. On the top deck of a hundred-foot-long houseboat, this guy was bustling about, doing whatever one does on a boat that size. He appeared to be alone. I imagined that one had to be doing something all the time on such a massive craft, or employing others to do it, but that was no excuse to submit everyone from here to Guild to his nostalgic pop-music tastes. I loved Jim Croce in high school, but I didn't want to listen to "Operator" forty years later in an otherwise peaceful natural setting. True, it wasn't all that late, a little after ten o'clock, so I turned away from the window, lay down, and sang along in my head. He turned it off around eleven o'clock, just as I was about to crack open my door and yell, "Turn that crap off!"

Next morning we lingered at the floating cabin, trading barbs with the fishing Ohioans next door, who were up long before me with their lines in the gassy water. It was tough to leave, but if we stayed much longer, I might never make it to Chattanooga and beyond. We got underway at midmorning and floated around the old powerhouse and campground, which hadn't changed in twenty years. It was full of RVs, no tents in sight, and at the very end, as at Cowford, was an RV with not one but two Confederate flags, a German shepherd, three motorcycles, and an upturned aluminum canoe. Someone I could not see shouted, "Good luck!"

And then we were off into the wild once again. The day before, an easy eleven miles, had been about as close to a gravy day on the trip so far, and part of that had to do with leaving the hardships and desolation of Guntersville Lake behind, and coming into the transformative scenery of the Tennessee River Gorge. The day after our floating-cabin stay promised to be just as idyllic, the weather warm and clear, current negligible, scenery spectacular, the lake narrow, with high bluffs rising on both sides. The sound sleep and the warm showers in the floating cabin had put me in a buoyant mood, and it didn't bother me much that across the way, on the north bank, it sounded like Thor's Hammer crushing rock—boom, boom, boom. Sure enough, the charts told me I was in the proximity of Signal Mountain Cement Company.

On Nickajack Lake in 1998, I fell victim to mischief that I attributed to supernatural beings of Native American origin, the Nunnehi, pranksters of Cherokee lore who lived at the bottom of the river. When I was making instant coffee one morning, my back to the river, the Nunnehi got ahold of my boat and pushed it out into Nickajack. I had to swim out fifty yards to retrieve it. They were still here, the Nunnehi, waiting for me on a day so beautiful it seemed nothing could go wrong. We'd pulled off on a low bank that did not quite come down to meet the water. Maggie had no trouble jumping out onto land and pulling the boat up with her lead. In contrast to Maggie, my getting into and out of the boat was pure geezer movement, a mix of creakiness and caution. I got out onto the bank, no problem, but getting back in resulted in Fall IV of the trip. I stepped into the stern from shore, and when the boat, floating in a couple of feet of water, moved away from me, I fell in a position that had me straddling the gunnel, inflicting a painful blow that rendered me helplessly nauseous for a few minutes. I also banged my right ankle, though I do not know how. My left foot, which had arrested my fall on the river bed, was wet, as was that entire leg. I ascertained that although Fall IV was painful and spectacular for the Nunnehi to witness, it would not result in permanent disability. Maggie, who had gotten into the boat before me, sat watching without comment as all of this unfolded. And from this emerged a Geezer Commandment: Thou Shalt Not Step into a Floating Boat.

Underway once again, I started searching my pockets for my voice recorder to describe what had just happened. I found it in the left lower pocket of my cargo shorts, soaked from the botched embarkation. I had just filled this device to capacity with my thoughts, thirty-odd hours of such ramblings. And now it would not turn on. My mind reeled in reverse gear 431 miles. I would be taking notes by hand, very soon, to recapture what I had recorded. I would be hoping and praying that my recorder would somehow resuscitate itself.

The Nunnehi prank altered the high tone of the day. We camped in a weedy clearing in Prentice Cooper State Forest and Wildlife Management Area, not far from an unseen (but heard) gravel road, a deer stand, a rope swing, a fire ring, and a full-sized grill. While I took notes, Maggie scavenged.

Our first campsite on Nickajack Lake, across from Raccoon Mountain, had been frequented by deer hunters.

She found a flip-flop that she seemed to regard as a priceless treasure, playing keep-away when I tried to take the nasty thing away. Across from us reared up Raccoon Mountain, around which the river would make a big U-turn, from east to due south, a course that would veer away from my ultimate destination: Knoxville. Here, the Tennessee staggered on its way to Chattanooga, lurching this way and that. The next day we would enter a segment known as The Narrows, which before the construction of the dams, confounded mariners with its whirlpools and rapids. In this area, early white settlers such as John Donelson, who was on his way to Nashville via the Tennessee and Cumberland rivers, were vulnerable to attack. The Chickamauga band of Native Americans, mostly Cherokee, were led by Dragging Canoe, who refused to acknowledge the 1775 Treaty of Sycamore Shoals and was determined to impede white settlement of the area. They killed thirty-three of Donelson's group. I was hoping for a different kind of reception as I approached Chattanooga.

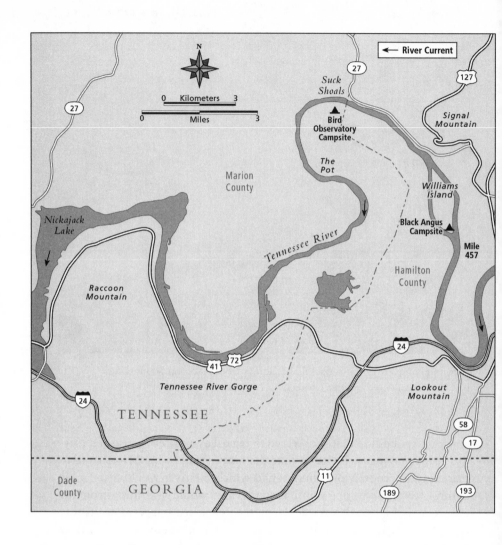

22

FITTING IN

Sometimes a smart dog like Maggie will surprise you and act outside the usual canine behavior patterns of romping, barking, chewing, eating, licking, and sleeping. On the bank of Williams Island, I sat in my camp chair, back to the river, and watched The Maggie Show. We were camped at a grassy, wooded area about eight miles downstream of Chattanooga. In looking for a site on the island, a couple of miles long, I'd passed up a bunch of good landing places where cattle had trampled the shoreline. When we stopped within sight of the island's upstream point, I thought we'd gone beyond a fence which would separate us from this herd of Black Angus. I was wrong, much to Maggie's delight. In an open field 100 yards away from our camp, the herd found us and trotted single-file down a slope to check us out. Maggie, on her fifteen-foot lead, formed the welcoming committee. She didn't bark and she really didn't herd, but she greeted each cow as it arrived in camp. She would feint as if to play with them, and they would flinch a little and jostle each other. She would run up to them as if they were large dogs and touch noses. Only one cow with a white face bellowed at Maggie and got a little rowdy. Some would trot back up to the open pasture and then file back down to greet Maggie a second time. Her tongue was hanging out she'd wrangled with such abandon. I thought it

On Williams Island, a few miles downstream of Chattanooga,
Maggie befriended a herd of Black Angus cattle.

would never end. About fifty Black Angus came down the slope to touch
noses. Some got kisses. They jostled each other trying to get at her. I was
enjoying it, but I started to worry a little about a stampede that would drive
us into the river. The canoe was below a high muddy bank that required
some acrobatic climbing up on roots to the flat ground above. I tried to be
firm but friendly with the cows. I asked them to go somewhere else for a
drink or whatever they wanted. After a while, Maggie got so exhausted the
cattle lost interest in her.

Lesson relearned that I'd forgotten: Never camp near cows; you will be
bitten on the back by savage flies.

After camping near Raccoon Mountain, we had two days to go about
twenty miles to Chattanooga for my rendezvous with Catherine. Thanks
to a former student, Ruthie Cartlidge, who had worked with Outdoor
Chattanooga, Maggie and I would have the privilege of camping at a bird
observatory managed by the Tennessee River Gorge Trust (TRGT). It was
about five miles from Raccoon Mountain, there was little current or wind,

Maggie considers disrupting this peaceful scene, the only church
we saw on the banks of the entire Tennessee.

and we had all day to get there, so I decided, for the first time on the trip,
to use the single-blade paddle which had propelled me on the 1998
downstream trip. It was liberating to have the short paddle in my hands,
switching from one side of the boat to the other when I felt like it. Something
about it seemed more natural, less of a strain on my shoulders and back.
Going slower, I scrutinized the scenery, more beautiful here than any other
part of the river so far, the narrow, winding lake more riverine, the thick
woods of the shorelines uninterrupted by human homes and industry. We
came upon a half-sunken volleyball net, one of the first signs of humanity
we'd seen since our campsite with the grill and the deer stand. It was fitting
to see recreational ruins in this part of the Tennessee, where the population
of campers and paddle-powered boaters was greater than in any other part
of the river system. After a couple of miles with the single-blade paddle, I
calculated that I was going about half the speed I normally do, so I switched
back to the two-blader and could immediately tell the difference in efficiency.
I recognized my compulsion to switch as a failure of sorts, even at the time,

but I couldn't bring myself to go so slowly when I didn't have to. I told myself that I'd reserve the one-blader for another contemplative morning.

We passed one of the campsites easily accessible by water that the TRGT had set up—Pot Point—a mown clearing with a table, wooden camping platform, and fire ring, all you needed for a secure night on the river. A sign posted a phone number for reserving it. I hadn't seen any fellow paddlers on this day, but the evening before, a couple of kayakers floated past our camp for an evening paddle downstream and then back up. This stretch of Nickajack reservoir was known as the Tennessee River Blueway, designated and mapped for people who wanted to paddle and camp. I felt like less of an oddball on this part of the river. In fact, I would feel privileged here, thanks in large part to Ruthie and the people she told about my journey, like Rick Huffines, executive director of the Tennessee River Gorge Trust. He agreed to let Maggie and me camp at the bird observatory, ordinarily reserved for people banding birds or researching them, not paddling up the river on a Don Quixote quest. On the phone, he told me how to find the takeout to the observatory and mentioned a hike of 300 yards to the shelters. I told him that we'd probably camp on the beach below because I didn't want to haul my gear up the trail. He said he'd normally not allow camping there, but he would make an exception.

This takeout was, without a doubt, the best of our trip. We glided into a small indentation in the bank, where the temperature dropped ten degrees the place was so deeply shaded. A creek trickled to one side of the beach. At its mouth, a hackberry tree had grown so that the trunk formed a low wall that extended five or six feet out from the bank, creating a tiny harbor. The beach was invisible from the river, impossible to find unless you knew it was there. Having arrived at noon after an easy five-mile paddle, I had an energy reserve that was normally depleted on river days, so Maggie and I hiked to the observatory shelters. What I saw and heard up there made me change my mind about camping on the beach below. First of all, the birds. They were not visible, but they were calling all around us from a tree canopy that soared as high as 200 feet, trees eighty to ninety years old. I lost count of how many different kinds of birds were chirping and cawing and whistling, at least twenty in those first few minutes. The place was full of what executive director Huffines called neotropical birds: indigo buntings, scarlet tanagers, yellow-throated warblers, and others who traveled back and forth from the tropics in South and Central America. Porch-like bird banding stations, built of rough wooden planks with screened walls, had shelving and tables inside, luxurious amenities for someone used to camping in the dirt. There was a fire ring, more than a cord of split wood, a picnic table, and a fancy elevated outhouse. I began to wonder if Huffines would let us stay here two nights, but there was no cellphone service at the top, and I had promised Catherine and my mother that I would make daily contact.

On one of my last trips to the beach to retrieve gear from the boat, I was dismayed to see a pontoon do a U-turn in the channel and pull right in to what I'd thought was my private beach for a day. This was the good ship *Gorgeous*, part of TRGT, which was in the process of educating a group of city kids about the river through a program called Bridge Chattanooga. They'd stopped here for a swim, and they weren't surprised to see a guy standing knee deep in the water poking at his cell phone. Rick had told them about me and Maggie.

Although I was alone in the woods, once again, I felt secure at the bird observatory that night, with none of the worries about an irate landowner rousting us out with a flashlight in my face. The sanctuary made me appreciate what an organization like TRGT does, here on the most beautiful part of the river. It helps prevent overdevelopment and exploitation of the gorge, purchasing land or forming partnerships with landowners to protect 17,000 acres for the public to enjoy, one of the vastest areas set aside on the river, helping to make Robert Kennedy Jr.'s idea of the commons a reality. TRGT monitors the ecosystem with water testing and bird counting, among other activities, to maintain and improve the health of the area and to educate humans about the river and the high bluffs rising from it. The organization makes it easy for people to connect to a beautiful landscape by encouraging "Leave No Trace" activities such as sunset kayaking trips. In my sampling of rivers and lakes all over the country, I have never seen such easily accessible and attractive campsites available for the public.

Huffines, who worked all over the Southeast during his twenty-six years with the U.S. Fish and Wildlife Service, articulated to me why this part of the Tennessee River was worth spending so much time and energy protecting. He called the gorge "an amalgamation of ecosystems." It is rare, he said, to see so many different habitats—over twenty—within a twenty-seven-mile stretch of river. He'd seen things in the gorge that "defy the textbooks": blueberry and blackberry bushes growing from the same soil, wood thrush and pine warblers thriving together, rough green snakes and eastern newts sharing the same slope. By studying the gorge, Huffines said, much can be learned about connectivity and adaptive pathways, as well as "anomalies within the gorge that can broaden our understanding of *how* they have adapted" (Huffines, Trevathan, 2018).

That afternoon, I walked over a mile up the dirt access road to the observatory. I didn't hike to the end of that road, but I was pretty sure that it had a locked gate at the entrance. I slept above ground, the screen protecting me from insects, the roof from rain and dew. The birds and other wildlife kept their party going all night, and something was scratching around underneath the shelter, which bothered Maggie for a while; I was able to ignore it and slept soundly through the night. It had only been a couple of nights since the floating cabin stay, but something about the observatory combined the best of the outdoors with minimal shelter in a compound that made me feel like I belonged.

Next morning, I left Maggie in camp and walked the trails, hoping to get one decent photograph of a neotropical bird before we left. A dizzying cacophony of fowl called from above, below, and all around.

"Twit, twit, twit," said something so many times that I began to take it personally.

It had to be on the ground nearby, so well hidden that I never even got a glimpse of it, much less a photo. I finally gave up taking pictures and sat down on a log to listen. I'd like to say that an indigo bunting glided down and perched on my shoulder, but that would be a lie. And it was okay that they stayed hidden in this wild place, where they could be observed and studied by experts. A rank amateur birdwatcher like me needed to get back to his business, paddling up the river toward the city.

Huffines later told me not to feel badly about getting skunked on a bird photograph.

"You need a ten to fifteen-thousand dollar lens for that," he said.

We had an eight-mile paddle that day to Williams Island, where Maggie made friends with the herd of cattle. For the last couple of gravy days, I began to feel almost normal as a canoer, going at a more reasonable pace and exploring more on the banks than I had been. I began to fantasize about living on Nickajack, the same daydreaming I'd done on Kentucky Lake. The parts of Nickajack that were populated seemed more like real neighborhoods than anything I'd seen on the river so far. We passed a small white church that looked as if it had been there many years. Mansions such as I'd seen on Wilson Lake, with cathedral-like atriums that rose above golf course lawns, were absent here. The houses on Nickajack blended into the landscape instead of rising up and dominating a hillside bulldozed of trees. People had trees hundreds of years old shading two to three-bedroom homes, modest boats moored at functional docks. Up on the right bank was my dream home, a log cabin with a tin roof and a front porch with a rocking chair and recliner on it. A maple tree shaded the entire house. It looked as if it had been there for decades. I didn't see anything new being built on the banks of Nickajack downstream of Williams Island.

I remember loving this part of the river twenty years before, but the current and wind pushed me down to Hales Bar Marina campground at such a pace that I only spent one night in the gorge. This time, going upstream and pacing myself because of my rendezvous in the city, I slowed down and appreciated good weather in a dramatic and mysterious landscape. Nights cooled down to the fifties, but the days were bright and warm enough for shorts and river sandals.

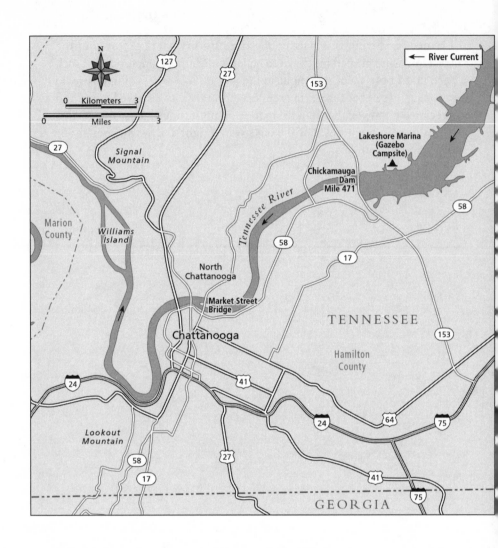

23

URBAN PADDLING

On the morning after Maggie's bonding with the Black Angus herd, the idyllic quality of Nickajack began to fade. For two miles, as I hugged the left bank, I paddled alongside I-24, which paralleled the right upstream bank, a half mile or so away from me. Traffic streamed in a continuous blur, a solid line of high-speed projectiles that made me want to stay on the river forever. A mile farther, I crossed the river and came alongside a scrap-metal salvage business where a crane scooped and clinched and sorted through shards of metal, a clashing, frictional, heavy-metal concert that canceled all other sounds except for the shooting range on the far bank. The shooting range, in a field next to a wooded hillside, seemed at odds with the urban industrialization of the salvage yard, though it was a noisy kind of rural as a lone shooter fired round after round from a pistol. Joining the party, the *Southern Belle* riverboat, a triple-decker modeled after nineteenth-century steam-powered sternwheelers, dominated the channel. People lined the rails shooting video and taking photos. I wondered what they thought of a shooting range so close to the water, and whether Maggie and me, parked on the shore, made it into the foreground of their Instagram captures of Scrap-Metal Mountain.

This noisy stretch notwithstanding, Chattanooga had remade itself into a river town in the best sense of the term. In 1998, after the transformation from polluted city to outdoor mecca was well under way, Jasper and I stopped at Ross's Landing near the Tennessee Aquarium, a wondrous place for learning about this river and others. We couldn't go inside, but we strolled around and shared a slice of pizza before traveling on downriver and camping among the Nunnehi pranksters. Twenty years later, it seemed to me that the city had progressed even further; it seemed built for the river, as it was originally, no doubt, now full of access points for recreational boaters, mainly geared toward paddlers. Ruthie Cartlidge, who had worked for Outdoor Chattanooga (OC), part of the city's organized effort to create and promote outdoor activities, had arranged for Phillip Grymes, of OC, to meet me at the Market Street Bridge Canoe and Kayak Launch, across the river from the aquarium.

A jury of turkey buzzards lined the ramp as Phillip walked down to greet us.

"That's never good," he said. The birds fluttered and preened but they did not fly away. The stench of death emanated from the shoreline.

The buzzard greeting committee was irresistible to Maggie, who leaped out a few feet from the bank, looping her lead around a dry bag and a towel and dragging both into the water, a grand entrance that scattered the staid buzzard crowd. Phillip helped me carry all my gear up the ramp to the OC supply shed, where I could stow it while taking a night off from the river with Catherine. He locked up our stuff and went back to his office, while Maggie and I walked through the city streets in search of a laundromat, the heat rising, summer-like, from the asphalt. It was surreal, dodging human traffic on the sidewalks, crossing streets along with herds of humans that streamed between vehicles emitting saunas of exhaust. We walked up to a White Castle drive-thru and bought a large ice water to share. My fellow clothes washers tolerated Maggie inside the laundromat, where she lay quietly on the hard, cool floor. Laundry finished, we went back and waited inside the OC headquarters until it closed at five o'clock, and then sat on the curb to wait for Catherine's arrival from Knoxville.

Sitting outside a public building with a soiled backpack and a panting dog made me appear worse off than I actually was. It made a good portrait for Catherine as she arrived in her minivan to drive us across the river to a hotel on a traffic-clogged Friday afternoon. The drive took us over an hour, for a distance I probably could have paddled in the same amount of time. We secured Maggie in her pet kennel in the hotel room and asked her not to bark; after she had roamed free on the banks of the river for the past six weeks, this was asking a lot of her. I think she may have been willing to sacrifice her freedom that evening for the reward of air conditioning.

Cat and I took an Uber to a beautiful old church where her work fundraiser was being held. I looked the part of the civilized escort in suit and choking tie, but my inner savage lurked just beneath the surface. The buffet table was crammed with delectable food—thinly sliced pork, roasted vegetables, pastry rolls stuffed with cream cheese, chicken kabobs, and cake. My only complaint was the size of the plates. I skipped the cake and filled the saucer with portions that pushed the limits of social acceptability.

After we listened to an unusually short but inspiring speech, the main event came onstage: a band of four vocalists, a horn section, two guitars, a bass, and drums. Therapists and benefactors arose from their tables to dance. The floor filled up with dancers of all ages. One woman was twirling and gyrating alone on the floor, taking up more than her share of space, I thought. Cat told me this was the dance therapist. Others were just as enthusiastic but lacked her repertoire; it was fun to observe, sitting in a chair next to Cat, while I gorged myself and drank bottled beer. The music was so loud we couldn't talk anyway. After a bit, I thought it was safe to return to the buffet for seconds. Nobody said anything. The band was so good they reminded me of Earth Wind and Fire. I danced a couple of times with Cat and drank a second bottle of beer. At this point, weariness set in, and I also began to worry about Maggie barking or somehow escaping her doghouse to ransack the room. We stayed until the Focus crowd began to thin, and rode in a van back to the hotel with other benefactors and therapy people, some of them singing songs they had been inspired to compose on the ride. Back at the hotel, I had my first dose of hypnagogia on this trip, a sure sign that the river had a hold on me, even though I'd traveled miles of pavement away from it.

Hypnagogia occurs when you're between sleeping and waking up, a liminal zone that I arrive at, most often, after I've been on an extended river trip and sleep indoors for a night, far from the river. That night in Chattanooga, after descending into a coma-like sleep, I sat up in bed and looked down to see the river flowing all around us in the hotel room. On one wall was a red light, and on another shone a green light, just like the navigational signals on a bridge. I imagined that I was passing under an interstate highway and that I needed to steer between the piers. A part of me knew that I was looking at a wall of a hotel room, that the red light was the fire alarm switch, the green something on the television. Another part of me was still on the river, trying to stay afloat, searching through the night to see what was ahead. I felt the river reality with great intensity and emotion, but somehow I knew, beyond that emotion, that I was in a hotel bed. I turned to Cat, who was in the "boat" with me, and said, "Where are we?"

She either said this or I dreamed it: "Oh, somewhere in Anywhere, Tennessee," in a sing-song tone.

Gradually, as it happens with these episodes, I came awake enough to reconcile the reality of my situation with the hallucinogenic river vision. I realized that I was in a hotel room bed dreaming about canoeing at night.

I love hypnagogia. I seek it out, but it is rare and it does not accommodate my will; long canoe trips seem to be the prerequisite. It is far more intense and authentic than the effects of the strongest hallucinogens, but short-lived. Its intensity and novelty have served to validate long river voyages as a transcendent, vital part of my life. It gave me hope that my little adventure, no matter how small-scale, no matter that I was exploring close to home, had a powerful effect on the part of my brain that controlled perception and memory and spirit. I'd do whatever it took to have another hypnagogic episode, including eating more chicken kabobs and bouncing around on a dance floor to the best band I had heard in a long time.

Cat dropped Maggie and me off at Market Street the next morning, and I gave her the shotgun to take back; I hadn't unwrapped it from the duct-taped garbage bags and was afraid to look at it, for fear I had ruined it.

"Now you will be unarmed," she said.

This was the truth. I did not have the Louisville Slugger baseball bat I took in 1998, and I left at home the throwing knives I had bought because it seemed like a good idea at the time. People made fun of my six Smith and Wesson knives with their black holster, and Cat said I should stop practicing on the tree in my backyard. She said it was bad karma to torture a tree.

I was not worried about my lack of weapons. Since passing through Nickajack Dam, I felt as if I had entered a friendlier zone of the river, full of people looking after me. I was among like-minded paddlers, hikers, birdwatchers, psychologists, most of them fellow tree huggers, I thought. I hadn't seen a canoe-eating cabin cruiser for many miles. The fishermen who snubbed me on Guntersville seemed harmless souls in retrospect; perhaps they were just shy. I could not blame them for being frightened of me and Maggie, having appeared from the darkness of that rocky shoreline. It seemed frivolous now, expecting people to return my greetings, a rural Southern ritual often false in its implied affability, its pretense of goodwill. On Nickajack in Chattanooga, people had just about stopped staring at us. We were on the verge of fitting in, particularly on that Saturday morning, among dozens of paddleboarders trying out boats that the retailer REI was lending out for free rides. I saw two canoers that day, big boys who were taking out after a short run, the only other canoe I'd seen in the water on the Tennessee, not counting the abandoned one back on Wheeler. After just

After locking through Chickamauga Dam,
Maggie and I sought refuge at Lakeshore Marina.

a few miles that morning, Nickajack lost most of its friendly charm as the sky turned gray; storms were due to arrive that night.

Phillip of Outdoor Chattanooga told me I could try camping at Lakeshore Marina, where he knew the owner, Steven. He couldn't remember his last name, but he told me the marina was upstream of the dam, in a cove off the left bank, and Steven was a nice guy.

The lock operator at Chickamauga was also nice, perhaps overly solicitous, I thought, in explaining things to me that I already knew. After I called him, he told me to wait under the railroad bridge while he discharged water from the lock. He instructed me that I could advance toward the doors after he turned the light from red to green. When I got inside the lock and paddled to the front as I had at the other dams, I almost tied up to a fixed bollard instead of the ones designed to rise and fall with the level of the water. He freaked out a little.

"No!" he shouted from the top of the wall. I had realized my mistake just as he yelled at me.

As we paddled out onto Chickamauga Lake, he said, "You did pretty good."

I resisted the urge to tell him that we were veterans of six locks on this river, that I had locked through all nine of them twenty years earlier. Boasting would probably not leave a good impression, and we were still trying to make up for the Pickwick blunder. Now was the time to find shelter before darkness set in and the storms broke loose.

I felt a little guilty, a couple of hours later, camped inside Lakeshore Marina's gazebo, just a day after sleeping in a hotel room, but I'd have been foolish to refuse. My tent fit in there neatly, and as the storms rolled through, Maggie and I sat in open air and enjoyed the pitter-patter on the gazebo roof, secure and dry, high above the big water. There was a porta-potty right next to us, a power source in the gazebo, a security light, and a water spigot a few yards away: hog heaven. Steven, the marina owner, asked that we not hang around too long the next morning because his customers tended to be high-end. He didn't say "high-end" but expressed it in sign language: holding his pinky finger out as if drinking tea from a cup. They might not like seeing a vagrant (my word) and his dog camped in their precious gazebo, he said.

Lakeshore Marina's gazebo sheltered Maggie and me from a steady rain.

I embarked upon Chickamauga Lake with some trepidation, remembering it not so fondly from Labor Day weekend, 1998, when it was buzzing with swarms of motorized watercraft, some of them cleaving large wakes. One gleaming white cabin cruiser roared into a narrow gap between me and a sailboat. Just before I had to start paddling to climb the wakes, the sailboat skipper looked at me, shook his head, and shrugged. What could we do about this maritime bullying? This time I would be traversing much of Chickamauga during the week, not on a weekend, and I hoped for calmer waters. What I got this time around were hints that beneath its friendly surface, the river could harbor unnatural conspiracies and suspicion. This departure from the friendly, scenic waters of Nickajack would make Chickamauga my unofficial favorite lake of the trip.

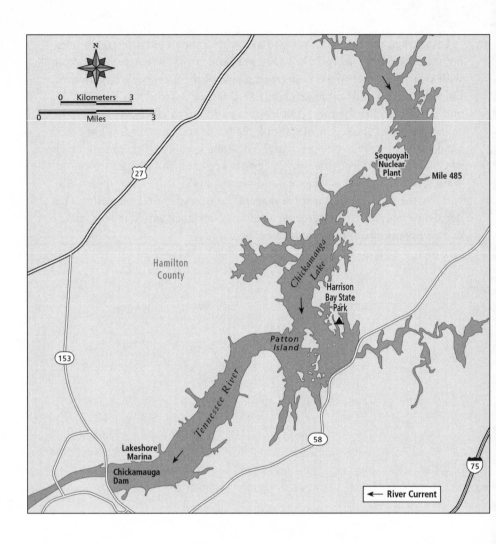

24

CONSPIRACIES

I passed Gold Point Marina that morning without recognizing it. It had probably changed in twenty years, as had most of the river's marinas and campgrounds—more spread out and upscale. In 1998, I'd pulled into Gold Point's cove in search of refuge from the turbulent Labor Day weekend waters. There, I met Scott Sullivan, who had a sailboat called the *Jolly Mon*. He drove me to Hixson for a cheeseburger and told me I "had to see" the movie *Captain Ron*. There was a boat-docking scene from the movie that he had re-enacted: he charged full speed at the dock, frightening the landlubbers into thinking the captain was asleep at the helm, and then he turned the wheel and slammed it into reverse to land the *Jolly Mon* sideways against the dock with hardly a bump. Scott introduced me to a canoer, marina worker, and former barge deckhand named J.D., famous for breaking the speed limit in a canoe (while being towed behind a motorboat). J.D., who also paddled standing up in his canoe, cocked his head at me and grimaced through his thick red beard when I told him that my wife was going to pick me up when I got to Paducah, Mile Zero, and bring me home to Knoxville.

"If you want to be like the real voyageurs, you'll turn around at Paducah and paddle upstream back home."

I wished that twenty years later I'd see J.D. pacing the dock so that I could show him I was finally following his advice, sort of. He was probably out there somewhere, in spirit, on this post-storm morning, the air clear and calm. Gliding along the left bank, Maggie and I passed a regatta of eight sailboats, stately in their circuit of the marked course out in the middle. On the other side of us, a man at the helm of a tiny johnboat—a SeaArk—put-tered out of a cove, his boat loaded down with five boys. They were staring at us.

"Got room for another one?" I asked.

He laughed and said he was getting ready to tow the kids on innertubes behind the tiny boat. "Did you lock through the dam?"

"That was our seventh."

A pause. "No way! That's killer!" He started a slow clap and all of the boys joined in.

Before he motored out into the middle of the lake, he asked if we needed anything, if he could offer us a tow. There had been times, a few weeks earlier, when I would have been tempted by this offer, but this was one compromise I would refuse. I would paddle the whole way, and I certainly didn't need a tow on a beautiful morning like this one, unless, of course, I wanted to break my speed record, in the style of the gonzo canoer at Gold Point. Meeting this bunch in the johnboat, so astounded at what we were doing, did affirm that we had accomplished something unusual and note-worthy. I don't know about Maggie, but I certainly did not expect applause for canoe camping, no matter how far we'd come. It was heartening and yet I knew there were hard miles ahead—200 of them and two more dams.

After noon, as the lake widened, the Chickamauga that I remembered from twenty years ago emerged, motorboaters zigging and zagging like water-bugs all the way across the lake. Then the wind started to create its own chop on our one-mile crossing to the right side. Back at Lakeshore Marina, Steven, the owner, assured me that I would get way past Harrison Bay State Park, but the oncoming boat traffic and the wind persuaded me to make camp there, a little beyond noon, after I'd paddled about ten miles. Why beat myself up on a Sunday, when the lake resembled a nautical freeway? I'd sit it out today and hit it hard starting tomorrow. It made me happy to be traveling at my own pace, in warmer weather, without a schedule or a place to be at a certain time.

The campground was packed, but since people were in the process of leaving, we procured a fine site near the water, on a rise looking down at a calm inlet where kayakers ferried back and forth and people fished off the bank. One couple glided back and forth in matching his/her sit-on-tops, an Australian shepherd standing on the deck of the man's boat. Just standing there, like a figurehead. Maggie, who was in the middle of an excavation project, happened to glance up from her trench. She commenced barking and straining at her lead, as if the deck dog's showing-off enraged her. The couple's boats came together, as if in a dance, and the Aussie stepped from one deck to the other, nothing to it, all of it a little performance. The dancing dog never acknowledged barking Maggie, not even a glance. I felt bad for her, as if she were my middle-school daughter, the victim of mean girls. Once they were gone, we forgot about it. A couple of tweenaged girls came over from the site next to us and asked if they could pet Maggie, who was now resting in the shade. The girls sat on the ground and hugged Maggie, who snuggled and licked and squirmed with delight. She still acted like a puppy, even though her body had matured into sixty-five pounds of muscle. When she went into berserk mode and started jumping up on the girls and knocking them sideways, the girls did not back away. They loved it. When their parents called them over and said it was time to go home, they said sad goodbyes to Maggie, whose tongue hung low as she watched them skip away. My dog might not have the cool obedience of the Aussie, the aloof grace to jump from the deck of one boat to another, but she had a charisma all her own and she made friends fast.

I set up the new hammock that Catherine had brought from my sister, Melissa, who had loaned me the one that I broke through, back on Pickwick. I took a shower. I organized and reorganized. Maggie napped. I bought a bag of ice. Took Maggie for a walk. By twilight I was exhausted and I hadn't even built a fire. Into the tent I crawled. The forecast said twenty percent chance of rain, not enough for me to put the rain fly over my tent. It was cooler inside without it. As Maggie and I began to negotiate our respective space inside the tent, a golden bee, on his back, buzzed on the tent floor in a frenzy of frustration. With a bandanna, I picked him up and lay him outside, proud of my sensitivity. Granola-man was I, caring for the least among creatures, even though my dog would have tortured the thing out of curiosity and probably have gotten stung on her black nose. I loved bees. The world needs more of them, and I was doing my part to make it so.

I dropped off into a righteous sleep until an hour later when Maggie woke me. She was emitting the low growl that meant business. Something was rampaging around the perimeter of camp, crunching leaves and branches as it circled us. I knew, even before I looked, what it was: my old nemesis, the one animal I hated almost as much as the horsefly or the gnat. Raccoon.

Lightning flashed to the north. I groaned and crawled out of the sleeping bag, resigned to completing two chores: scaring off the raccoon and setting up the rain fly. I told Maggie to be quiet because everyone around us had gone to sleep by now, a little after ten o'clock, the designated quiet time in the campground. She grumbled and lay back in her corner. I slipped on my shoes, outside next to the tent door, and stood, then crumpled to the ground at the sharp explosion of pain on the sole of my right foot. In the dark, I did not see the culprit, but I knew who it was: the bee whose life I had saved. Either that or a copperhead. I had never felt such exquisite pain, and I cursed loudly and yelled "ow, ow, ow" as I hopped around camp on one foot with my shoe in my hand. From a tree near the lake, my dreaded enemy's eyes glowed with pleasure. To my right, in a gully, his partner in crime paused in his leaf-stirring revelry to stare at the human spectacle. I limped around and found some pebbles to sling at them, first at the tree raccoon, and then at the other one making all the noise. They barely moved.

Something stank. Somebody was burning garbage in a campfire. How rude. People shouldn't have a fire, I thought, if they don't know any better than that. And then I figured out that it was my own fire pit, which must have had some live embers left over from the previous camper. I'd tossed my own plastic bag of garbage into the pit, and it was aromating the entire state park, drawing in the raccoons, who had lured me out of the tent to get stung on the foot. I sat down and applied ice to my swollen, throbbing foot, the same one with the big blister on it that had finally healed after two weeks. Lightning kept flashing, as if to mock me further. On the radar, a small but intense red patch festered twenty miles away. If I did not put up the rain fly, it would storm. If I did, it would not. So I did. Painfully.

I was convinced that the whole evening was a conspiracy masterminded by the raccoons, in cahoots with the small, potent bee, who had pretended to be in distress. I wondered what the kayaking couple with the perfect dog was doing. Not this. It was near midnight, and, having awakened all of the recreators with our silly skirmish, we would owe apologies the next morning. Or we could get up and leave before anyone else awakened, our usual routine.

The next day, the Harrison Bay drama behind us, I sank into the trance that lake paddling often brings, losing myself in the repetitive motion, thoughts wandering across the broad surface with no particular focus, forward and backward in time, from place to place, people arising from the gray surface and then dissipating like swirling mists. I have never feared boredom; it never occurs to me. If this is boredom, I thought, give me more.

We passed the cooling towers of Sequoyah Nuclear Plant at a respectful distance.

Flat water paddling in the middle of a lake lulls the mind into a pleasant stupor akin to sleep. Through the late-morning haze emerged the towers of Sequoyah Nuclear Plant, less than subtle relief in the featureless lakescape.

In 1998, I stopped to chat with a couple who sat outside together on a swing in front of a brick rancher just upstream of the plant. They remembered the old river, before Chickamauga Dam, and they told me about watching deer swim across the lake here. They weren't bothered by the nukes, they said. Didn't even think about it. Twenty years later, the house was still there, and it looked the same, except I'm pretty sure it was empty. I lingered off the bank and saw no signs of life. Twenty years and the couple was gone, life moving them elsewhere, either across that final river or to another place, to wait out their days. I began my crossing to the right bank, where Grasshopper Creek Campground would be, about sixteen miles away.

Glancing over my shoulder every now and then at the cooling towers, I wondered what Sequoyah, inventor of the Cherokee syllabary, would think

On a bright Sunday morning, we encountered a fleet of eight sailboats navigating a course in the middle of Chickamauga Lake.

about having a nuclear plant named after him. I imagined him shrugging his shoulders, unsurprised at the appropriation, at the mindless progress of civilization. Tellico Dam, upstream, had drowned sacred burial grounds and villages on the Little Tennessee River. Much lay beneath these waters, history good and bad, ruins of boats and dwellings, once-fertile fields, the decaying remnants of capital crimes and lesser mischief, much of it undiscovered, secrets forever concealed. Maybe treasure lay under the mountains of silt and mud that gathered in reservoirs unable to properly flush themselves. Conquistador Hernando de Soto passed through these parts in search of gold. Like other compatriots of his, he would fail in his quest for riches. When he died, his men concealed it. They waited for nightfall and slipped his body into a hollow log, which they pushed into the Mississippi, anxious to preserve the illusion that he was immortal. The log would twirl and twist in the churning muddy water, taking the conquistador to his final resting place somewhere downstream. I liked to think that conquistadors lay below the hull of my boat on the bed of this river, in the deepest part of the old channel, their armor shielding bare bones and skull, a sword tip poking up through centuries of silt for carp to prod. Perhaps, in twenty more years, my ashes would settle to the bottom of this river to mingle with the adventurers of old, scoundrels and heroes alike.

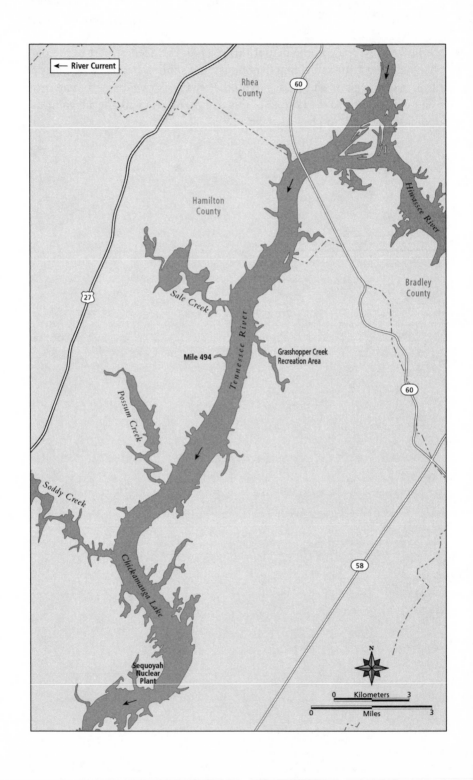

25

COMEUPPANCE

I did not require a settled campground that evening, but I thought it would be nice to try again, after the raccoon and bee conspiracy of the previous night had left me short of sleep. Grasshopper Creek, a private campground, sounded fun, like a playground; I held no grudges against grasshoppers. I remember holding them in my hands summer days, amazed at the energy they unleashed when I released them. Today turned hot as summer, in the eighties, and around midday I pulled up on a narrow gravel bar to cool off in the water. We'd come a long way, it seemed, from the narrow gorge and its dramatic beauty. Here the flatwater coves held the normal flotsam of logs and limbs, plus the detritus of reservoir leisure, the heavy human population living on the banks and using the lake, leaving its parade of plastic that bobbed against the shoreline. I jumped in anyway, among the limbs and bottles and cans, desperate for immersion. Maggie splashed around up to her chest. No matter how much I coaxed her, she hadn't gone swimming since the incident at Pickwick Dam. The trauma had robbed her of that pleasure.

Soon after my swim, my sister texted me and asked if I had my life jacket on.

"Why would you ask that?" I replied.

"Just checking."

I'd taken it off fairly early that hot day and stuffed it behind me for extra padding. I knew better than to go without it, and I tried to set a good example for other boaters, but the flat water had induced that hypnotic trance in me, and it had been empty of barges and pleasure boats. What harm would it do to paddle without the PFD?

How she knew to pester me about this, I do not know. It was uncanny. What other transgressions had she ascertained from Hopetown, over 400 miles downriver? Did she somehow hear me swearing after the bee sting? As if to expiate for all of my river sins, I put the sweaty jacket back on, but I also turned my phone off.

By the time I paddled sixteen miles to reach the vicinity of Grasshopper Creek, Maggie and I were sapped by the heat, ready to be out of the boat and lazing around in the shade on a carpet of mown grass. To reach the campground, we had to paddle about a quarter-mile off the main channel, up a sheltered cove. The grounds, on a knoll, seemed crowded to capacity with RVs. Our search along the bank for a vacant spot was fruitless, so I paddled back to the boat ramp to get out and investigate. A guy in a golf cart coasted to a stop at the ramp, right about where we were planning to disembark.

"Do you have any sites free?" I asked from the boat.

He cupped a hand around his ear, as if he couldn't hear me.

"I said, 'do you have any campsites to rent'?" I wanted to make sure he didn't think I wanted to camp for "free," so I didn't use that word again.

He stared at us a beat before answering, an old lizard with his billed cap pulled down low over his eyes.

"We're all booked up for the next three weeks."

My turn to wait a beat or two, for more of an explanation, perhaps. How could this place be booked for that long? I'd gone past far more spectacular scenery just in the last week, and it wasn't as if there were some kind of resort-level luxury to humble Grasshopper Creek, your average country campground. I hoped he might take pity on us and find that hidden, unofficial spot like Wade had discovered back on Wheeler. I would pay, no problem. But there was no concession coming from this guy; he wasn't even going to waste another sentence on me.

"Well, thank you for checking," I said.

We paddled back out into the main channel and headed across the river on a tip from Phillip, the Outdoor Chattanooga guy, who said there was a "beach" in this area. Overheated and put out by being turned away after wasting the energy it took to get to Grasshopper Creek, I doubted there was anything resembling a beach on the other side, but I paddled toward a pale strip of land that looked like it might have possibilities. I made up my mind that once I got camp set up and cracked open a warm beer that I would call Grasshopper Creek and confirm my suspicions about the codger in the low billed cap. I thought he was lying and I wanted to catch him in it. Hell hath no fury like an overheated canoer denied a campsite.

The distant tan strip didn't pan out as the fine-grained white beach of my fantasy, but just across the cove from the beach mirage was a gravel bar, an expansive bit of real estate, flat and weedless, better than a beach, all things considered. Even though others had camped here, it was fairly clean, and in our initial recon, Maggie and I trekked up a dirt track that led into empty, undeveloped woods, seeing nothing there to be concerned about on a weekday. A cursory glance confirmed the absence of "No Trespassing" signs. I concluded that the snubbing at Grasshopper Creek had been a blessing, but my fury still simmered, and I needed to satisfy my curiosity with a phone call.

"Hello," I said. I tried to sound chirpier than the haggard grouchy geezer he'd seen in person an hour ago. "I was just wondering if you had any campsites free tonight."

"Let me check," said the codger. I recognized his voice. Funny that he had to check now. A few seconds passed, and I began to suspect that he was lying now, that he wasn't checking anything but the grime under his fingernails. "It looks like we've got one," he said.

He made it sound like he'd found a twenty-dollar bill at the boat ramp: pleasantly surprised. I was elated but not for the reason he thought. My suspicions had been confirmed. He lied to us earlier because he didn't like our wilted, down-on-our-luck demeanor. We were tired and smelly and we didn't have a motor. My boat was stained around the waterline and my gear was in disarray. My dog whined. No room for you!

"You're sure you've got a campsite available?"

"Yes, we do." He was getting excited.

"That's funny. I was over there an hour ago in a canoe, and you told me there were no campsites available for three weeks."

A beat or two passed, enough for it to sink in. "We had a cancellation. Come on back over."

No way would I paddle away from this sweet gravel bar and pay this guy to camp in his overcrowded park just to take a shower in a slimy bathhouse and maybe buy a sugary canned drink and some chips. I think he knew that. At the same time, I had a gut feeling that he was lying about the sudden cancellation, and I wanted to rub it in just a little bit more.

After being turned away from Grasshopper Creek Campground,
we found a comfortable gravel bar and camped for free.

"I'm not coming back over there," I said. "You lost some business by
lying to me earlier."

Silence. I hung up and took a long pull from my warm beer. Satisfaction.
And now I was alone, watching the sun set.

Perhaps that's what frightened him about me: my being alone. Even with
Maggie, I understood that some found this threatening and abnormal—the
lone drifter, free of conventional responsibilities, unmoored in the world to
drift where he wanted. It relaxed me, not to have to talk for long periods,
to bask in the peace of the darkening cove in front of me, fish feeding on
the surface, small circles appearing and disappearing in their wake. I'd
start a fire with free wood when I felt like it. Or not. No expectations, no
worries about what my neighbors thought. Clothing optional. Whooping
and hollering okay, too. Singing badly. It was enough, for me, to sit and
contemplate the little cove and the woods around us, particularly after all
of the company I'd had the past week. I'd be meeting friends the next day,
and these periods of solitude sharpened the pleasure of sharing the landscape
with people who understood the allure of quiet slow travel over flat water.

A pair of fishermen drifted past us near sundown, and we stared at each
other without speaking for a few minutes. I was in my camp chair eating

dinner from a bag, and Maggie gnawed on a piece of driftwood ten feet long.

The guy at the motor said he used to camp on that gravel bar when he was younger. A lawyer owns the land, he said. They drifted onward, up into the cove. Next morning, as I paddled east toward the Hiwassee River confluence, the newly-risen sun made me look sideways against its bright eye. Approaching a small boat, I was surprised to see the two guys from the evening before, talking and fishing. They nodded at me, like ghosts in the fog, and onward we traveled, toward the mouth of the Hiwassee and beyond, to Blue Water RV Resort and Marina, a place I was returning to after a gap of twenty years. Then, I had landed in a picnic area with my dog, Jasper, and waited for Julie, my wife at the time, to pick us up and take us into Dayton for a dinner at an Italian restaurant and a night in a motel room. The next day at Blue Water, I met commercial anglers Bill and Kathy Sligh, who had just come in with a boatload of fish, mostly carp and catfish. Kathy stood in the middle of the fish pile in rubber boots, a cigarette in one hand, the other holding up a sixty-pound channel cat for me to photograph. They told me about their lives on the water, mainly the hardships like government regulations and inconsiderate sport fishermen and powerboaters who destroyed their nets. Bill had almost drowned in an accident below Nickajack, where I'd seen the paddlefish. In 1998, the meeting with Bill and Kathy had come relatively early in my downstream trip, and meeting people who fished for a living, who knew the river like nobody else I'd talked to, gave me momentum on a weekend that had been brutal in its heat and powerboat turbulence. They complained about it as much as I did, and it made me feel as if I were part of an older culture, even though all I was doing was paddling.

Coming the other way toward Blue Water, now, I wondered how much of it would remain, whether I would fill in the blank spaces of my memory of twenty years ago, or if it would be unrecognizable, as so many other places had been. Bill and Kathy wouldn't be there. I knew because I called Kathy before this trip and learned that Bill had died. Perhaps the place, the swampy, weed-clogged cove and the little boat ramp, would remain the same to honor him and the day he'd pulled a load of fish from Chickamauga and found somebody who marveled over his description of a life's work about as close as to the river as you could get.

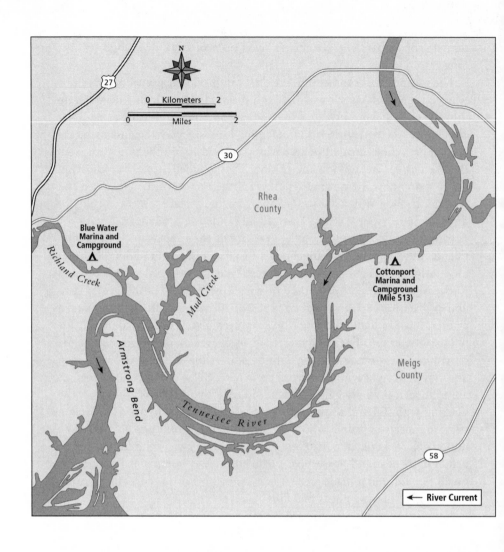

26

GOOD COMPANY

Because I launched so early, I foiled the plans of my friends, Maryville College biologist Drew Crain and chemist Terry Bunde: they wanted to paddle downstream and meet me on my way to Blue Water. By half-past noon, I was paddling up Richland Creek toward the marina, just after Bunde had pulled into a campsite in his 1997 Nissan pickup with camper top. Sticking out of the bed of his truck was a faded blue fiberglass canoe, a boat he had bought in the 1970s for one hundred dollars. (I'd paid $600 for mine, used.) Bunde, retired from his professorship at Maryville College and now working as a consultant, divulged the price of all his gear, and put us to shame, even Drew, a self-professed penny pincher. These two, veterans of many outdoor excursions with me, met us at the boat ramp and helped carry gear up a steep incline to the campsite fifty yards away. A tall, husky fellow, taking out his bass boat and eyeing my soiled rig, in disarray, paused to ask what I was up to. I said I was canoeing the length of the river going upstream.

"You've got bigger balls than I have!" he roared.

The anatomically graphic metaphor aside, his compliment flattered me but was also a little embarrassing because so many people were around to hear it. Last time I'd been here, Blue Water had been a swampy little cove with a deserted boat ramp. Now, there was a marina and store, the campground was packed with RVs, and a procession of bass fishermen waited in line to put their boats in; except for patches of grass here and there, everything seemed to be paved. I remembered a weedy field and a low area shaded with trees. Now houses lined the bank across from the campground. Was this even the same place? Had to be.

At our campsite, in full view of the fishing pier below, where my canoe was moored, Bunde handed me a cheeseburger from Wendy's and showed off the variety of beer he'd brought. With a big grin on his gray-bearded face, he urged me to open one of the Leinenkugel "Paddler" lagers. I did not resist. It was well after noon.

"I almost brought some Perrier," he said. This was an allusion to our trip on the Sequatchie River when he made fun of the beverage I'd brought: fizzy French water in dainty green ten-ounce cans.

When I told Barron, the campground manager, over the phone what I was doing, he was glad to make an exception to Blue Water's no-tent-camping policy, and he reserved us the campsite nearest the ramp. The site was in full sun, and it was a hot April day, but my friends had come prepared, and soon we had manufactured our own shade with Drew's canopy. They set up a tent that looked big enough for ten and welcomed me and Maggie in as guests. I declined and popped up our dome home. Maggie, tethered to a nearby tree, had greeted Bunde with a dog punch below the belt that doubled him over. I explained to him that she was part boxer, and from then on, he kept his guard up. We were surrounded by RV campers with small fluffy dogs, many of them voicing their high-pitched disapproval of Maggie. We were conspicuous campers out on the point of this RV city, with a barking, leaping mutt, two tents, and my gear spread out all over the grass. Nobody except the small dogs seemed to care.

Sport fishermen trolled the banks of Richland Creek in their gleaming bass boats, and some motored on out of the creek to the long islands in the main channel. I could not conceive of commercial fishermen pulling out here with a boatload of squirming carp and catfish. Everything seemed spic and span compared to the time I met Bill and Kathy Sligh, all of it upgraded, in a sense, homogenized to be consumer-friendly. The Blue Water website, with its flyover portrait, presented the comprehensive makeover: a log cabin marina clubhouse and grill with a party-friendly covered deck; a swimming pool with spurting fountains; cabins, lakehouses, and a lodge. The overhaul had started in 2010 and lasted six years. It wasn't just my memory playing tricks on me. And even though I mourned the transformation of the laid back, low key Blue Water into the upscale recreational empire, I could not have asked for a more welcoming place to meet friends in terms of convenience, amenities, and activities to observe and keep us entertained when we began to bore each other with the same old stories.

Bunde took me to the Walmart in Dayton. My list featured one geezer item: Ibuprofen. But I came out of there with a couple of bags, including a bone for Maggie and two cans of sardines that Bunde talked me into buying, not the higher-priced stuff that I reached for at first, but the bargains on the shelf below. Even after the cheeseburger, I was hungry, and being in a store always seemed like a last-chance event that required stocking up.

Back at camp, Bunde was displaying his outdoor gear. "This is the best thing that came out of my time in Vietnam," he said. He held up an army-issue poncho liner.

"He almost didn't bring a sleeping bag," Drew said. He was using a pedal pump to inflate a mattress that would keep him a foot off the ground. Bunde couldn't believe the size of it. Though I was ashamed to announce the fact that I'd spent over 300 dollars on my sleeping bag, I did not regret a cent. It had kept me warm and dry on the coldest, dampest, loneliest river nights. That night, among the Blue Water community, I slept well, though I did have one of my floating tent dreams that always woke me up. I had to sit up and look out the tent door to make sure I was on terra firma and the dam

After camping with me and Maggie at Blue Water RV Resort and Marina, Drew Crain and Terry Bunde paddled upstream for a stretch.

hadn't broken and flooded the marina. I hold Drew partially responsible for these dreams; before the trip, he sent me an advertisement for a tent designed to float down a river, though I'd had these dreams long before the product came out.

Next morning, much later than my usual stealth camping departures, we paddled out of Richland Creek onto the main channel alongside a swampy island. Bunde and Drew made an odd pair in the old canoe. Drew, wearing a white visor (homage to Steve Spurrier), went without sunglasses, as always, and Bunde had a fancy pair that looked like giant insect eyes, his pony tail looped through a brimmed khaki Tilley hat that looked brand new. I knew, without him saying so, that he got the hat at one of his church's rummage sales. At school, Drew was famous for wearing bow ties; Bunde, whose field was chemistry, taught a class on the music of the sixties and seventies. He played guitar and sang folk songs. In everyday life, Bunde quoted John Prine. Each of them had this in common on that bright cool morning: they were giddy about being on the big water. Drew shouted when he saw a bald eagle across the lake. Together, the two scientists consulted each other about the composition of a rocky bluff about a half mile away, a layered wall of tan and gray that slanted diagonally up from the water. A great blue heron lifted off from the bank a few yards ahead and squawked at us. Both of them followed its flight as it swooped all the way across the lake. Bunde kept looking over his shoulder for fear that a barge would sneak up on us. This was good for me to see, all of this enthusiasm and vigilance. I'd seen dozens of eagles and great blues, and I didn't tire of it, but at the same time, since I had only Maggie to share such sightings, I had become less vocal about them. Hearing my friends' remarks helped spur me onward in the voyage and renewed my observational acuity. Losing one's self in the monotony of flat water paddling, seeing but not seeing as you turn inward and let thoughts roll like an old filmstrip—the past, the hypothetical future, things you've forgotten, things you wish for and things you fear—this meditative state had superseded my scrutiny of the outside world for the past few days on Chickamauga, and having Drew and Bunde along shook me out of it.

Bunde caught a fish, of course, one of the bluegill he'd been tracking by scent. ("I smell those blue gill beds," he kept saying in camp.) Drew caught one, too, and he later claimed that both were keepers, though I never saw either fish, and no photographic evidence exists to support such a claim. My rod stuck out like a slanted flag pole from my stern, my lazy trolling-mode of fishing, and I gathered weeds with my Little Cleo spoon. I encouraged my friends to keep going with me to Cottonport, my next planned stop, but after a couple of hours, they turned around and headed back to the

Leaving Blue Water RV Resort and Marina and headed to Cottonport,
Maggie and I were in for an easy paddling day. Photo Credit: Terry Bunde.

marina. Each of them had obligations back on land. When they were fifty
yards away, one of them delivered a parting shot: "It's a lot easier going
this way!"

Getting to Cottonport made for an easy day—about five miles—but I had
to stop there because of such fond memories from 1998. Bob Armstrong,
the owner back then, treated Jasper and me like royalty, such a welcome
respite after a few hot and thirsty days of improvised camping. Bob invited
us into his trailer, served me grilled hamburgers, and put on *Titanic* for us
to watch, a movie I would have nightmares about later on, even though I
got so sleepy sitting on Bob's couch that I had to quit watching and return
to camp about the time it looked like Leonardo DiCaprio's character would
drown below decks. I had no reason to expect such special treatment this
time around, and I doubted that Bob, who was in his sixties and not in
good health in 1998, would still be there, but the place had the same laid-
back feel to it when I pulled up to the bank next to one of the small fishing
piers that extended from each campsite. Up at the store, which also housed
a restaurant, young Zach Andrews, who now owned the place with his

brothers, said this when I asked about available tent sites: "You can pitch a tent anywhere you find a flat spot."

"Wow. Really?" After being turned away at Grasshopper Creek and experiencing the upgrades at massive Blue Water, Zach's attitude seemed too good to be true. I'd come to expect letdowns from revisiting 1998 campsites, at least a discombobulation from the way memory distorted reality. At Cottonport, the look of the place and its positivity seemed to have survived the passage of two decades. It was as if I'd found a piece of the memory puzzle that fit exactly into the blank space where it belonged.

"The best site is the last one," Zach said. "There's a couple of RVs nearby, but you've got a lot of room there and it's right on the water."

"Just camp anywhere you like and here's our best spot" was something I hadn't heard the whole trip, and it was even more unusual for just twenty dollars.

"You're not into wild parties, are you?" he asked.

This made me laugh. "I'm usually asleep by nightfall."

"Well, you can drink here, but we don't want campers getting drunk and rowdy."

"That's good," I said. "That will help me sleep." I told him that my friends David Wilburn and his son Jordan would be joining me. Before he changed his mind about me, I paid up and paddled upstream to set up camp.

The landing for the canoe required a steep climb up a wall of riprap, but other than that, the site had a fire ring, stacked wood, a fishing pier, and a picnic table, all well-shaded. Several yards away, a guy was running a weed-eater near his RV. Claude, a semi-retired, transplanted Floridian, lived in this RV with his wife. He killed the weed whacker when he saw me. "I just moved that table there and trimmed all around it," he said. "Figures that somebody would camp there." He was smiling, yellow-toothed, face pitted and pocked, long frizzy hair in a ponytail. Claude looked like he may have, in his day, been the rowdy partier that owner Zach worried about.

He'd moved up here from Florida to escape the hot weather, he said, and he spent his days fishing, watching "Jerry Springer," and "whatnot." He said I was welcome to the wood he'd stacked next to the fire ring at my site, and he had more if I needed it. I asked about drinking water, and he escorted me to his neighbor's RV, where we unscrewed his water hookup and filled up my tank.

"He won't mind. He's in town working."

I explained about Maggie's barking and left her in camp to do the long-overdue laundry. Two old guys were sitting at the bar counter eating lunch. I call it a bar, but the Andrews brothers did not sell beer. I found out from

Hitchcockian cormorants pretended to ignore us from their perch
above Chickamauga Lake.

these guys that Bob Armstrong had died in 2010, that when the brothers
bought the place five years ago, it was known for being Party Central, a
hotbed of drinking, drugs, stabbings, and shootings. Since the brothers took
over, there had been no trouble. Bob had told me a similar story in 1998,
about how he'd had to clean up the place when he bought it and stop people
from fighting and partying too hard.

I was salivating over the menu on the wall above the little opening to the
kitchen, and I asked the old guys what I should get when I came in for sup-
per with the Wilburns. They recommended the Bubba Burger, about what
I expected them to say. But then came other recommendations: the Philly
steak sandwich, the salads, the fish, the chicken. They pretty much went
through the entire menu, no help for me. One of them said he didn't like
onion rings, so he couldn't recommend them. Zach, in the kitchen, piped up
and said that the fried shrimp were really good. They would close at 8:00,
he said. I called David and told him to hurry up and get here.

Wilburn, as everyone calls him, had been a rafting guide on the Ocoee for
twenty-seven years. On the job, steering a big rubber boat full of tourists

down a hellish storm of whitewater, Wilburn had seen about everything: unscheduled swims in said whitewater, freakish weather, and aberrant behavior from customers and fellow guides. He'd even survived a heart attack while guiding, requiring an airlift to a hospital. The summer after, he was back to guiding, and he talked me into a run. Never have I seen anyone guide a boat so effortlessly, with such calm, through passages with names like Table Saw, Broken Nose, and Double Suck, all worse than the names imply. As he steered, he gave us soft-spoken instructions using understated humor like this: "We're going to drop 247 feet, but not all at once."

He and Jordan, who would graduate from high school in a couple of days, came in two vehicles because they planned on running a shuttle and camping with me at least one night after Cottonport. Unable to decide between the shrimp and the salad with fried chicken in it, I ordered both and did not regret the gluttony of the double order. I needed the salad for roughage, and everyone knows that seafood is healthy, that you can't fry the goodness out of it.

As we were paying the bill for our meal to one of Zach's employees, she looked at Jordan's long hair, sticking out the back of his cap and hanging down his back. "There's lots of girls who would give anything for your hair," she said.

He said thank-you, taking it for a compliment. I thought it set a strange tone for the rest of our time on Chickamauga. Jordan fished that night from our private pier, while David told me river stories. His worst day on the river, he said, involved a family who insisted on taking the trip, even though they were so far over the weight limit that the life jackets supplied by the outfitter weren't guaranteed to buoy them if they fell out. As if to test the jacket, one of them jumped out at an inopportune time (right before a rapid) and another one jumped in right afterward, to "save" him. The third one bopped up into the air and hurtled toward David, backside first.

"The last thing I remember before going under was that big half-moon blocking out the sky."

He had other stories, just as harrowing. I thought it telling that the day of the big people he considered to be tougher on him than the day he had the heart attack. He'd told me he was at peace with whatever happened that day, and also that many people helped to take care of him, a switch from his usual role of caretaker, cheerleader, paddling coach, swim coach, pilot, and skipper.

Formerly the site of untold mayhem, Cottonport was silent that night, everyone following the rules to extremes. We didn't hear a sound from the RVs after 8:00. It was so quiet we felt compelled to whisper. The next morning, David and Jordan left to drop David's pickup off at the picnic area above Watts Bar Dam, where we planned to stay overnight, and I waited in camp for them to return in Jordan's truck. After a while, I got impatient and launched. I texted them, and they said they were fine with catching up with me, Jordan in his sit-on-top kayak, and David in his canoe, an Old Town like mine.

I was looking forward to a couple of easy days on the water with the Wilburns, but I was afraid the flat water would bore them, Wilburn an old-school whitewater canoer as well as a rafting guide, and Jordan an up-and-coming guide. I figured not much could happen on water that would surprise David, but in the next day, the dammed-up river would offer up some sights that surprised the three of us, hinting at a darker side of the Tennessee than I'd seen so far.

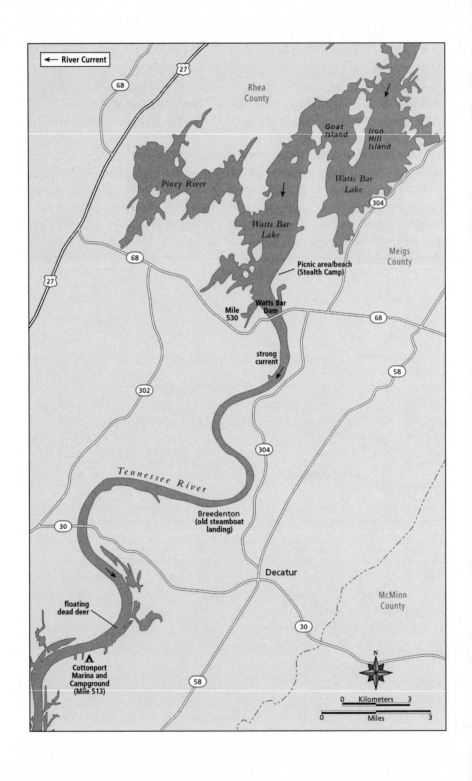

27

"THIS MAY SOUND STRANGE, BUT..."

I kept looking over my shoulder for signs of David and Jordan, and after two hours, I started to worry. Had they turned the wrong way on the river? If you were looking for current to indicate up from downstream, you could easily become confused on a segmented river like the Tennessee, and if they went downstream, I wouldn't see them again that day. After the socializing of the past two days, I wasn't ready to be alone with Maggie; I'd been having a few laughs, enjoying myself like a normal canoer. Laughing and carrying on alone in a small boat with a dog, no matter how beloved, just wasn't the same. I kept checking for a text from the Wilburns. Nothing. Then something distracted me from my phone activities, something emerging from the water that I'd never seen before. It first appeared as a swath of light brown fur drifting just above the surface. And then the entire deer appeared. It floated sideways, its head twisted around as if it were staring at me through the water. This deer, a buck, was whole, not field dressed by a hunter, and it hadn't been dead long. I didn't touch it, but I paddled all around it and could see no signs of decomposition. I half expected it to revive itself and swim away, a resurrection that would have given me a heart attack. I'd seen plenty of dead animals on the water, but something about the deer, so beautiful and whole, even in death, created a sense of foreboding and dread that day, particularly since I was getting more and

more concerned about the Wilburns. I felt responsible for them, my quest
having been the reason for their visiting Cottonport and taking a paddling
tour of Chickamauga Lake with me.

After a couple of hours, when I was within the shadow of the Highway
30 bridge, I looked back and saw them gaining on me. We pulled over for
lunch at a crumbling concrete boat ramp, and they told me that since Jordan
wasn't making good headway in his kayak, they decided that both of them
would get into David's canoe and tow the kayak; coming to this decision
had delayed them. It never occurred to either one of them to check their
phones, a negligence I gave them credit for.

At the ramp, I opened one of the discount sardine cans that Bunde had
talked me into buying, the one with mustard sauce. Something had happened
to the little fish; it was all yellow mush, nothing identifiable. I took a bite
or two and put the rest in my trash bag, the strong smell turning me into a
target for scavengers such as my masked friends, raccoons. I took some of
the beef jerky that David offered. Much better.

We had the river to ourselves: no boats, no bank fishermen, not even a
barge appeared. On the banks, no houses or farms were in evidence, just
flat, scruffy land covered with small trees, bushes, and weeds. The nearest

Jordan and David Wilburn, whitewater rafting guides, paddled a bizarre stretch
of Chickamauga Lake with us and locked through Watts Bar Dam.

town was Decatur. Jordan, who had been fishing constantly, hadn't gotten a bite, and I began to wonder if the lake was cursed, if we had wandered into some dead zone, more desolate than the parts of Wheeler, in Alabama, that had made me uneasy and longing for a settled campground. I spotted a boat ramp on the charts where I thought we could pull over for a break, but David pointed to the opposite bank at a wall of riprap and a ramp next to one of the first rocky bluffs of the day. It was strange how this place just seemed to appear, no sign of it on any of my maps. It wasn't a blank spot in the sense of what Alexander MacKenzie and Percy Fawcett searched out in their quests to fill in the maps of the Earth, but after hours of empty lake and the unsettling tone of the day, it may as well have been in remote Amazonia, this boat ramp. Not only was it uncharted, but as we would soon find out, this place's history, what had transpired here, would surpass anything we could have conceived in our imaginations.

The Wilburns sped off toward the ramp ahead of me and Maggie, much slower in our freighted boat. Drizzle began to fall as soon as our boats scraped concrete. Up above lay a half-acre gravel parking lot, empty of vehicles, on the bank a pizza box and a few empty beer bottles. About the time we got out of our boats to stretch our legs, a beat-up maroon Thunderbird pulled into the lot. Seeing that we had company on this desolate day did not thrill me. Misanthropic bile arose in my gut, prompting suspicion toward some local coming down here to give us grief, when all we wanted to do was make a quick pit stop. I had no reason to believe he would be belligerent, other than my tribal protectionism and the way that the dim day had created darkness inside me.

A gangly kid in a baseball cap and sneakers got out of the T-bird and walked toward us. He seemed to age as he got closer. In his mouth he held a thin cigar with a white plastic tip on it, and the hair that sprouted from under the cap was graying. Not a kid at all. This was Travis, from Decatur, who said he came down here a lot "just to look around." The man who owned the property had put up two or three No Camping signs near shaded flat places that would have served us well for a night's stay. Travis said the man had seventy acres that he was selling for seven million dollars. We were looking around us, as if to survey this valuable land, when Travis spoke up.

"This is kind of gruesome."

The Wilburns and I glanced at each other through the drizzle, which was waxing and waning in the still air, as if someone above were easing a spigot back and forth.

"I found a human arm down here," Travis said. He said this with a slight tone of wonder in his voice, almost as if he'd reported seeing a pod of dolphins breaching the waters of upper Chickmauga Lake. The human arm reference came up five minutes after we'd met friendly Travis, without any warning about the shift to the macabre. We stood in silence as he continued.

He said he notified the authorities, and the "people in the black Suburbans" took the arm and determined that it was an "animal bone."

Travis said, "I'm a hunter and I know that was no animal bone. There was still some flesh on it. It was a human arm."

Downstream a ways was a slough where he said his uncle used to dump couches and old appliances. This was disturbing enough to us philosopher canoers who preached "Leave No Trace," but he didn't pause to let us comment on the ethics of large-scale dumping into public waterways.

"They found a naked woman in that creek without a head."

"Did they find out who it was?" I asked.

"Never did. Would you all like to go on a tour?"

We all hesitated before replying, down there at the water's edge, not far from our boats, but I think we felt obligated, as if it would be rude to refuse Travis' invitation. He was so friendly, his tone at odds with the disturbing fragments of stories. I think David voiced his assent with more conviction than Jordan and me, and then he stayed behind at his boat to dig out his cell phone for photos. Travis led Jordan and me up the slope and lectured us about the area in his affable, disarming manner, as if he were a character who had walked out of an *Andy Griffith* episode directed by David Lynch.

Travis said one of his high school teachers used to bring classes for tours of this place, an old steamboat landing. We followed him past a tree with two "No Trespassing" signs nailed to it, one black with red lettering, the other red with white letters. Whoever posted these signs must have thought one wasn't enough to communicate the message that we were ignoring. We turned a corner and climbed a mown slope toward a two-story Victorian style house with big porches and ornate trim. The second-story wrap-around porch was sagging, and much of the white paint was peeling, but the tile roof looked fine, as did the two chimneys. On top, between the chimneys, was a widow's walk with a rusty iron fence around it that wouldn't reach your knees if you were a widow pacing around up there looking for the steamboat to arrive.

This used to be an inn, Travis said. He stepped onto the front yard, ahead of us, far beyond the tree with the signs. I kept thinking, the way the day has gone, the owner will pull up here any minute. Travis didn't care that we were trespassing. He pointed out a broken window in what looked like an attic above the second story and said this: "Huh. I don't remember that window being broken." I don't know what flashed through Jordan's mind after that comment, but I was thinking to myself: what could be in there that broke out the window? Travis' tone of wonderment and what he chose not to say added to the macabre aura that he had been developing from the time he met us at the boat ramp. It was as if he'd taken over his high school teacher's role as tour guide and local historian, only his specialty was raising questions and making innuendos that made shivers go up my spine.

After the exterior tour of the inn, we followed Travis up a path partially blocked by a mound of gravel meant to keep out four-wheelers. He led us to a closet-sized building at the end of a walkway that extended out over the river, the place, he told us, where steamboats would moor. Later on, David told me that Jordan came up to him at this point and whispered, "Dad, we have got to get out of here."

The rain began to fall harder, but we were somewhat sheltered from it under the leafy canopy of the old trees that rose above us over the path.

"What's down there?" David asked Travis. He pointed down a pathway beyond the pile of gravel that followed along the side of the bluff.

"I never go past this point," Travis said.

What he left unsaid—why he wouldn't go down the path at this place he visited often, just to look around—created another blank spot in the historical web of insinuation he was weaving.

As we stood there next to the rusty tower where steamboats had tooted their whistles and passengers disembarked to spend their night in the creepy inn, Travis shared some personal history. He was 35, divorced twice. He told us how his car got dented up. He'd fallen asleep on his way back from a late football game with one of his former wives. He was describing this to us, and we were wondering if the ex-wife was okay after the car wreck, when a truck pulled up into the lot and parked. Travis said it was the landowner, and we used this as an opening to depart. Instead of getting out or acknowledging us in any way as we walked down to our boats, the landowner just sat in his idling truck. Travis walked past and did not greet him, either. We said a quick farewell and paddled upstream toward Watts Bar Nuclear Plant in rain that got heavier and heavier. Finding shelter next to the bank under the steamboat landing made sense, but like Jordan, David and I were ready to get away from the creepy boat ramp for fear of what else we'd discover about the place, about Travis, or about the anti-social landowner.

A couple of guys in a bass boat sped straight at us and slowed down. One of them stood up and announced, "Big storm coming!" They pointed in the direction we were going with urgent motions.

We just kept on paddling. What could we do but endure it?

Rain fell so hard we could see only a few yards ahead, and we stayed close to the bank, under trees when possible. Thunder jarred the landscape. After about a half hour, the storm passed and the sun beat down. We pulled off about a mile from the dam at a boat ramp. I'd forgotten to reel in my fishing lure, and I was backpaddling in an attempt to get it loose from a snag. Maggie, excited by our proximity to shore, was prancing around in the bow. David and Jordan sat at the bottom edge of the ramp below a guy who was blocking access to the water, having set up a private fish cleaning station from the back of his truck. He and his buddy were tossing entrails and fish heads into the riprap, and turkey buzzards flapped all around us, waiting to feast on the offal. In the middle of all this activity, I was trying to call the lock operator about our impending arrival. Maggie went ahead and jumped on the bank, still tethered on her lead, and jerked the boat against the rocks in her effort to explore inland. I managed to inform the lock operator that we'd be there in two canoes in a half-hour.

David and Jordan had never locked through a dam, and this was the extent of my instructions to them: paddle to the front of the lock and wrap a rope around one of the mooring bitts that will rise as the lock fills up. When the big doors open and the operator sounds the horn, I told them, that means we can paddle out onto Watts Bar Lake.

This was the dam I had locked through before the trip, just to see if they would allow me to go through upstream in a canoe. The operator said he'd given me a "slow lift" to minimize the turbulence, and after I told him about my upcoming trip, he said I sure would see a lot of interesting things.

As the Wilburns and I approached the lock, the doors opened without us having to pull the cord or call again. This was a good sign; the operator was watching for us, just as he said he would. I was thinking we'd get through this no problem and then we would probably be able to get away with camping at the picnic area above the dam.

As soon as we got through the big lock doors into the chamber, the operator began yelling at us. We could understand nothing because he was so far above us—about seventy feet—and the wind was roaring. He seemed kind of stressed. David thought he was telling us to tie up to the third bitt.

"Both of us?" I asked.

"I think so."

This was not really possible. David tied off to that bitt and I called the guy.

"Did you tell both of us to tie off on the third bitt?" I asked.

"No, you tie off at four," he said. This was about the middle of the chamber, counter to all the locks up to this point, but I did as I was told. I thought it might have something to do with the stiff tailwind kicking up. He had already started the process of lifting us.

"Make sure your boat is flat against the wall," he told me over the phone. Then he ended the call and leaned over the wall to yell at David and Jordan. It was so noisy in the chamber I could not understand anything being said. David texted me: "Send me the lock operator's number. He's trying to tell us something, but we can't understand him."

I was able to twist around enough to see that David had tied off with a rope near his stern, so he was unable to hold his boat flat against the wall, but by the time I realized this, we were almost finished. I was ready for it to be over. While the tension in the lock rose during all the yelling, a turtle and a dead carp surfaced over and over again in the well-like opening where my mooring bitt was housed. These corpses did a water dance that spread an overwhelming stench.

The lock operator was waiting for us beyond the doors. He was really nice about it, but he said we needed his phone number handy when locking through. I don't know why he was telling me this since I'd just called him. And then he tossed down at us a rolled-up copy of how to lock through a dam. One of them missed and blew away, and the other one hit Maggie in the head and dropped into the boat.

"Thanks," I said. I paddled as fast as I could away from that dam, toward the swimming area at the TVA picnic area. I could hear David behind me, having a conversation with the lock operator. It did not sound rancorous.

David had kept his cool during the entire ordeal, but Jordan was a bit shaken. They'd seen their first nuclear plant from the water and locked through their first dam, all within an hour, and Jordan had known from the start that there was something wrong during the lock through. The operator had been yelling for David to moor his canoe so that it was flat against the wall. He was afraid that the boiling currents in the chamber would capsize him, tied up like he was, from the stern. This was something I should have told him. I also should have given him the dam's phone number. Little did I know that these omissions would turn a simple operation into a stressful experience for all.

In 1998, Jasper and I had camped at the picnic area, a shady hill with tables, a pavilion, and bathrooms. I had a photo of him posing with the cooling towers of the nuclear plant in the background. I felt pretty sure that David and I could get away with camping there; Jordan was heading back to Maryville, but first he and David had to drive back to Cottonport for his truck. I sat on the dog food bucket near the canoes and waited, conspicuous in my inactivity and lack of a vehicle, an aging vagrant who happened to be lugging a bunch of stuff and in charge of a dog. The boat ramp and the picnic area were busy. Fishermen put their boats in the water and pulled them out. Three young women in swimsuits, with two shirtless men in long pants tagging along, pranced over to the ramp from the swimming area around the bend. They had tall cans of something that made the girls converse at high volume in multisyllabic profanity: "motherfucker [noun], motherfucking [noun]." Somebody's toddler was with them; it was unclear to whom he belonged. One of the men fished on the pier at the farthest point distant that he could manage. Two of the girls rollicked on innertubes in the water where people had been launching their motorboats. In my experience, the water quality around boat ramps and marinas was less than optimal for swimming, the nautical traffic emitting fumes and leaking gas and oil. The air was turning chilly, and I put a jacket on, but it did not deter these girls from launching themselves off the pier. They made splashy entrances into the gassy water and then did it all over again. I doubt there were any fish brave enough to come within 100 yards of these whooping, chortling bathers. The third girl, sober enough to stay out of the water, came over to me and asked if she could pet Maggie. I warned her, but she insisted, adding that she had "like seven dogs at home." She began to name the breeds of those seven when Maggie jumped up and left a four-inch welt down the inside of her left breast. This had no apparent effect on her. She leaned over so far that both breasts were on the verge of falling out of the swimsuit top, and Maggie licked her face while I looked away.

"Thank you!" she said. Then she walked back toward the fishing pier. I think the toddler was hers.

At some point, drama erupted between the loudest girl and her boyfriend. She said something about having bailed him out of jail, I got that much. I think she'd found something incriminating on his phone (making me thankful, once again, that there were no phones like these in my youth). He got his device back from her, shrugged, and walked away, back around the bend to the swimming area. He wore pants that he had to hold up with one hand as he walked. I assumed he'd forgotten his belt.

One of the girls fell off her float and said, "My titty fell out!" Then, "Oh I hope that old man up there [me] didn't hear me say that."

That pissed me off, her calling me an old man, never mind the accuracy of the designation. I didn't need it confirmed in such a rude way, and I glared at her, like any self-respecting geezer would, and inwardly seethed at being left out of the fun. I might be old, I could have said, but at least I wasn't drunk in public, out making a spectacle of myself. I'm glad I kept this to myself because it sounded more prim and proper than I wanted to be.

By dark, they had left, and all seemed quiet by comparison. Jordan and David came back with double cheeseburgers from Cottonport, so big we could barely fit them into our mouths. I had the onion rings, my vegetable for the day, and tried to convey the spectacle of the drunken young people, but it came out flat compared to all that we had experienced that day. David did not want to camp illegally in the picnic area, despite my assurances that we could get away with it. He said that the story I planned to tell authorities about not being able to go anywhere else didn't hold up because his truck was parked up near the entrance.

After Jordan left, David and I got into our boats, paddled about fifty yards around the back side of a peninsula, and found a narrow landing for the boats. We stumbled around in the dark setting up camp among scrubby bushes that tripped us and little trees with spiny low branches that reached out to snag our clothes and scratch our flesh. In the morning, fishermen cast lures at the rocks below our tents. We paddled back to the ramp and David walked up to check on his truck. He said that it was "still there," but out of the several vehicles parked in the lot overnight, only his had been chosen by a convention of turkey vultures as a hangout.

David would paddle the first couple of miles with me on Watts Bar and then turn around to go back to his truck. The highlight of this short paddle was a small island taken over by cormorants, the small black waterfowl known by Europeans as the "crow duck." The island looked like it had been firebombed, the trees all bare and bleached white. Cormorants kill the trees where they nest by breaking off their branches and covering them with guano, which sounds like a horrible way to die. David said the island looked like something out of Hitchcock. And then, having invoked the American master of horror movies, he said, "So long, I've had a great time." That weekend he'd be back on the Ocoee, guiding tourists down the hellstorm of whitewater, probably happy he wasn't locking through a dam.

The weather had turned hot, this first week of May; it was as if I'd traveled through all four seasons on this trip. Up ahead, I had no idea where I would stay next, and I would be alone in my deliberations. Maggie never offered much help in this area.

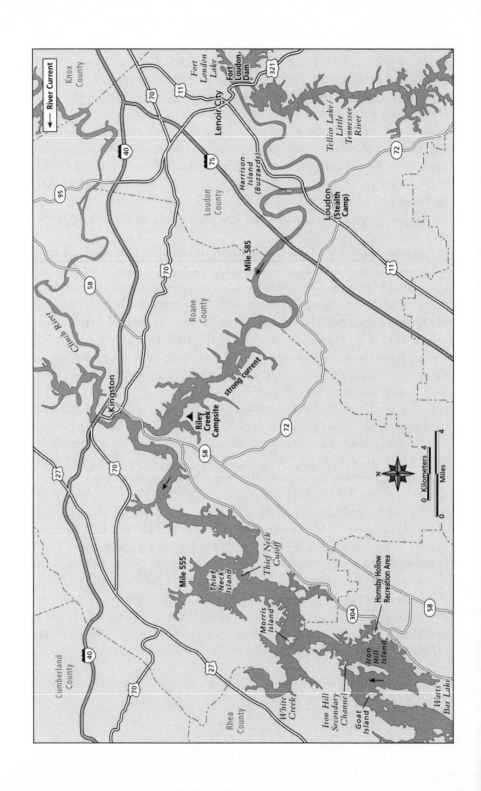

28

NIRVANA IN THE DOLDRUMS

Back in 1998, I entered Watts Bar Lake singing along to Merle Haggard's "Big City," an anthem of longing for rural life in the wide-open West. After the boat-wake tempest of a Fort Loudoun Lake end-of-summer weekend, Watts Bar had been a welcome respite, the river turning from urban to rural the instant I locked through Fort Loudoun Dam on a Monday morning. This time, in 2018, coming off the weirdness of Chickamauga, I entered Watts Bar with my guard up. I was truly on the home stretch now, a little over 100 miles from the end of the journey, and my vigilance originated from worry about what catastrophe would rise up next, to stop us here, on the verge of finishing. It seemed like we had endured about everything the river gods could throw our way: rain, wind, cold, heat, and various misfortunes of our own doing. After having the good luck to be around friends during the Chickamauga weirdness, I felt as if we might be due some adversity. I feared it was time for the adventure pendulum to swing the other way, toward misfortune with consequences. This pendulum theory I based upon past experience on trips like this: bright days followed storms, benevolence followed psychopathy, ease followed suffering. And vice versa.

People often ask me what was the most unusual thing I'd seen on the Tennessee River. Now that I'd undergone the strangest historical tour ever and seen a floating ghost deer; now that I'd seen my dog jump out of the boat inside a lock; after I'd spotted the same cargo ship that had wrecked the bridge my uncle had jumped from, I'd have to say that my strangest night on the river was the last one on Watts Bar, at the boat ramp of Loudon City Park, a few days after David Wilburn invoked Hitchcock and paddled away.

Maggie and I had once again failed to find a campsite at our planned destination, Harrison Island, about a half-mile downstream of the hamlet of Loudon, not far from where David worked, at Kimberly-Clark, "making toilet paper," as he put it. I paddled along the side of the island facing away from Kimberly-Clark and Loudon's other industries that lined the east bank, which became the north bank on this part of the river, crooked as a writhing snake held down by a stick. We were twelve miles downstream of Fort Loudoun Dam, which was generating now, in the evening, so the current was strong, and the water had risen high up the banks of the island. There was no room for a man and his dog to camp on Harrison Island, not even a place to land until we reached its upstream tip, a sand bar just above the water line, with room enough for a tent. Alas, it was already taken by occupants I would not intrude upon: buzzards ruled the sand bar, dozens of them perched and preening in silent, longing contemplation of a live human and a dog floating past. Onward we went, paddling hard in the fading light, under the Southern Railway Bridge and the Loudon County Memorial Highway Bridge, ferrying toward the right bank, away from the factories on the left. We had no choice, in this current, in the dark. We had to stop at the city park and we had to spend the night there.

The current from the dam's generators was stirring up food for the fish, and several anglers lined the pier next to the boat ramp to take advantage. In the time that I was getting out of the boat and securing Maggie, somebody caught a striped bass, someone else a bream. I stumbled toward the pier with Maggie jerking me forward and asked the nearest fisherman if he thought we'd get run off if we tried to camp here.

He didn't answer right away.

"People can fish here all night, can't they?" I asked.

He nodded. "Probably won't even notice."

I moored the boat to a smaller pier on the other side of a hillock from the boat ramp. The spot was partially hidden from the road above that led to the ramp. I considered setting up camp at a picnic table above the busy fishing pier, but the security light and overflowing garbage can discouraged me. I asked the fishermen, as a general group, if they minded watching Maggie while I walked to the convenience store a half-mile away to buy some fried chicken.

The fish were biting at Loudon City Park, where Maggie and I spent the night.

One of them said, "No problem."

After devouring the convenience-store chicken, I set up camp on the pier next to my boat, sleeping pad laid out on the walkway planks under the stars. Truly, I had reached some higher level of vagabondage. Just for show, I had my rod and reel ready in case the cops came and wanted to arrest me. I could even tell them, without lying, that I'd caught a couple of striped bass from the pier earlier, hard-fighting fish so small that no self-respecting fisherman would keep them as evidence.

The Loudon City Park wasn't the best campsite of the trip, not by a long shot. For one thing, the dew was so heavy that it soaked my sleeping bag. Maybe the dew had been as heavy elsewhere, and I just hadn't realized it under the protection of my tent. Maggie was in a constant state of agitation because the boat ramp and the fishing pier stayed busy through the night. From across the river floated laconic dispatches by a factory voice over a loudspeaker intercom, the messages garbled, as if in some alien code. Trains rattled past the factories every hour or so, their whistles filling up the night. When I finally dropped off into a restless doze, a strange noise awakened me. Strange and familiar. It was the sound of a mewling kitten, only louder, and it was coming from the water. All of the fishermen at the pier across the way were gone. Maggie, asleep, didn't seem to notice the mewling as it got closer and closer. Why would a kitten be in the water? I couldn't fathom. I brushed off the beads of dew from my sleeping bag and fell into another doze. A bit later, something was bumping my boat: bop, bop, bop.

I sat up and spotted the source of the bopping, an animal I'd been seeing the entire trip, from Day One: a beaver, only this one was about a half-foot long, and instead of making that big plunging noise and disappearing below the surface, like his parents always did, he continued ramming my boat with his head and making that strange, almost human, mewling sound, deeper and more resonant than a kitten, now that he was closer. When he grew tired of ramming my boat, he circled around the pier. Now he'd gotten Maggie's attention, and she wandered to the edge of the walkway and touched noses with the critter. There may have been some licking, too; usually her greetings involved the tongue. I called her off, worried that she might harm the kit, who had apparently lost its mother. Nothing I could do, right? I lay back down and dropped off again. Fishermen would arrive here early, I knew, and it would not be feasible to sleep here much past dawn. This place was apparently one of Loudon's social hubs.

When I woke, I could not find Maggie. It was after sunup and a few fishermen were already on the main pier. Maggie, who had stretched her lead to its maximum length—about twenty feet—was up on top of the hillock, making friends with what appeared to be a cat. Nothing made sense in Loudon, so I accepted this at first, knowing full well that Maggie would make friends with anything. I got up and snatched my end of her lead and pulled, afraid she'd get scratched by a mean town cat making her usual rounds. As I reeled in Maggie, I saw that her new friend was no cat; it was a raccoon who had wandered up to the grassy patch next to the boat ramp. It didn't take long to realize that this raccoon was not well. After a while, he lay down, despite the fact that people were all around. One guy had been baby-talking to him; others steered clear, including a woman who was so frightened of him that she cowered behind her fishing companion, down on the pier a dozen yards away from the sick animal. Another guy walking up to the pier didn't see the raccoon until he was right up on him: "What the. . . ?" he said.

"There's something wrong with that raccoon," I announced to the group in general. "I'd stay away from it if I were you guys." He had wandered over by the trash can now, blocking the walkway to the main fishing pier. I don't know why I thought people would listen to me, the guy who had spent the

This raccoon, who joined us at Loudon City Park the morning after our night there, probably had canine distemper.

night on the public boat dock. My opinion didn't carry a lot of weight, and the fisherman who had been baby talking to the raccoon, caught a small fish—a shad—and tossed it to the raccoon, who grasped it in his paws and began to eat.

"He's got parvo," said the guy who fed it. "Poor guy."

This was a very specific diagnosis that I did not question. Maggie, meanwhile, was dying to renew her friendship with the afflicted raccoon, who was most likely infected with canine distemper, something that humans could not contract from him but dogs could. Maggie had been vaccinated, but I wasn't taking chances. As soon as I could, I got the boat loaded and ready to leave Loudon, the place of strange animals. As we paddled past the main pier, one of the fishermen asked me what I was doing. I told him about paddling the entire river going upstream, that I was on the home stretch. I didn't want to come off like I was bragging, but I may have sounded a little proud of myself.

He gave me the slow head shake of dismay and pity. "If I was in a canoe," he said, "I'd sure as hell be paddling downstream."

I hadn't the energy to tell him I'd already done that twenty years before. I'd just open myself up to more ridicule. Onward we went, Maggie and me, toward the last dam of the trip.

Despite the prevalent opinion that I was going the wrong way, I'd covered a record distance on Watts Bar a few days earlier, when David Wilburn said farewell. For twenty-seven miles we traversed the heat and humidity of Watts Bar's broadest section. I have to come clean about this. On that part of Watts Bar, there are three shortcuts that enabled me to cover what I'll call twenty-seven chart miles, as measured by the Corps of Engineers on the navigable channel for barges. In my little boat, I was free to go where the barges and cabin cruisers could not: Iron Hill Secondary Channel Cutoff, which saved me having to paddle the five miles around Iron Hill Island; then there was Half Moon Cutoff, an inside passage to the east of Morris Island, saving me a couple of miles; and finally, wonderful Thief Neck Cutoff, inside the main channel's five-mile near-circle around Thief Neck Island. My actual miles that day might have been around fifteen, average for the trip under normal circumstances.

That evening, we camped on a small island ruled by geese, who weren't happy about our presence. We stayed anyway, and they flew away, honking their displeasure. Our first island campsite in a while, this one had a gently sloping gravel beach that had been trashed by humans and geese. Across the

Maggie made herself at home on Government Island after a long paddling day on Watts Bar Lake.

way about fifty yards, the shore was lined with fine houses, and we were in plain sight, but nobody seemed to mind that we were there.

Next morning, I caught up with Ken, a native Minnesotan, as he paddled his daily lap from his house to a navigational buoy. He'd been paddling his blue kayak the evening before and spotted me camping, on what he told me was known as Government Island. He and his wife had retired and recently bought a house on Watts Bar, he said, to escape the cold weather in his home state. Ken and his wife had tried finding a place on Kentucky Lake, but it seemed too remote for his wife, too far from a population center like Chattanooga or Knoxville. Ken did not betray any judgment of this, but he started talking about roughing it up on the Boundary Waters of Minnesota, how much he loved being isolated in the wilderness. Many people, he said, don't get it.

"My brother's idea of roughing it is a hotel with less than forty-seven channels," he said.

Ken said his wife loves television, especially reality TV. "This is reality," he asserted, gesturing to encompass our surroundings.

I've always tried to avoid assessing my experiences in the outdoors as more "real" than other people's amusements, or more authentic, which I think is what Ken was getting at. It's hard to avoid that kind of judgment, the feeling that living a life closer to the elements, more remote from technology, was somehow more real. I sympathized with this notion, though I harbored skepticism about it. He'd had his earbuds in, listening to National Public Radio when I hailed him, and my cell phone was in the dry bag in front of me, turned off but accessible. Ken and I weren't at home watching an adventure channel, nor did we bear any resemblance to Alexander MacKenzie traversing the Great North and looking for a trade route to the Far East. We were maybe closer to Mackenzie than the guys on TV traveling the world on jet skis, or the people watching the program about the guys on jet skis with multiple sponsorships, but I wasn't sure that what we were doing was more "real." If anything, it got less real every day, as constant and complete immersion in technology became more the norm than pulling a paddle through the water ten-thousand strokes a day.

I didn't say anything about this to Ken, whose sentiments about the outdoors made us kindred spirits. We mused about why people throw trash in the Tennessee River. I'd camped and paddled in Minnesota, I told him, and it was clean where I went. He nodded. In the Boundary Waters, he said, you saw no signs of humans, not the case here on Watts Bar, not by a long shot. Ken wouldn't say anything bad about the Tennessee Valley, his new home, but he did say that littering the waterways seemed a cultural attribute that

Minnesotans lacked. He put his ear buds back in, and we headed in opposite directions.

The fields of flotsam on Watts Bar got worse as I headed for the confluence with the Clinch River and my goal for the day, Riley Creek Campground. For a few miles after seeing Ken, I paddled through acres of driftwood punctuated by plastic bottles that had contained sugary, chemically laced drinks and petroleum products. Some of it might have gotten washed into the river by rain or blown in by the wind. I'd also heard of dams flushing trash from one reservoir to the next, a practice that would work to the detriment of Watts Bar, if the intent was to make Fort Loudoun Lake less trashy than its more sparsely populated neighbor.

There's no good answer to why we trash our rivers in the South; I've been all over the country, and it's a problem in this region more than anywhere else. I hadn't seen anyone throw trash into the river on this trip, but it had to get there somehow, the result of ignorance or negligence. Who knew? Trash was part of the reality that Ken and I paddled through, something that the adventure shows tried to hide from viewers. It was something to work on, this tendency of our culture to tolerate abuse of our natural resources. You could fight against it by joining groups like the Tennessee Riverkeeper and the Little River Watershed Association, who not only organize cleanups but also educate people about the value of keeping waterways clean, about the benefits of being outdoors on a pristine river. It's a good fight, cleaning up a river and keeping it that way, and we should hold ourselves accountable for rivers that are part of the commons.

Martin Knoll, TenneSwim's U.S. project director, who accompanied swimmer Andreas Fath down the Tennessee, said that the river contained pretty much what he'd expected in terms of the contaminants he'd tested for, with the exception of the far greater than normal presence of microplastics. In terms of what he could see, Knoll mentioned that the segment below Kentucky Dam, approaching the Ohio, seemed to have more litter than anywhere else. I can't imagine what it would be like to swim through the flotsam fields that I paddled through that day, a complex stench rising from it. If Fath had slogged through a version of this, it seems that Knoll would have mentioned it.

I stopped for lunch at the Clinch River confluence, on a beach bordering the Southwest Point Golf Course, across the Tennessee River from the town of Kingston. The Clinch's mouth was vast here, an expanse of water four miles downstream from the steam plant where in 2008 the failure of a solid-waste containment area had spilled over a billion gallons of coal ash slurry into Watts Bar Lake. The spill destroyed homes, killed wildlife, and created a mess that covered 300 acres in the area near the confluence of the Emory and Clinch rivers. Barriers were set up to prevent contamination of the Tennessee River. As of early 2017, the Environmental Protection Agency said that Watts Bar Reservoir water quality had returned to pre-ash-spill conditions, according to data that included analyses of fish communities, insects, tree swallows, and sediment quality. As of 2018, TVA was in the process of converting from wet storage of ash to dry storage, though some, such as the Southern Environmental Law Center's senior attorney, Amanda Garcia, said that TVA "continues to dump coal ash into unlined pits that pollute groundwater, rivers, and lakes, and continues to leave millions of tons of coal ash in unlined, leaking pits" (*Knoxville News-Sentinel* July 25, 2018). Of further concern was President Trump's rollback of Obama's deadline for steam plants to stop dumping coal ash into unlined ponds. In November 2018, workers who had participated in the Kingston spill cleanup won a lawsuit against Jacobs Engineering, the contractor that TVA hired to clean up the mess. They claimed in the lawsuit that the company did not keep them safe, the work endangering their health as a result. As of October 2019, forty-four of those workers had died, and more than 400 were sick.

After lunch I took a hard right away from the mouth of the Clinch, following the Tennessee, which seemed a narrow channel here, counterintuitive to what you'd expect at the confluence of a tributary and major river. If I hadn't had the charts, I would have turned up the Clinch here, thinking the Tennessee bent left instead of right. After I paddled under power line derricks that crossed the entire river, I turned into Riley Creek Campground by early afternoon and hauled my gear up a hill to the RV pad I had reserved by phone. The gravel pad, complete with picnic table, water, electricity, and lush shade trees all around, unfortunately faced westward toward the open lake. We had to keep inching uphill to stay in the shade away from the hot sun's descent. We sweated until twilight.

When I first got there, I walked up to say hello to Lynn, the camp host, who was assembling an outdoor canopy beside his RV. I asked where I could get some ice. Instead of telling me, he got into his golf cart, scooted to the campground manager's place a half-mile away, and delivered my ice to me at my campsite. I later asked him how far away a store might be because I wanted to stock up on granola bars and paper towels. He said he'd drive me, no problem.

Lynn cranked the air conditioning in his truck and drove me three miles to a gas station with a lunch counter. It was three o'clock and they had stopped serving lunch—except for pizza. Lynn said he didn't mind waiting in the truck, so I ordered a pepperoni and mushroom and shopped around as they cooked it. I hadn't eaten a pizza since the beginning of my trip, and this was one of the best I'd ever had, and I'd had a lot of them: crisp crust, not too greasy, tangy sauce, and fresh meat and mushrooms. It may have been frozen and thawed, but even if I'd known that, I wouldn't have changed my rating of it. Lynn wouldn't take a piece. I ate half of it in camp and put the rest on ice for breakfast. I'd work it off, no problem.

Lynn said he thought the river was in better shape than it had been twenty years ago, during my other trip. He'd retired from Oak Ridge National Laboratory and said that the lab had been more careful about what it put into the water since he'd worked there, first as a chemical operator—which is what my dad did in Calvert City, back on Kentucky Lake—and then on cleanup crews. He mentioned "puddles of mercury." The river, he repeated, was a lot cleaner than it was twenty years ago. I noted that Watts Bar had more advisories against eating fish caught there than any other lake. You weren't supposed to eat catfish or striped bass, for example. Despite what he'd seen at his job in Oak Ridge, which was on the Clinch, Lynn said he'd been eating catfish from Watts Bar all his life, as had many of his acquaintances, and he'd never feared getting sick from it.

Though Watts Bar had been a mixed bag, not the glorious transition from urban to rural I'd experienced twenty years ago, my last half-day on it, after the night in Loudon City Park, restored my faith in the power that landscape retains over our efforts to alter and control it. As I paddled upstream toward Fort Loudoun Dam, my progress more labored while approaching another of the behemoth structures on which we depend for cheap power, the landscape had up until now become more riverine. The frequency of the rise and fall of the river usually carved out high muddy banks and left behind rotting, unlucky fish, but for some reason, the final stretch of Watts Bar was an exception to this ugliness. Industry lined the left bank, but on the right bank, we were greeted by cattle, horses, donkeys, forested bluffs, and lakehouses under the deep shade of old trees. A woman sat in a chair on a dock, reading a book. A book! Giant, lush trees cast shadows across a third of the river. Two cabin cruisers approached us, having just locked through the dam, and both of them slowed down for us. Now, we still had twin tsunamis to jump, and we witnessed the disintegration of the shoreline and the murky siltation which always followed the passage of these boats, something the captains never saw, but what a contrast in etiquette to what happened to us back on Kentucky Lake, in the cold weather, backed up against the rocky cliff. Could the warmer weather have improved the dispositions of the big boat pilots?

Donkeys and cattle came down to greet us before we locked through
Fort Loudoun Dam and left Watts Bar Lake behind.

It was working for me. Honeysuckle blossoms suffused the air with sweet-
ness, and a sycamore bloomed down near the water's surface, a flower I'd
never noticed before. A deer stared at me from a mown yard, and great blue
herons, my kindred spirits, congregated in this area. Primroses cheered up
the deep green shoreline, and even the thorny locust trees that had tortured
me back on the stormy Kentucky Lake campsite flowered in a friendly way,
big white clusters that hung heavy like grapes.

After the haywire lockage at Watts Bar Dam, I approached Fort Loudoun
with caution. This had been the first dam I'd ever locked through in my
life, and it would be the last of this trip. I reassured Maggie and asked her
to be still. Our final rising was calmer than any other dam, barely a hint of
turbulence, and the doors opened to the last reservoir, Fort Loudoun, the
most prosperous of our trip, the busiest, most populated segment. Here, on
the last fifty miles, with no more dams to negotiate, with old friends and
new awaiting us, I wondered what could go wrong to halt our progress so
close to the end.

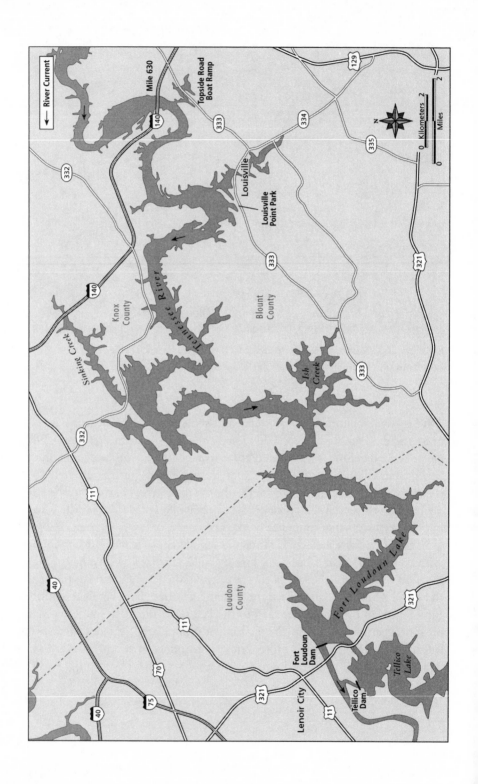

29

SO CLOSE AND YET

Twenty years earlier, as I lay down to sleep at Yarberry Peninsula Campground, three miles upstream from the dam, the ground beneath me undulated like a cheap waterbed. No earthquake, this was a sort of residual muscle reaction to my day on the water, ten miles of bouncing over thousands of boat wakes. Day Two of my downstream trip was as turbulent and frightening as the beginning of this trip, each end of the river ruffled up, but for different reasons: Paducah's waterscape wind-whipped, white-capped, and cold, and Knoxville's 1998 version warm and as crowded as an interstate with no lanes and no laws. This time, as the doors of the dam opened up, the reservoir was smooth and featureless, ominous as a sleeping, inscrutable giant, a gray expanse spreading out three or four miles across.

My goal that day was the boat dock of old friends: Phil and Tammie Zacheretti, who lived seven miles from the dam. Maggie and I hugged the north bank, and the river took us on an irregular looping course that headed in an easterly direction. Phil and Tammie, sweethearts since high school, worked in the movie theater business, and their lakehouse was decorated with posters of classic movies: Newman and Gleason, Bacall and Bogart staring back at you. In high school, my slacker friends and I would harass Phil as he worked late at the drive-in and at Murray's only theater, a twin screen called the Cheri/Capri. Little did we know as we chomped our pop-corn that Phil, in his usher uniform, had long-term aspirations that turned into a fulfilling career path.

And here I was, still a slacker, in essence, sweaty and exhausted from a sleepless night at a city park, paddling a stained and battered plastic canoe on a big wide lake with mansions looming from remote hilltops. One of the first houses we passed on Fort Loudoun Lake made me think of old money: a three-story white stucco, with white wooden railings and an exterior stair-case, all in need of paint, no lawn or dock fronting it, just a steep decline with brush, dogwoods, cedars, and one big shade tree. Though I abhorred the kind of work that restoring an old house would require, I wanted to be on a ladder painting this one, turning to stare at the lake before loading my brush every few minutes. I had fantasized about owning a lakefront home on Kentucky and Watts Bar and Nickajack lakes, but here in Knox County, I'd be better off dreaming of a caretaker job, perhaps living in an apartment above the boathouse. On this part of the river, I began to see not just houses for sale, but "estates." One place, a 16,000-square foot house on six acres, set back a quarter-mile from the water on a treeless hillside, was priced at 2.4 million dollars. Maggie and I stopped at a shaded boat ramp attached to this property, and I took a quick swim. If anyone came down to ask us what we thought we were doing, I'd say we were having a look at the property and wanted a lakeview perspective. "The boat ramp needs some work," I might add.

Farther up the river, on the main channel, sprawled estates with white-fenced horse pastures out front, one of these for sale, too. Yarberry Peninsula, on the other side of the lake, in Blount County, looked like a bulldozer had been at work to make room for more RV sites; the shaded pine hillside that I remembered was gone. I felt fortunate that we didn't have to try our luck at Yarberry, and that I had a friend with a double-decker dock on the Knox County side, where I could camp under a roof during the coming storms. Phil and Tammie were insisting that Maggie and I stay in their house. I was tempted but I had a couple of reasons for requesting the dock. One, I didn't want to have to worry about Maggie rampaging through the house eviscerating Phil and Tammie's throw pillows. She had matured on the trip, somewhat, but she retained her savage hatred of pillows, an instinct that compelled her to tear off a corner and pull out the stuffing. She hadn't stayed in anyone's house since Chris Alexander's back on Kentucky Lake, where she'd driven his three dogs crazy, and then herded the neighbor's cattle the next morning. Phil and Tammie had a sedate old dog named Domino, and they had a lot of pillows that would look like ripe fruit to Maggie. The other reason for declining a stay inside? It seemed a bit like cheating, here on the last few miles, to sleep in a bed; it might spoil me. I wouldn't be roughing it, exactly, camped on a swanky boat dock, but at least we would be outside, on the water, and if a storm came up, as forecasted, we'd be in a fairly safe place.

The Zacheretti's spoiled me with a great dinner of barbeque and key lime pie, a breakfast of bacon, sausage, eggs, and biscuits, and embarrassing stories from high school told in front of Catherine, who had come for dinner. I slept better on the gently floating dock than I had for a week. It was difficult to leave this sumptuous outpost the next morning to enter the heart of darkness that awaited me: the urban river. My target that day would be Louisville Point, a public park and boat ramp that prohibited camping, though by now I was confident in my stealth-camping skills. At the same time, I was hoping that Drew Crain, my biologist friend, had the connections to get me permission to camp in the yard of one of his friends. Yes, it had come to this in the final days: asking to camp in people's yards.

I'd caught a few bass on Watts Bar Lake using my hands-free tactic of throwing a lure behind the boat and propping up the rod behind me. On this last stretch I trolled with more consistency and was having some luck. Striped bass, more than any other species, were attracted to the Little Cleo spoon that fluttered behind my boat. I caught a largemouth bass while talking to a fisherman at Chota Bend; he tried to ignore it. That evening, after a storm blew through, I was trolling near Louisville Point and saw something I'd never seen before in all my years of inept fishing. I was paddling at a pretty good pace in the cool tailwind that followed the storm, and something hit the Little Cleo hard enough that the butt end of the rod, resting on the bottom of the boat, rose up and banged the reel against my ankle bone. It took five minutes to get him up near the boat. I knew it was something fairly big, to be fighting so hard, zigging and zagging and diving as I fiddled with the drag on my cheap little reel. The water was fairly clear, and I got him up to the boat and identified him as a striped bass, a good-sized one. Then a catfish twice as big as the bass darted up right behind him as if to take a bite out of him. I pulled him out of the water, rescuing him, I imagined, just as he was about to be eaten. As if to contradict me, he shook his head and escaped back into the water before I got a good look at him. I wondered if the big cat was waiting for him. Maybe they were just playing.

Before the storm, in the swirling wind, Maggie and I had been interviewed by a young reporter from a local TV station. I shouted into a clipped-on mic over the wind and the thunder, and I do not think I made much sense, but the producer did an amazing job of editing. John Becker, a WBIR anchor

Maggie did not appreciate me interrupting her navigational
session by showing off this largemouth I caught on Fort
Loudoun Lake.

who visits my journalism classes and talks about paddling with me, had a
good laugh with his co-anchor when the story aired. Then he gave viewers
the slow, sad head shake, code for "Trevathan not right in head."

Jeff Pewitt, Drew's friend who lived at Jackson Point, a couple of miles
upstream of Louisville Point, found us a place to stay that was even better
than his yard. He motored up to the Louisville boat dock in his bass boat
and gave us directions to the place. I paddled past a grand hacienda with a
tennis court in the front yard, and on the opposite bluff was what I would
call a French-style mansion that seemed to have grown out of the dense forest
far above the lake, its pale stucco contrasting with the deep green all around

it. Jeff's place was on the Blount County side up a fjord-like slough off the main channel. He and his wife Karen came out on the point and directed me to what looked like a gazebo on the other side of the fjord from their house. But this was no gazebo; I would be dock-camping again in another swanky double-decker. Jeff told me that the owner, who was out of town and happy to let us camp on his property, had built the major-league boat slip but no house yet. Jeff started a driftwood blaze in the friend's fire ring and talked until nearly dark, when it began to sprinkle. Camped under a roof again, I didn't care how hard it rained. I loved the sound it made on the metal roof, the feeling of being dry but not walled-in, and I was grateful for the kindness of friends.

The next day, which I calculated to be our second to last on the trip— about thirty miles from the takeout—I knew we had run out of friendly boat docks to camp on. Where we would reside on the final night was a mystery to be solved. I was aiming for Looney Island, and I mentioned my plan to a friend, Vince Vawter, who met me at the Topside Road boat ramp. Vince, a newspaperman turned novelist, owned a kayak with pedals. He voiced serious doubts about my prospects of camping on Looney Island, which was overgrown, he thought, seeing it as he had from Alcoa Highway, a busy four-lane that ran between Knoxville and Blount County, where I lived. But why would I listen to Vince about where to camp? I was almost finished with this trip. Was I not an expert on the various camping venues that the Tennessee offered? From islands to flat rocks at the river's edge to private boat docks, public boat ramps and city parks, I felt like I'd done it all. Turns out, I hadn't.

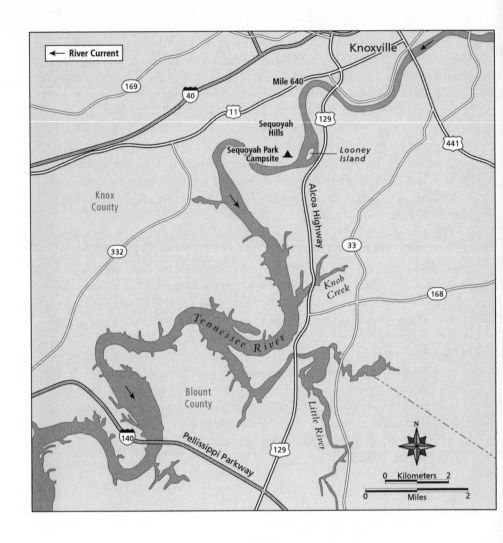

30

A FAR PEACE

After the late breakfast with Vince, I paddled under Pellissippi Parkway, a four-lane connecting west Knoxville with Alcoa and Maryville, the bridge a mammoth structure that I'd driven over hundreds of times. We were about three river-miles away from Knoxville proper. The shore on both sides had that mix of urban and rural that has always fascinated me about the Knoxville area. On my right, a bluff thick with trees rose 200 feet straight up from the water, so steep I wondered how the tree roots could grip the slope tightly enough to stay in place. On the other side loomed opulent homes whose boats lived in structures bigger than professors like me did. In front of one home was an elaborate brick castle with copper turrets and a water wheel, what I guessed may have been a playground. Turns out that this was a "medieval village" in the yard, and the whole shebang was for sale at the reduced price of $1.5 million. Beyond the bridge, it seemed that we traveled back in time a hundred years. On the left bank was a dairy farm with an ancient dilapidated barn, and on the right at Jones Bend, Peninsula Hospital, a mental health facility, where most of the shoreline was wooded and undeveloped. Between tree trunks, teenage hikers appeared and disappeared, unaware of our presence on the water. We paddled past a riverside garden that a young man was watering, and he told us this was Peninsula Village School. Soon after, we crossed the mouth of the Little River, whose headwaters sprang from high in the Smoky Mountains, sixty miles away. I had paddled the tamer sections of this river many times and had rented a house ten miles upriver from its mouth. In fact, it was while driving alongside the Little River for the very first time, when I was looking for a place to live in the Knoxville area, that I first got the idea to buy a canoe and paddle it from east Tennessee to western Kentucky.

Maggie and I hit a long straightaway that headed north, Knox County now on both sides of the river. On the west side, newer houses, built in the last thirty years, sat up on higher ground, Cherokee Country Club atop the highest bluff. Some houses on that side had property that sloped down to a flat expanse of mown grass, emerald now, in the warming spring. No one was outdoors. Absolutely no one was fishing on this part of the lake, on this beautiful day. The east bank houses were more modest, and switching to that side made the paddling more interesting for a touring canoer. The homes were older and more diverse in size and style, built closer to the water. People sat outdoors next to vegetable gardens in folding aluminum lounge chairs made with green and white nylon strapping, like my grandparents had owned. Many of these east bank docks housed canoes, kayaks, and sailboats that looked well used.

Back over on the west bank again, we skirted Sequoyah Park, a long strip of land that runs parallel to Cherokee Boulevard, at the perimeter of one of Knoxville's most exclusive neighborhoods. According to the Kingston Pike Sequoyah Hills Association, this neighborhood has been "one of Knoxville's oldest premiere residential sections" for seventy-five years (KPSHA. 2008–2017). For about a year, I'd worked as a caretaker at a residence on Cherokee Boulevard. One of my jobs was to get on a tall stepladder and trim a row of Bradford pear trees that ran along the front of the estate next to a wrought iron fence. The trees were to be trimmed so that they resembled tall-boy beer cans—at least that's the metaphor I concocted while on the ladder in the heat. Now, I was skirting the riprap shoreline, looking for a place to let Maggie out before scouting Looney Island for a campsite. It seemed important to have a great campsite for our final night on the river.

One side of the island faced busy Alcoa Highway, and the other side looked out on Sequoyah Park and the fine houses on the ridge beyond. Looney Island epitomized urban wilderness, an exemplar of what the city of Knoxville was in the process of creating farther south, with dozens of miles of trails you could hike and bike.

The river curved north at Looney's Bend, named after pioneer Moses Looney, who in 1796 acquired the 700 acres that would become Sequoyah Hills. Looney, originally from Wales, arrived in Virginia before the Revolutionary War. A member of the militia, he was captured by Cherokee in 1781. I wondered how he would feel about the legacy of his land, what had become of it, and the fact that the neighborhood that came to be was named after the famous Cherokee scholar, who would have been a young man during Looney's heyday. I doubt either Looney or Sequoyah could imagine the traffic on Alcoa Highway, much less the idea of motorized transport; they might not even understand the concept of "wilderness" as we use it today, to distinguish areas that are free from human improvements, such as pavement, buildings, and denuded landscape.

Turns out Looney Island was wilder than I thought it would be, the banks dense with vegetation all the way around it, no place to land a canoe. I saw no signs of weedeater usage, not even evidence of a sling blade, no human footprints having stomped down a parcel of weeds. Looney himself might have recognized this piece of urban wilderness, so wild that it prevented access. I was in a bit of a fix now, with daylight fading, just a mile or so from downtown Knoxville, eleven miles from our final destination: Holston River Park. After having paddled seventeen miles, I was done for the day. All I wanted was a place to sleep where I wouldn't be bothered. That way, I could arrive at my final destination, fresh and rested, and whoever showed up to welcome us wouldn't feel sorry for me or Maggie. I could claim that the trip had rejuvenated me and look as if it were actually true.

At Sequoyah Park's boat ramp, a gaggle of construction workers inside a corral of orange tape were digging deep into the ground. People were walking and running all around, and one guy, sitting in the back of his van working on a laptop, said he thought the police would run me off for sure if I tried to camp here. I asked him about camping because his setup made me think he was going to stay there overnight. He assured me he was not. A man carrying a twenty-foot long white kayak walked down the ramp and launched. I backed out of there at the same time and commented that his boat looked pretty fast.

He told me that he was a kayak racer out for a practice run. This guy, Paul, said he'd won a race from where we were to Fort Loudoun Dam and that he was preparing for a seven-day, one-thousand-mile race down the Yukon. This information humbled me. I told him it was taking me seven weeks to go seven-hundred miles, and he had the good manners not to guffaw. He said he thought surely I could find a camping spot nearby, and then he paddled on, surging ahead of me. He veered off to the park's bank up ahead and motioned me over.

"I bet you could camp here," he said.

The bank was low riprap, not too steep, with a place to land the canoe and tie it off. Although the "campsite" was right next to a walking trail, it was separated from Cherokee Boulevard by a narrow but dense strip of woods. I pulled up the canoe and unloaded some of my gear, not wanting to make it too obvious that I planned an overnight stay just across the road from Knoxville's swankiest neighborhood. Maggie and I reconnoitered. The boat ramp and its parking lot were a five-minute walk away, and the trail continued the other way for 200 yards and circled back around. Returning to our site near the water, we sat and waited for dark. Some dog walkers strolled past. One of them, with a Great Dane, said that paddling the whole river might be something he'd like to do. I said that he should do it, that it was a lot of fun.

"Where do you sleep?" he asked. He eyed my boat and the gear I'd unloaded. The tent was up on the bank, in its bag.

"That's the biggest challenge," I said. "Finding places to sleep." I wasn't going to confess my intentions to him for fear he might be with the Neighborhood Watch or the like. Maggie was about to dislocate my shoulder trying to get at the pony-sized dog, so the guy walked on. Five minutes later, another dog walker stopped and said he'd tried to get his friends to paddle with him to Chattanooga in a homemade raft.

"You should do it," I said.

A weariness came over me talking to these inquisitive dog walkers. I had pretty much finished my trip, I thought, and now, camping illegally on the final night, I began to realize how tired I was, how ready I was to sleep in a bed, under a roof, with walls around me. I was tired of explaining myself. I'd talked to a reporter on a phone interview earlier that day. She had also interviewed me before I began the trip, when I had big plans and was trying to appear confident and knowledgeable, when the plumper version of myself really had no idea what awaited me, no idea if I could carry out what I had in mind. I didn't know about the guy in the green kayak who went down the river and back every year. I didn't know whether I could lock through the dams or even approach them going upstream. I had no idea how Maggie would do. Now, the slimmed-down, river-whittled version of me was still in love with the river but worn out and ready to reach my destination. Tomorrow night, I told the reporter in response to her asking what I wanted to eat, I would order pizza and watch the Chicago Cubs baseball game on television.

At dark, I began setting up my tent, stealth-style, as close to the brushy thicket as I could get. With one more night remaining on the river, this would be the last place for the fabled meth addicts of the Tennessee River to show up, at what appeared to be the optimal place. I was in the middle of a city and I was on an urban trail. One could smoke some meth here, if so inclined. Perhaps some demented teenagers would happen upon us after we dropped off into dreamland. Catherine and I, on one of our first dates, were taking a walk one night in Concord Park, five miles downstream from this campsite, in the suburbs, when up ahead of us, near the river's edge, I saw something odd, something that didn't seem possible. But yes, we were looking at a kid holding a great blue heron upside down, by its feet. It looked like something out of a Looney Tunes cartoon, the roadrunner captured by the demented offspring of Elmer Fudd. We stared from fifty yards away, slowly approaching. He let the bird go, and I wondered aloud if these were some kind of vampire kids. I never thought it possible to snatch up these majestic birds. And the big question, the most disturbing thing about seeing a kid torturing a heron: why?

Now, camped in the park, I sat on the dog food bucket and ate my last dehydrated meal. Across the river, sirens screamed up and down Alcoa Highway, a bad wreck for sure. Two ambulances had sped past, then several cop cars. This seemed a marker, this car wreck, that my time on the river was ending. The dangerous highway and the horrible but commonplace car accident reminded me of the life off the river that I was returning to: speed, crowds, exhaust, asphalt—things I had not missed.

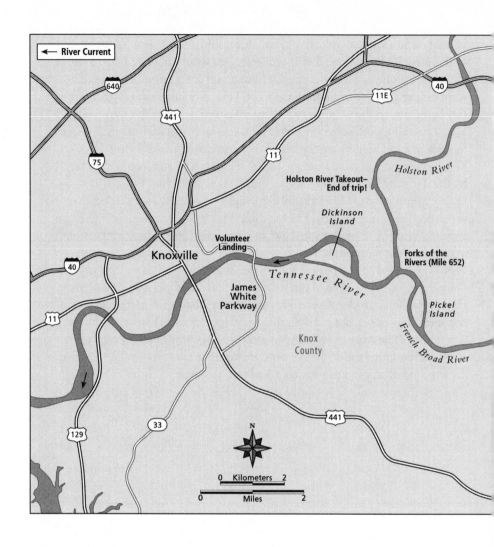

31

FULL CIRCLE

Nobody rousted us that night—not the cops, not the Neighborhood Watch, not the teenage vampires or the tweakers—and I woke Maggie just before first light to break camp and paddle our last twelve miles. In the low-angle light of the new day, the big old houses on the left bank, Crescent Bend, looked glorious. We paddled past Thompson Boling Arena and Neyland Stadium, basketball and football lairs for the University of Tennessee Volunteers. Once, I'd paddled to a Florida-Tennessee football game among the Vol Navy cabin-cruiser traffic and took refuge from the wakes up Third Creek. I thought I'd happened upon a dead body, decomposed to a swollen ripe greenish tint, but it turned out to be a life-sized Shrek doll floating face-up, next to a log. A few years after that, I paddled to the last Boomsday (Labor Day) fireworks display in Knoxville. Watching from water level near a bridge pier, I flinched over and over as the apocalyptic performance turned the river bright red, the sky transformed into eruptions of sparkly light.

Today, the river looked as clean as it had in the other sizable city on the river, Chattanooga, no flotillas of plastic or large-scale trash like the refrigerator back on Guntersville. I'd participated in annual Ijams River Rescue cleanups, sponsored by TVA and other organizations. In early April, when the river is lowest, at winter pool, volunteers clean up public areas from

Mile 652 all the way down to Turkey Creek, near Mile 616. What we found always surprised me: tires, boats, construction cones, appliances, automobile parts, shoes, underwear, outerwear, syringes, Tennessee Vol paraphernalia, disposable lighters, and millions of cigarette butts. I always left these cleanups feeling like we'd accomplished something but also dismayed at the volume of trash and a little resentful that we were having to clean up after others.

Starting out at his base of operations, Ijams Nature Center, River Captain Jake Hudson regularly patrolled the stretch I was canoeing that day, from Sequoyah Park, where I'd camped, to Forks of the River, where I was headed. In a pontoon with nets and sometimes a helper from Americorps, Jake cleaned up trash in this high-profile segment of the river. A 2014 *Knoxville Mercury* article by Patrice Cole informed readers about Jake. At the time, he said the river had gotten better in the decade he'd been patrolling it. He has had to haul out everything from dead cattle to parts of docks and partially submerged trees, all of which are hazards to boaters. In his time on the river, Jake has noticed that with the decrease of trash, there's been an increase in people fishing, boating, and swimming. Indeed, going further back in the river's history, to the 1950s, when Cormac McCarthy's novel *Suttree* was set, the riverfront has greatly improved compared to the murky, smelly, languid waterway where the main character, Suttree, a commercial fisherman, resides in a shantyboat.

Paddling the urban river on a weekday, the lone boater, I just wanted to get through downtown, but of course an east wind rose up against me. I'd promised people that I'd be at Holston River Park by noon, and by 9:00, despite the current and wind, I thought I'd beat that easily, that I needed to slow down so that I would not cheat friends and reporters out of the high drama of my arrival. Drew Crain and Mark Ellison would be there to transport me, my smelly, hyperactive mutt, and my boat and gear back home to Maryville.

Past the Gay Street and Henley Street bridges, I hugged the right bank below rejuvenated South Knoxville, where microbreweries and riverfront condos had sprung up near Ijams Nature Center, the focal point of the urban wilderness project that was spreading its tendrils throughout the county. I paddled beneath a monumental wall of riprap that marked Suttree Landing, a fairly new park named after the McCarthy novel. Jack Neely, writing for the Knoxville History Project, opines gently that McCarthy's descriptions of the riverfront would not be of great use to the chamber of commerce. McCarthy and his protagonist clearly have a deeply rooted affection for the river, but his descriptions of it are closely observed and truthful in their grittiness, portraying an urban river that seemed more like a trash repository than a recreational asset. In the opening of the novel, we get our first view of hungover fisherman Suttree at work, as well as our first view of the Tennessee: "With his jaw cradled in the crook of his arm he watched idly surface phenomena, gouts of sewage faintly working, gray clots of nameless waste and yellow condoms roiling slowly out of the murk like some giant form of fluke or tapeworm. . . . A welt curled sluggishly on the river's surface as if something unseen had stirred in the deeps and small bubbles of gas erupted in oily spectra" (McCarthy 1979).

Lovely. Later in the novel's version of the river are rabid bats, a corpse being retrieved with a grappling hook, and houses floating down the river in a flood. It has a certain literary charm, this bygone river, and certainly some of those things still might emerge from it, but I'd rather be reading about this version than paddling it. Suttree Landing looked like a nice, clean place to stroll, picnic, launch a boat, or just to sit and watch the river flow.

When I got to Island Home Park, where I'd launched for that last Boomsday, I got out and sat at a picnic table to eat a scoop of peanut butter spread across my last tortilla. Then I cleaned the trash out of the boat and deposited it in the park's garbage can. I had on my cleanest dirty cargo shorts and my fanciest shirt, a lightweight gray plaid button-up. The left sleeve had a small, ragged hole where I had snagged a fishing lure that I was showing to Phil Zacheretti. Bragging about how many fish I'd caught with the Little Cleo without even trying, I had managed to catch myself in front of Phil as we stood on his dock, and the carp the Zacheretti's fed surfaced from the depths all around us, their mouths open for a handout.

I relaunched at eleven o'clock, confident that I'd be at the park by noon, as promised. I was about four miles away. It was on this familiar section, near the small airport on Dickinson Island, where a sweet sadness about ending the trip began to wash over me. The river seemed to reciprocate my feelings by rising up against me with stronger and stronger current. This spring had been wet, and the lakes had been high this trip, the dams spilling, but nothing like what happened in March 1865, long before TVA.

Jack Neely calls the "Great Freshet of 1865" Knoxville's greatest natural disaster. The word "freshet," Neely observes, was an innocent-sounding term for flood, and this one was a doozy. Heavy rains for five straight days, as well as melting snow from the mountains, flooded all roads into and out of Knoxville. The city's only bridge, built three years earlier, was washed away.

The deluge completely submerged the large island I was struggling to paddle past. Above me, a black helicopter kept circling; at one point, it hovered above me beyond the point of good manners, I thought, and I considered making a gesture to express my feelings. Later, when I saw this was a sheriff's chopper, I was glad I'd let it go. I'd gotten this far on the river without once flipping someone the bird, an achievement, something I couldn't say at the end of the 1998 voyage. Past the island, I paddled along the far left bank, away from Ijams Nature Center, where I used to take Maryville College students every January. Here, as part of my nature writing class, I turned them loose on their own to wander the trails, my two requirements that they walk alone and turn off their cell phones. They usually responded well to this exercise and wrote journal entries about startling observations and thoughts that emerged in the absence of electronic connectivity. And here I was, checking my phone every few minutes in case someone texted me and asked where the heck I was, because I was falling behind schedule.

In 1965, according to Neely, the city purchased the original twenty acres from the Ijams family, avid birdwatchers, hikers, gardeners, and canoers. Harry and Alice Ijams canoed from Knoxville to Chattanooga—the right way, going downstream—on one of their wedding anniversaries in the early 1900s. It took them seven days, a pretty good pace, though that trip predated Fort Loudoun, Watts Bar, and Chickamauga dams, so they probably rode some pretty good current the whole way, on the old river. The nature center has since grown to 315 acres, and is adjacent to Knoxville's Urban Wilderness, 1,000 acres and expanding, set aside through the Legacy Parks Foundation for hiking, mountain biking, and generally partaking of the outdoors.

I paddled harder past Ijams, determined not to try the patience of those awaiting my arrival at Holston River Park. The Forks of the Rivers—where the French Broad comes in from the south to meet the Holston—marked the official end (or beginning) of the Tennessee, an unassuming confluence featuring a railroad bridge over the Holston and a wildlife management area on the final mile of the Tennessee's south bank, networked with trails shared by hunters, hikers, and cyclists.

I continued up the Holston, alongside Boyd Island in a creek-like stretch where trees loomed overhead, nearly blocking out the sky. I had to paddle hard for a little over a mile to make it to within sight of the little boat ramp. Maggie, her lead still hooked onto the thwart, leaped from the bow and dragged the boat a good ways up the concrete ramp. She was putting on a show for the small gathering.

A few people stood at the end of the ramp, cameras up, plus one guy trying to fish from a platform above the river. Drew handed me the cup of coffee I had requested. Later, he said that I seemed really relaxed and unhurried;

We arrived to a small but enthusiastic contingent at
Holston River Park, the terminus of our journey up the
Tennessee River. Courtesy of Scott Keller/The Daily Times.

he thought I'd be paddling hard toward the finish. And here I thought I had
been paddling hard.

Mark had a big, spotless white pickup truck with a crew cab and a metal
rack over the bed. He makes his living as a nurse, so you'd think he might
have a serious, even grim personality. I know I would. Not so. When I first
met him at the Maryville College tennis courts, he wore skimpy, tight gym
shorts and striped tube socks pulled up to his knees. Sporting a headband,
he was going for a John McEnroe look, except that he is built like a college linebacker, taller and bulkier than Mac. Now, working together, Mark

and Drew took what seemed to me quite a while to tie on my boat, while I watched, sipping coffee. After they ignored a few of my suggestions, they finally secured it. On the half-hour ride to Maryville, I wondered why Mark kept all four windows down in such a fancy truck that had to feature some impressive air conditioning. I didn't ask, but at some point, one of my bene-factors mentioned that Maggie and I stank. Just like that. At least that's the word I remember hearing. I also remember that I did not care since I had descended on the evolutionary scale to roughly the Cro-Magnon period. Drew hinted at our devolution at the boat ramp, when he held up Maggie's life jacket between his thumb and forefinger and said, "You might consider burying this when you get home."

I don't remember much about the rest of the day, other than unloading the gear in my driveway and leaving it spread out all over, then turning up the air conditioner in my house and ordering a pizza. I didn't care that the Cubs game got rained out. Sleep came fast and hard, and I thought it would be dreamless because I was so tired, but it turns out the Tennessee wasn't quite ready to let me go.

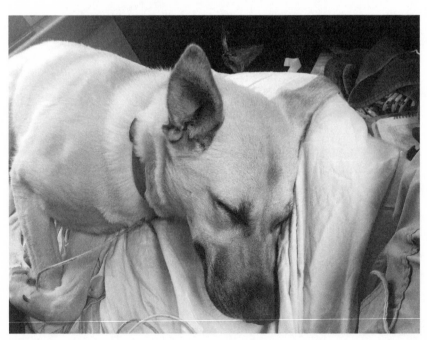

Maggie got comfortable in the back seat of Mark Ellison's truck and dreams of hogging the couch at home.

I'm in the boat with Maggie, feeling around the edges of it for the water, darkness all around us. We're passing under a monumental structure, once again, as in the Chattanooga dream, an interstate highway, I think, with massive concrete piers between which we have to navigate. Now, I'm paddling with my hands, and I see the venetian blinds of my bedroom, thinking I have to peek through the slats to see the shoreline and get my bearings. Again, as in the earlier hypnagogic dream in Chattanooga, it's a struggle to see and perceive where I am and where I'm headed. It's stressful. It's exciting. I look down from the bed and see Maggie on the floor of the bedroom, and I'm still within the dream, and my bed is the boat. The shadows on the wall ahead of me I perceive as the bridge piers of the interstate. The ceiling is the bridge span above us. My awareness of my location is like a stream divided by an island: the drama of the dream going by one side of the island and my emerging consciousness of being in my house for the first time in two months, the opposite passage. I know where the bedside light is, but still the venetian blinds seem like the gateway to the shore. Only turning on the light takes me out of the river's realm. The stream is no longer divided. Is the trip really over? What does it mean for it to end? Why am I always passing under an interstate highway in these nightmares?

32

~~~~~~

AFTERWARDS

W hen I told people about my plans for the upstream trip, they divided into two camps: those who liked the idea and thought it would be "fun"; and those who said they admired the attempt, but that it seemed risky, difficult, and crazy, especially for someone my age. Now, after finishing the trip, instead of having to justify what I was getting ready to do, it was time for me to explain what it all meant, what I had learned about the Tennessee, the people I met, myself, and my dog.

Twenty years had aged the river—the waterway and the landscape—in ways I could not have predicted. New houses were popping up, particularly from Watts Bar Lake on toward Knoxville; I noticed more new houses and ongoing renovations on Fort Loudoun Lake than any other. At the upper end of Watts Bar, a new resort development was under way, a few suburban mansions built on lots cleared of trees, other houses in the works, the marina attached to the development sprawling and almost empty of boats. Some places had changed so much that I didn't recognize them, mainly the marinas and campgrounds where I'd stopped in 1998. Most of them had become more upscale, with more facilities, bigger campgrounds designed to accommodate more RVs, with a corresponding decline in primitive sites, if they even existed any more. Blue Water Resort, near Dayton, was the most prominent example of this kind of renovation. Cottonport, just upstream from Blue Water, was the exception: a campground and marina that retained its unique, laid-back character from twenty years earlier. A few towns seemed different; Clinton was bigger and busier, no longer the sleepy little hamlet where I'd climbed up rickety steps from the river and ravaged a diner's buffet. Saltillo, the west Tennessee town where I stopped with Jasper, was unrecognizable, partly because the ferry we rode in 1998 was gone. I missed plenty of landmarks, having to favor one shoreline over the other, and I'd forgotten details from the 1998 trip, blank spaces in my memory that I had attempted to fill in on this trip. Despite the changes, the river had retained its essential character from the version I'd canoed twenty years earlier.

Much of what looked different this time around resulted not only from my going the "wrong way," but also from my start in early spring instead of late summer as I had in 1998. I wanted to see late winter on Kentucky Lake, my favorite time of year there, and I wanted to see the gradual blooming of spring as I headed south and east. Turns out, winter extended into spring, and although I loved the subdued look of the Land Between the Lakes in mid-March, I got all I wanted of winter's chill after the first 200 miles. Spring's onset did not come gradually. It arrived suddenly and then passed, as we went from a cold, rainy March and first half of April to an unseasonably warm remainder of April and May. Nevertheless, going this time of year meant less boat traffic, fewer people on the water in jet skis, pontoons, and seaworthy cabin cruisers. In general, this meant less noise and fewer wakes to jump, and those who did pause to talk—people fishing or working on the river, and those who lived on it—tended to be more interested in what we were doing, mostly more sober than the late summer crowd, and more knowledgeable about their home reservoir, if not the river as a whole. Jasper and I met many helpful and generous people on the 1998 trip, but overall, in 2018, the people we met as well as those I already knew who were part of this trip, exceeded my expectations in terms of generosity. Maybe being older has its advantages; as you accumulate years, you collect friends. One of the best things about paddling a river like the Tennessee, so close to home for me, was the fact that people could join me for a day on the river or in camp. People enriched this journey beyond my expectations.

More than in 1998, I had feared that the contentiousness of the political climate might extend to the river trip, that there might be people who would look askance at a tree hugger in a green boat with the leisure to paddle a canoe for two months. But there were no political arguments. It seemed that in the conversations I had with people, there were more immediate, concrete things that interested us: fishing, birdwatching, food, river history, and of course, the crazy weather. If people were suspicious of me and my

Drew Crain and Mark Ellison loaded my boat and gear
into Mark's truck without much help from me.

motives, they never said so. I found that I stopped caring about—and didn't
miss—listening to current events or watching cable news networks.

I assumed there would be more pollution on this trip, that I would see
more trash after twenty years had passed, and more people lived on and
used the river. I didn't comb every bank and I didn't tabulate the number
of bottles and cans stacked up in the coves, but I took some photos, and
I made note of trashy places as well as the clean zones. Guntersville Lake,
though one of my favorites, won the prize for having the most large-scale
trash, and the coves of Wilson, the smallest reservoir, were clogged with more
inorganic flotsam than any other lake. That said, I do not think that the river
was more trashed than twenty years ago. Martin Knoll, the geologist who
accompanied speed swimmer Andreas Fath down the length of the river
in the summer of 2017, said the Tennessee was in "pretty good" shape. It
never stank, he said, or had much of a film over it, even in industrial sections
like the Decatur area. They took water samples throughout the trip, testing
for 173 chemicals and seventeen metals; all were within EPA guidelines.
The one exception was the unusually high concentration of microplastics.
Knoll's and Fath's entourage, which consisted of a good-sized support team
that had positive news coverage and publicity out of in front of them, got a

friendly reception from people all the way down the river. Knoll did admit that "weekends were hard" with all the boat wakes. Perhaps most telling about the river's health: Fath swam it in thirty-four days, and he never got sick to his stomach or contracted any infections. (Knoll, Trevathan, 2018)

Canoeing the river a second time made me more grateful for an organization like the Tennessee Riverkeeper, its staff busy at work finding pollution that's less visible, discharges that industries might be trying to hide. Through this nonprofit, I met people who were passionate about keeping the river clean and about educating the public on the challenges facing the Tennessee. Likewise, the Tennessee River Gorge Trust (TRGT), formed in 1981, was helping to protect the most beautiful part of the river, downstream of Chattanooga. Rick Huffines, the director, saw his organization's role as an overseer of the gorge; he wants people to camp and to boat on Nickajack, but he also wants to protect it by being aware of what activities people are engaged in there. The TRGT does studies at places like the bird observatory to monitor the health of the gorge, using the birds as an indicator species. Also in Chattanooga is the Tennessee River Rescue, an organization that picks up trash every year in three counties along the river, including some tributaries. Event coordinator Christine Bock has noticed, since the formation of the organization in 1988, "declines in the amounts of garbage we are removing from some of the zones," but is not about to let up in her organization's vigilance and caretaking of the river: "It would be nice to find ourselves out of business one day, but right now that seems like wishful thinking" (Bock, tennesseeriverrescue.org n.d.)

The sixty-year-old version of myself seemed to hold up fairly well on this trip. I lost twenty-five pounds—going from 190 to 165—and although I needed to catch up on sleep at the end, I felt good. The afflictions I had earlier in the trip—aching hip and shoulder, split open fingertips—simply went away because during those first two weeks, I was often put in a position where I had no choice but to paddle and to paddle hard for long periods of time, without stopping. This functioned as a sort of boot camp for me, forcing me to go beyond what was comfortable and toughening me up for the rest of the trip. My fingertips finally healed, my muscles got used to repetitive motion, and I gained endurance on the paddling treadmill that became my gym. By the end of the trip, my hands were sore, and for months afterwards, I had a small knob in the middle of my right palm, and when I clenched that hand, the pinky finger would catch in a bent position, as if it needed some WD-40 in the middle joint.

I went in for an annual checkup soon after returning. My cholesterol, the main physical concern, according to my doctor, was lower than it had been in ten years. The nurse practitioner said the weight loss probably contributed to this.

"How'd you lose all that weight?" she asked.

"I canoed up the entire Tennessee River and ate dehydrated food for seven weeks."

She made me repeat this.

"You are crazy." She said this a few times during the examination.

Before the trip I had listened to an episode of the radio program *On Being*, with a segment titled "Running As Spiritual Practice." Marathon runner Ashley Hicks spoke of the meditative quality of running long distance. A shoe salesman told her, before a marathon, to remember: "The blessing is outside your comfort zone" (Hicks, Interview: July 06, 2017).

About the same time that I was getting ready for my trip in March 2018, Minnesotan Will Steger, 73, was also preparing for a one-thousand mile, seventy-day solo trek into the Canadian Arctic. In this same episode of *On*

This photo on the last day of the journey shows what two months of paddling upstream and living on dehydrated food can do for you: I lost twenty-five pounds, lowered my cholesterol, and couldn't unclench my right hand for a few months. Courtesy of Scott Keller/*The Daily Times.*

Being, he talked of the spiritual nature of the expedition, the regenerative quality of "being in the moment" for long periods of time; on some travel days, he might continue for fourteen hours. Steger would probably not see another person on this trip, and he didn't take books other than his journal. He differentiated the expedition's hardships from the stresses of everyday life: "In the wilderness, your mind is totally free . . . and there's a lot of strength and power in that" (Stowell 2018). Steger's solo expedition into the Barren Lands ended successfully in late May 2018.

Running differs from paddling in many ways, as do hiking long distance and trekking, though the repetitive, long-distance nature of each activity can lead to that meditative state where you can lose yourself, where time seems to stop. This state of mind is hard to come by, for sustained periods, in everyday life, when you're working and preoccupied with deadlines and making sure that others meet deadlines. It requires a departure from routine, an adaptation to the rhythm of waking with the chirping of birds and sleeping hard after a day of exertion, exposed to the elements.

Before this trip, I wasn't afflicted with anxiety or depression. I wasn't having a mid-life crisis. I'll admit to being a bit burned out at my job, ready for a prolonged break. I could have done something like go on a writer's retreat in New England or hang out at my sister's lake-house for a few weeks. I could have chosen to stay at home and write a novel about a canoer and a dog. But I've come to understand something since that first trip twenty years ago: every few years, I need to plan and undertake a long adventure and live outdoors for a chunk of time. Like Hicks's shoe salesman told her, pushing yourself and going beyond what you thought you were capable of can renew you physically, mentally, and spiritually. If I've changed at all in twenty years, it's in realizing this about myself. Somewhat at odds with that notion of enlightenment through hardship, I also realized on this trip that I could allow myself some ease and comfort, that I didn't have to push so hard all the time, didn't have to be consumed by the desire to cover miles. If there was an opportunity to rest from the river, I took it. I wasn't going to paddle through day-long rains. I would paddle five miles in a day if I wanted to and not feel guilty about it. It was my trip, after all, and I decided what the rules were.

By the end of the trip, at Holston River Park, I knew I had completed a challenge of my own creation, and I was grateful for the clarity and simplicity of finishing what I had started.

While the trip was arduous, sometimes harrowing, Maggie and I did have fun, as Catherine had suggested. Maggie alarmed and frustrated me at times, but she also made me laugh and helped me to remember that she was making the best of a situation that she didn't choose for herself. Looking back on it, the trip offered more than just a few chuckles; there was fun in the sense of the profound calm that comes after a close call with disaster and of beauty that arises unexpectedly, outside of one's control. There's fun, also, in being curious about what's around the next bend.

I do well to remember that paddlers like Verlen Kruger, who traversed over 100,000 miles during his life, and Kira Salak, who paddled the Niger River alone, constructed journeys to unfamiliar, sometimes unwelcoming places, across miles that dwarf my journeys. But I want people to know that you don't have to be the first or the fastest or to paddle the farthest, to benefit from a journey like this. You make your own journeys on your own terms, and it should not matter how old you are. It should not matter what kind of shape you're in or how tough you think you are. Age is more than just a number, in contradiction to the positive cliché, but it shouldn't be a barrier to testing ourselves and taking risks. There were times when I felt badly about causing loved ones to worry, and despite texting my mother and girlfriend almost every day, I knew that they probably had dark thoughts about what I might be up against on a given day. By the end, I think they learned to accept that these little journeys are part of who I am, that I need them in my life, that I seek them out. I was a little surprised when my sister reported that my mother was a lot more worried about Maggie than she was about me.

I had filled no vast blank spaces on the map of the world, as did Alexander MacKenzie and Percy Fawcett. The Tennessee is a known entity these days, dominated by human engineering, each mile charted, its depths measured in predictable rises and falls, the temperature taken and posted online each day. Yet, in spite of these tabulations, despite my personal history with this river, I feel that if you look long enough at any field, mountain or forest, at any body of water, moving or still, you will see something new, something you hadn't considered before. If there were blank spaces to be filled on this trip, they involved memory and perspective. Rivers, like us, are always in flux, changing course, rising and falling, influenced by forces outside our control. To know them, we have to rely on memory, on looking back, but also on going forward, advancing toward the blank spaces that remain inside us. What better way to fill in those spaces than on a river, dipping a paddle beneath its surface, with a minimum disturbance, and then telling the stories that emerge from the passing of time and the coverage of distance?

After finishing our expedition, Maggie and I didn't take the canoe out for a couple of months. When we did, on a Sunday in late July, we went to Breedenton, the name of the place where we'd met Travis and toured his little world of historical and criminal relics. I wanted to further investigate this place that had seemed so mysterious and dark that day, to see if it retained that essential character on another day, in another season, arriving by car instead of by boat. Maggie was so eager to be on the water that as soon as I parked, she jumped out the half-open back window of the Subaru, a feat for a big dog like her. The boat ramp was at the end of a mile-long gravel road, past a wastewater treatment plant. The ramp was deserted at noon on Sunday, so it retained that sense of desolation that had been established on our first visit. Maggie and I launched and floated up to the base of the lighthouse tower, in the shade, and read the water level numbers on it. Up in the bushes, someone had flung aside a pair of white leggings, spread-eagle in a tree that hung over the water. I expected Travis to pull up in his T-bird any minute. The day was bright and crisp, unusual for July, a contrast to the dark, drizzly May afternoon of our first visit. We paddled downstream about a half-mile, alongside Butcher Bluff's rock walls. My intent was to paddle up the creek where Travis said the headless body was found, but when I heard loud voices from the boat ramp, I turned around and paddled back. Three cars had pulled into the lot. When I got there, a guy about my age and a slender young woman oohed and aahed over Maggie sitting up in the bow with her life jacket on. We discussed the weather and how lucky we were to be outside in it. At the ramp, a thin young man and a girl of about ten were wading out into the water. Another young woman, a little plumper, possibly in the early stages of pregnancy, walked up as I got Maggie in the car and said, "I wish I could get my boyfriend to mind like that." I asked her if she used a leash. She repeated this to her boyfriend, the thin guy wading in the water. Back at the boat, the plump girl and her boy-friend insisted on helping me carry the canoe to the car, but I fended them off. I had a system, and having help just complicated things. The boyfriend and an older man left in one of the cars, and I was there with all the girls, who were fascinated with Maggie.

"Look at her pee!" said the slender girl, pointing at her.

Maggie, unfazed, finished her business and accepted the adulation without jumping up on her admirers. Everything about the tone of this place had changed, not just because of the bright, haze-free July day. Arriving here where Travis had told his dark tales and meeting new people who had no tales, made Breedenton seem benign, just another place on the river where you could put in a boat, park and have a picnic, or go for a swim.

Maggie and I walked up the path to the dark tower, where Travis had led David and Jordan and me, and it seemed a completely different place. It lacked the mystery that Travis had infused it with. Only the memory of that day brought back Breedenton's essential character, which came into greater relief only after David and Jordan and I made our escape. We had paddled toward the dam in the hardest rain of the trip, thunder clapping hard in our ears, lightning electrifying the blurred-out landscape. After the storm passed, a transcendent moment arose, unique to that time and place, to the sequence of events that day: the sun burst out, hotter and brighter than any other time during the entire trip, illuminating us and our surroundings, comforting us with its warmth. The air had that cleansed look and feel that follows a storm, and the shadowy narrative that Travis had woven seemed worlds away. I was grateful for moments like these and others: the fishermen's voices arising from the fog before I could see them near the Hiwassee confluence, the landing on the gravel bar at Bruton Branch after Maggie's jumping out of the boat inside the Pickwick lock, the miraculous emergence of the lighted pier, in the twilight, at the Bridgeport city park. These moments were only possible in a canoe, with a dog like Maggie, going the wrong way on the Tennessee River.

BIBLIOGRAPHY

Alldredge, J. Haden, et.al. *A History of Navigation on the Tennessee River System: An Interpretation of the Economic Influence of this River System on the Tennessee Valley.* Washington, D.C.: United States Government Printing Office, 1937.

Bock, Christine. "About Us." *Tennessee River Rescue.* Chattanooga, TN: Tennessee Aquarium, partner. n.d. www.tennesseeriverrescue.org.

Capps, Andrew. "Microplastics hit home: Tennessee River among the most plastic polluted in the world." *Knoxville News-Sentinel*, Feb. 8, 2019. www.knoxnews.com.

Castner, Brian. *Disappointment River: Finding and Losing the Northwest Passage.* New York: Doubleday, 2018.

Cole, Patrice. "A Day with Jake Hudson on Fort Loudoun Lake." *Knoxville Mercury*, August 3, 2016. www.knoxmercury.com.

Crocker, Brittany. "EPA rolls back protective regulation enacted after 2008 Kingston coal ash spill." *Knoxville News-Sentinel*, July 25, 2018. www .knoxnews.com.

Davidson, Donald. *The Tennessee.* Vol 1. Knoxville: University of Tennessee Press, 1978.

Etnier, David A. and Wayne C. Starnes. *The Fishes of Tennessee.* Knoxville: University of Tennessee Press, 1993.

Foote, Shelby. *The Civil War: A Narrative.* Vol. 2. New York: Random House, 1963.

Gaines, Jim. "Tennessee Valley Authority's coal ash conundrum continues as lawsuits, cleanup issues loom." *Knoxville News-Sentinel*, Oct. 5, 2018. www.knoxnews.com.

Grann, David. *The Lost City of Z.* New York: Vintage Books, 2010.

Groom, Winston. *Shiloh, 1862.* Washington, D.C.: National Geographic Society, 2012.

Hicks, Ashley. Interview, "Running As Spiritual Practice". *On Being* August 18, 2016. Minneapolis, MN: Krista Tippett Public Productions, 2014–2020.

Huffines, Rick. Interview by author, 2018.

Joseph, Timothy. "Stop Silver Carp in Tennessee." Video. Accessed April 18, 2020. https://www.facebook.com/watch/?v=238529757320955.

Kennedy, Robert Jr. Speech, for Tennessee Riverkeeper, at Huntsville Botanical Garden, Huntsville, AL. April 18 2018.

Kingston Pike-Sequoyah Hills Association. "Neighborhood Information: History." Knoxville, TN: KPSHA. 2008-2017. www.sequoyahhills.org/history.

Knoll, Martin. Interview by author, 2018.

Lough, Kyser. "Cherokee Park Renovation Celebrated." *Murray Ledger and Times*, Sept. 16, 2010. Murray, KY. www.murrayledger.com.

McCarthy, Cormac. *Suttree*. New York: Random House, 1979.

Means, Rebecca and Ryan. *Project Remote*. https://www.projectremote.com /defining-remote/.

Neely, Jack. *Knoxville History Project*. Knoxville, TN: KHP. n.d. https://knoxville historyproject.org.

———. "Ijams Nature Center." *Knoxville History Project*.

———. "Knoxville's Greatest Disaster: The Freshet of 1867." *Knoxville History Project*.

———. "Sevier Avenue." *Knoxville History Project*.

Peterson, Phil. *All Things Are Possible: The Verlen Kruger Story: 100,000 Miles by Paddle*. Cambridge, MN: Adventure Publications, Inc., 2006.

Savannah Topix Forums. This chatroom is no longer accessible online. Referenced by https://savannahtn.edefeed.com/topic/savannah-general-news/alternative -to-savannah-topix-forums/.

Soniak, Matt. "Why Some Civil War Soldiers Glowed in the Dark." *Mental Floss*. April 5, 2012. www.mentalfloss.com.

Stowell, Scott. "Minnesota explorer Steger will take unprecedented solo trek in Canadian Arctic." *Star Tribune*, March 1, 2018. Minneapolis, MN: Star Tribune Media Company, LLC. 2014. www.startribune.com.

Tennessee Aquarium. "Animals & Exhibits: Fish: Paddlefish." June 8, 2017. *Tennessee Aquarium*. Chattanooga, TN: tnaqua.org. 2020. www.tnaqua.org. Accessed: April 1, 2019.

The Tennessee Encyclopedia of History and Culture. Nashville: Rutledge Hill Press, 1998.

Trevathan, Kim. "Ben Montgomery's 'Grandma Gatewood' Reveals the Full Story of an Appalachian Trail Pioneer" in *Outdoors, Voice in the Wilderness, Knox Mercury*, February 8, 2017. Knoxville, TN: Knoxville History Project, 2015–2017. archived at: www.knoxmercury.com.

Weil, Andrew. *Healthy Aging: A Lifelong Guide to Your Well-Being*. New York: Anchor Books, 2007.

Weil, Elizabeth. "Alone at Sea." *The New York Times Magazine*, March 22, 2018. www.nytimes.com.